D1479791

CMP

ALLE · ZEIT · WACH
1842

Acknowledgement for the front cover illustration is made to Isykon Software GmbH for the use of Figure 23, page 202, from their system description on PROREN 1 & 2.

Computer Aided Engineering Systems Handbook

Volume II

Editors:
J. Puig-Pey
C.A. Brebbia

Computational Mechanics Publications
Southampton Boston

Springer-Verlag Berlin Heidelberg New York
London Paris Tokyo

J. PUIG-PEY

Escuela de Ingenieros de Caminos
Universidad de Santander
Avda de los Castros
Santander
Spain

C.A. BREBBIA

Computational Mechanics Institute
Ashurst Lodge
Ashurst
Southampton
SO4 2AA
U.K.

British Library Cataloguing in Publication Data

Computer aided engineering systems handbook.
Vol. 2
1. Engineering — Data processing
I. Puig-Pey, J. II. Brebbia, C.A.
044′.02462 TA345

ISBN 0-905451-49-X

ISBN 0-905451-49-X Computational Mechanics Publications Southampton
ISBN 0-931215-25-0 Computational Mechanics Publications Boston
ISBN 3-540-17936-4 Springer-Verlag Berlin Heidelberg New York London Paris Tokyo
ISBN 0-387-17936-4 Springer-Verlag New York Heidelberg Berlin London Paris Tokyo

Library of Congress Catalog Card Number 87-70842

Printed in Great Britain by Unwin Brothers Ltd, Old Woking, Surrey

PREFACE

This is the second volume of a set containing the most up to date Computer Aided Engineering systems available to the engineer. These volumes concentrate on those systems which are well established and can be used for solving problems of the mechanical engineering type.

In selecting the systems included in the set we have taken into consideration systems which are not only comprehensive and up to date but are also well supported. The present emphasis on Computer Integrated Manufacturing (CIM) underlines the importance of interfacing different computer codes and most systems presented here have the capability of being used in conjunction with other codes.

The usefulness of the Handbook is enhanced by a set of tables which classify the codes according to general capabilities, graphics, applications, geometric building elements, interfaces and hardware. The tables refer to systems included in Volume I as well as this volume.

The first volume includes the following systems:

AUTOCAD™2, BEASY™, BRAVO (Solids Modelling I/II™), CADDSTATION/CADDS 4X: SOLIDESIGN™/IMAGEDESIGN™/ CVMAC/CVNC/AUTOMEASURE™, CADRAW, CAM-X, CIS MEDUSA™, COMPAC, DOODLE™, DORA/SID, EASYDRAF^{2}™/ ATTRIBASE™/EASYDATA/EASY^{3}™, EUCLID, FAM, GIFTS, HOLGUINCAD ADC-400/ADC-420, ICEM, MENTAT

The Editors

CONTENTS

HOW TO USE THIS HANDBOOK

This Handbook has been put together in an effort to help CAE systems users to select the best available package for their particular requirements. The Handbook consists of a set of volumes, the second of which, i.e. this one, contains 19 well known systems each of which is described in a separate chapter. These chapters explain in detail the different capabilities of the systems and their range of applications.

In order to help the reader in the search for the best suited system, a set of tables has been compiled presenting in a schematic way the capabilities of each system. There are seven tables describing the packages or containing information of direct relevance to the user.

TABLE I

This table describes the general capabilities of each system such as whether the system has solid modelling, the possibility of providing sculptured surfaces or integral properties calculation. The table also points out those systems which have interfaces with analysis codes and can mesh the solid into boundary or finite elements.

Other applications reported in the table are interference analysis, mechanisms and kinematic representation, parametric design and tolerance representation, most of them of importance in mechanical engineering design.

TABLE II

Table II indicates to the user the different types of graphics representations which are contained within the system, such as 2D and 3D colour graphics, shaded display and automatic hidden line removal. Text on drawings, dimension facilities and listing or bill of materials are also important facilities which some systems present. The table also points out those systems which can be interfaced with a user-made element library.

TABLE III

Applications of the systems are presented in Table III, classified in accordance with conventional topics such as mechanical engineering – including stress analysis, fluid mechanics, heat transfer, plant design, piping sheet metal and mould design; naval; aeronautical; electrical; electronics; architectural and civil engineering applications; with a separate category for survey and urban planning.

TABLE IV

This table refers to the primary geometric building elements of the systems. They are classified in accordance with three main categories, i.e. solid modelling, surface representation and curve modelling. Within the solid modelling category the systems are classified according to the following definition techniques: wireframe modelling, analytical modelling, sweeping, boundary representation or construction solid geometry (CSG). Surfaces can be represented using patches, splines or in other precise manners, using quadratics, applying general rule or sweep descriptions, having the possibility of using surfaces of revolution and representation of fillets. Curve modelling is subdivided into those representing elementary curves and those which use splines or piecewise curves representation.

TABLE V
Table V describes the interfaces of the CAE systems with analysis codes or user provided programs. The systems are first subdivided into open and closed packages. Then the type of permissible input is described, i.e. menu, tablet or text typing.

The table also stresses the availability of extended documentation, if the system has a user's group, the programming language and the type of analysis systems interfaced to the CAE package.

Finally the systems can be interfaced within the CIM process through interfaces with NC programs or automatic ROBOT Action packages, and can have tool paths and robot action simulations.

TABLE VI
This table simply describes the types of hardware on which the systems can be run.

TABLE VII
It gives details of availability of the packages, and presents addresses, telephone and telefax numbers.

VOLUME I This volume contains the same type of information on other CAE systems, including AUTOCAD™2, BEASY™, BRAVO (Solids Modelling I/II™), CADDSTATION/CADDS 4X: SOLIDESIGN™/IMAGEDESIGN™/ CVMAC/CVNC/AUTOMEASURE™, CADRAW, CAM-X, CIS MEDUSA™, COMPAC, DOODLE™, DORA/SID, EASYDRAF^{2}™/ ATTRIBASE™/EASYDATA/EASY^{3}™, EUCLID, FAM, GIFTS, HOLGUINCAD ADC-400/ADC-420, ICEM, MENTAT

TABLE I

GENERAL CAPABILITIES

SYSTEM	SOLID MODELLING	SCULPTURED SURFACES	INTEGRAL PROPERTIES CALCULATION	INTERFACE WITH ANALYSIS	INTERFERENCE ANALYSIS	FEM/BEM MESHING	MECHANISM REPRESENTATION & KINEMATIC SIMULATION	PARAMETRIC DESIGN	TOLERANCES REPRESENTATION
ANSYS	*			*		*		*	
ANVIL-5000	*	*	*	*		*			
AUTO-TROL SERIES 7000 SERIES 5000	 * 	 * *	 * 	 * *	 * *	 * 	 * 	 * *	 *
CADVANCE SOLID VISION SYSTEM 25/PRISMA	 * *	 * *	 * *	 * *				* *	*
DIAD/DGM/C-DATA/ C-PLAN/GNC/C-TAPE								*	
IDEAS GEOMOD/ SUPERTAB/SYSTAN/ GEODRAW	*	*	*	*	*	*	*	*	*
INTERGRAPH	*	*	*	*	*	*	*	*	*
MECHANICAL ADVANTAGE 1000/MA1500/GPX			*	*	*	*	*	*	*
PADL-2	*		*					*	
PALETTE				*	*				
PATRAN	*	*	*	*	*	*	*		
PIGS/DOGS/ BOXER/PAFEC FE	*		*	*		*			
PRIME MEDUSA/ GNC/PDGS/SAMMIE	*		*	*			*	*	
PROREN 1 & 2	*	*	*	*	*		*	*	
ROMULUS-D	*	*	*	*	*			*	*
SABRE-5000	*	*	*	*	*	*		*	
SYNTHAVISION	*		*		*				
TIPS-1	*	*	*	*	*	*			
UNIGRAPHICS II/ UNISOLIDS	*	*	*	*	*	*	*	*	*

OTHER SYSTEMS ARE AVAILABLE IN VOLUME I

TABLE II

GRAPHICS

SYSTEM	2D	3D	COLOUR DISPLAY	SHADED DISPLAY	AUTOMATIC HIDDEN LINE REMOVAL	TEXT ON DRAWING	DIMENSION FACILITY	LISTING / BILL OF MATERIALS	USER-MADE ELEMENTS LIBRARY
ANSYS	*	*	*	*	*				
ANVIL-5000	*	*	*	*	*	*	*	*	*
AUTO-TROL									
SERIES 7000	*	*	*	*	*		*	*	*
SERIES 5000	*	*	*	*	*		*	*	*
CADVANCE	*	*	*			*	*	*	*
SOLID VISION	*	*	*	*	*	*	*	*	*
SYSTEM 25/PRISMA	*	*	*	*	*	*	*	*	*
DIAD/DGM/C-DATA/ C-PLAN/GNC/C-TAPE	*	*				*	*	*	*
IDEAS GEOMOD/ SUPERTAB/SYSTAN/ GEODRAW	*	*	*	*	*	*	*	*	*
INTERGRAPH	*	*	*	*	*	*	*	*	*
MECHANICAL ADVANTAGE 1000/MA1500/GPX	*					*	*		*
PADL-2		*	*	*	*				
PALETTE	*	*	*	*	*	*	*	*	*
PATRAN	*	*	*	*	*	*			
PIGS/DOGS/ BOXER/PAFEC FE	*	*	*		*	*	*	*	*
PRIME MEDUSA/ GNC/PDGS/SAMMIE	*	*	*	*	*	*	*	*	*
PROREN 1 & 2	*	*	*	*	*	*	*	*	*
ROMULUS-D		*	*	*	*	*	*	*	*
SABRE-5000	*	*	*	*	*	*	*	*	*
SYNTHAVISION		*	*	*	*				
TIPS-2		*	*	*	*		*		
UNIGRAPHICS II/ UNISOLIDS	*	*	*	*	*	*	*	*	*

OTHER SYSTEMS ARE AVAILABLE IN VOLUME I

TABLE III

APPLICATIONS

SYSTEM	MECHANICAL	FLUID MECHANICS	HEAT TRANSFER	PLANT DESIGN	PIPING	SHEET METAL	MOULD DESIGN	NAVAL	AERONAUTICAL	ELECTRICAL	ELECTRONICS	ARCHITECTURE	CIVIL	SURVEY & MAPPING	URBAN PLANNING	OTHERS (SPECIFY)
ANSYS	*	*	*		*			*	*	*	*		*			
ANVIL-5000	*					*	*		*							
AUTO-TROL SERIES 7000	*					*	*	*	*	*						
SERIES 5000				*	*					*		*	*	*	*	
CADVANCE	*			*	*	*		*	*	*	*	*	*	*	*	MANY
SOLID VISION	*			*	*							*	*		*	
SYSTEM 25/PRISMA	*			*	*					*		*	*	*	*	
DIAD/DGM/C-DATA/ C-PLAN/GNC/C-TAPE	*															
IDEAS GEOMOD/ SUPERTAB/SYSTAN/ GEODRAW	*		*				*	*	*		*	*	*		*	
INTERGRAPH	*			*	*	*	*	*	*	*	*	*	*	*	*	
MECHANICAL ADVANTAGE 1000/MA1500/GPX	*	*	*	*				*	*		*	*	*			
PADL-2	*															
PALETTE	*			*	*	*		*	*	*	*	*	*	*	*	
PATRAN	*	*	*		*		*	*	*				*			
PIGS/DOGS/ BOXER/PAFEC FE	*									*		*	*	*		
PRIME MEDUSA/ GNC/PDGS/SAMMIE	*					*						*				
PROREN 1 & 2	*					*	*			*						
ROMULUS-D	*						*	*	*							
SABRE-5000	*					*	*	*	*							
SYNTHAVISION	*											*	*			
TIPS-1	*	*	*				*									
UNIGRAPHICS II/ UNISOLIDS	*			*		*	*		*	*	*					

OTHER SYSTEMS ARE AVAILABLE IN VOLUME I

TABLE IV

GEOMETRIC BUILDING ELEMENTS

SYSTEM	SOLID MODELLING					SURFACES						CURVE MODELLING	
	WIREFRAME	CELLULAR MODULES (ANAL. MOD.)	SWEEPING	BOUNDARY REPRESENTATION (B. REP.)	CONSTRUCTION SOLID GEOM. (CSG)	PATCHES, SPLINES, PIECEWISE	QUADRATICS	GENERAL RULED	GENERAL SWEEP	REVOLUTION	FILLETS	ELEMENTARY CURVES	SPLINES, PIECE-WISE CURVES
ANSYS	*	*	*	*	*	*			*	*	*	*	*
ANVIL-5000	*		*	*	*	*			*	*	*	*	*
AUTO-TROL SERIES 7000 SERIES 5000	*		*	*	*	*	*		*	*	*	*	*
CADVANCE SOLID VISION SYSTEM 25/PRISMA	* * *		 *	 * *	 *					 *	 *	* *	*
DIAD/DGM/C-DATA/ C-PLAN/GNC/C-TAPE												*	
IDEAS GEOMOD/ SUPERTAB/SYSTAN/ GEODRAW	*		*	*	*	*	*	*	*	*	*		*
INTERGRAPH	*	*	*	*	*	*	*	*	*	*	*	*	*
MECHANICAL ADVANTAGE 1000/MA1500/GPX	*												
PADL-2					*								
PALETTE								*	*	*		*	*
PATRAN		*				*		*	*		*	*	*
PIGS/DOGS/ BOXER/PAFEC FE	*				*			*		*		*	*
PRIME MEDUSA/ GNC/PDGS/SAMMIE	*		*	*	*	*		*	*	*	*	*	*
PROREN 1 & 2	*		*	*		*		*	*	*	*	*	*
ROMULUS-D			*	*		*	*		*	*	*	*	*
SABRE-5000	*		*		*	*	*	*	*	*	*	*	*
SYNTHAVISION					*								
TIPS-1	*		*	*	*								
UNIGRAPHICS II/ UNISOLIDS	*	*	*		*	*		*	*	*	*	*	*

OTHER SYSTEMS ARE AVAILABLE IN VOLUME I

TABLE V

INTERFACES

SYSTEM	WITH USER								WITH ANALYSIS (SPECIFY)
	OPEN PACK	CLOSED PACK	INPUT			EXTENS. DOCUMENT.	USER GROUPS	PROGRAM LANGUAGE (SPECIFY)	FEM
			MENU	TABLET	TEXT TYPING				
ANSYS			*		*	*	*		*
ANVIL-5000			*	*	*	*	*	GRAPL FORTRAN	NASTRAN,ANSYS MOLDFLOW
AUTO-TROL SERIES 7000 SERIES 5000			 * *	 * *			 * *	 FORTRAN,EAGLE FORTRAN	PATRAN NASTRAN,ANSYS
CADVANCE SOLID VISION SYSTEM 25/PRISMA	* * *		* * *	* * *	 * *	* * *	* * *	 FORTRAN IGL,FORTRAN,C	 SABA
DIAD/DGM/C-DATA/ C-PLAN/GNC/C-TAPE			*	*	*	*		FORTRAN	
IDEAS GEOMOD/ SUPERTAB/SYSTAN/ GEODRAW	*		*	*	*	*	*	FORTRAN	NASTRAN BEASY,SINDA ABAQUS,ANSYS SUPERB
INTERGRAPH	*		*	*	*	*	*	FORTRAN C	MANY
MECHANICAL ADVANTAGE 1000/MA1500/GPX			*	*	*	*		MAINSAIL	
PADL-2	*				*			FLECS FORTRAN 77	
PALETTE	*		*	*	*	*	*	FORTRAN C PASCAL,BASIC	SEVERAL
PATRAN	*		*	*		*	*	FORTRAN 77	22 Translators
PIGS/DOGS/ BOXER/PAFEC FE			*	*		*		FORTRAN	*
PRIME MEDUSA/ GNC/PDGS/SAMMIE			*	*		*	*	FORTRAN	NASTRAN,ANSYS PATRAN,FEMGEN
PROREN 1 & 2	*		*	*	*	*	*	FORTRAN 77 C	FEMGEN others
ROMULUS-D	*		*			*	*	C	SUPERTAB PATRAN
SABRE-5000	*		*	*	*	*	*	FORTRAN C PASCAL etc	VARIOUS
SYNTHAVISION			*	*				FORTRAN	
TIPS-1	*							*	*
UNIGRAPHICS II/ UNISOLIDS		*	*	*	*	*	*	FORTRAN GRIP	ANY

OTHER SYSTEMS ARE AVAILABLE IN VOLUME I

TABLE V (CONTINUED)

INTERFACES

WITH ANALYSIS (SPECIFY)		WITH OTHER SYSTEMS					WITH CAM			
							AUTOM. GENER.		SIMULATION	
BEM	OTHERS	COMMUNICATION PACKAGE	IGES IMPLEMENT.	GRAPHIC STANDARD	DATABASE SYSTEM	COMPATIBILITY WITH OTHERS (SPECIFY)	NC PROGRAMS	ROBOT ACTIONS	TOOL PATHS	ROBOT ACTIONS
		*	*			*				
			*				*			
		*	* *		* *		*		*	
		* * *	* *		* * *	dBASE III plus UNIFY				
					*	SEVERAL SYSTEMS	*		*	
*	OPEN INTERFACING CAPABILITY		*			INTERLEAF MOLDFLOW	*		*	
		*	*	*	*	20 CAD Translators	*	*	*	*
*	DRAFTING	*	*		*	BEASY, ROMAX PATRAN, ADAMS				
		*	*		*	SEVERAL	*			
1 Trans.	FINITE DIFF.	*	*			12 CAD Trans.				
					*		*			
		*	*		*	GNC COMPACT PDGS APT MRPII	*		*	
			*		*	VDA	*		*	
		*	*		*					
	MOULD ANALYSIS	*	*			FORD, CHRYSLER, BEZIER, GM VDA etc	*		*	
*							*	*	*	*
		*	*		*	MOLDFLOW	*	*	*	*

OTHER SYSTEMS ARE AVAILABLE IN VOLUME I

TABLE VI

SYSTEM	HARDWARE
ANSYS	ALLIANT, APOLLO, CONTROL DATA, CELERITY, COMPUTERVISION, CONVEX, CRAY, DATA GENERAL, DIGITAL EQUIPMENT CORPORATION, FLOATING POINT SYSTEMS, HARRIS, HEWLETT-PACKARD, HONEYWELL, IBM, PRIME, RIDGE, SILICON GRAPHICS, SUN, UNIVAC. Subsets of ANSYS available on IBM PC/XT, PC/AT & compatibles
ANVIL-5000	IBM, DEC, DG, APOLLO, SUN, SILICON GRAPHICS, HP, PRIME
AUTO-TROL SERIES 7000/5000	DEC - GPX, VAXSTATION 2000, APOLLO DN3000/4000, IBM PC/AT
CADVANCE SOLID VISION SYSTEM 25/PRISMA	All IBM PC/XT/AT Compatibles All IBM PC/AT Compatibles Masscomp, DEC, IBM PC/AT Compatibles and others
DIAD/DGM/C-DATA/C-PLAN/GNC/C-TAPE	APOLLO, DEC, ICL, PRIME
IDEAS GEOMOD/SUPERTAB/SYSTAN/GEODRAW	DEC, APOLLO, SUN, HP, IBM (System called CAEDS). GENRAD, + 60 Graphics Devices
INTERGRAPH	DEC BASED INTERGRAPH
MECHANICAL ADVANTAGE 1000/MA1500/GPX	DEC/IBM, DEC
PADL-2	DEC
PALETTE	DEC, APOLLO
PATRAN	APOLLO, CDC, CRAY, DATA GENERAL, DEC, HARRIS, HP, IBM, TEKTRONIX, SUN3, SILICON GRAPHICS, CELERITY
PIGS/DOGS/BOXER/PAFEC FE	APOLLO, DATA GENERAL, DEC, HARRIS, HP, ICL, NORSK DATA, PERKIN-ELMER, PRIME
PRIME MEDUSA/GNC/PDGS/SAMMIE	PRIME
PROREN 1 & 2	DEC, IBM6150, Nixdorf Targon, PRIME
ROMULUS-D	APOLLO DN-SERIES
SABRE-5000	HP9000
SYNTHAVISION	APOLLO, DATA GENERAL, DEC, IBM
TIPS-1	PRIME, HITAC, IBM, FACOM, DEC, UNIVAC
UNIGRAPHICS II/UNISOLIDS	DATA GENERAL, DEC, IBM

OTHER SYSTEMS ARE AVAILABLE IN VOLUME I

TABLE VII

AVAILABILITY OF THE PROGRAMS

ANSYS	*Contact:*	Mrs. C. Ketelaar, Swanson Analysis Systems Inc., Johnson Road, P.O. Box 65, Houston, PA 15342-0065, U.S.A.
	Telephone:	(412) 746-3304
	Telex:	510-690-8655
ANVIL-5000	*Contact:*	Mr. W. Betts, Manufacturing & Consulting Services Inc., 9500 Toledo Way, Irvine, California 92718-1895, U.S.A.
	Telephone:	(714) 951-8858
	Telex:	(910) 595-2790
AUTO-TROL SERIES 7000/5000	*Contact:*	Mr. B. Jones, Auto-Trol Technology Ltd., Neville House, 42/46 Hagley Road, Egbaston, Birmingham, B16 8PL, U.K.
	Telephone:	(021) 455-7277
	Telex:	335662

CADVANCE/SOLID VISION/ SYSTEM 25/PRISMA	*Contact:*	Ms. K. Kershaw, ISICAD Inc., 2411 West La Palma Avenue, P.O. Box 61022, Anaheim, California 92803-6122, U.S.A.
	Telephone:	(714) 821-2600
	Fax:	(714) 821-2529
DIAD/DGM/C-DATA/ C-PLAN/GNC/C-TAPE	*Contact:*	Mr. P. Drath, CADCentre Ltd., High Cross, Madingly Road, Cambridge, CB3 OHB, U.K.
	Telephone:	(0223) 314848
	Telex:	81420
IDEAS GEOMOD/ SUPERTAB/ SYSTAN/PRISMA	*Contact:*	Ms. A. Baker, Structural Dynamics Research Corp., CAE-International, York House, Stevenage Road, Hitchin, Hertfordshire, SG4 9DY, U.K.
	Telephone:	(0462) 5711
	Telex:	826580 SDRC UK

INTERGRAPH	*Contact:*	Mr. N. McCleod, Intergraph GB Ltd., Delta Business Park, Great Western Way, Swindon, SN5 7XP, U.K.
	Telephone:	(0793) 619999
MECHANICAL ADVANTAGE 1000/MA1500/GPX	*Contact:*	Ms. L.J. Popky, Cognition Inc., 900 Tech Park Drive, Billerica, MA 01821, U.S.A.
	Telephone:	(617) 667-4800
	Fax:	(617) 667-2155
PADL-2	*Contact:*	Miss T. Beloin, Cornell Programmable Automation, Cornell Manufacturing, Engineering and Productivity Program, Cornell University, 104A Kimball Hall, Ithaca, New York 14853-7501, U.S.A.
	Telephone:	(607) 255-2000

PALETTE	*Contact:*	Mr. M.J. McLean, Palette Systems Inc., Two Burlington Woods Park, Burlington, MA 01803, U.S.A.
	Telephone:	(617) 273-5660
	Telex:	948502
	Fax:	(617) 272-4660
PATRAN	*Contact:*	Mr. J. Newcomb, PDA Engineering, 2975 Red Hill Avenue, Costa Mesa, California 92626, U.S.A.
	Telephone:	(714) 540-8900
PIGS/DOGS/ BOXER/PAFEC FE	*Contact:*	Mr. I. McKenzie, Pafec Ltd., Strelley Hall, Main Street, Strelley, Nottingham, NG8 6PE, U.K.
	Telephone:	(0602) 292291
	Telex:	377764 PAFECG

PRIME MEDUSA/GNC PDGS/SAMMIE	*Contact:*	Mr. J. Bennett, Prime Computer (UK) Ltd., Mount Farm, Milton Keynes, MK1 1PT, U.K.
	Telephone:	(0908) 79673
	Telex:	826157 PRMBEDG
PROREN 1 & 2	*Contact:*	Dr. Fritsche or Dr. Harenbrock, Isykon Software GmbH., Kohlenstrabe 55, D-4630 Bochum 1, West Germany
	Telephone:	(0234) 45905-0
	Fax:	(0234) 4595-17
ROMULUS-D	*Contact:*	Mr. D. Pascoe, Evans & Sutherland, Interactive Systems Division, P.O. Box 8700, 580 Arapeen Drive, Salt Lake City, Utah 84108, U.S.A.
	Telephone:	(801) 582-5847
	Telex:	389492

SABRE-5000	*Contact:*	Mr. A. Popiolek, Gerber Systems Technology International - UK., G.S.T. House, 4 Priory Road, High Wycombe, Buckinghamshire, HP13 6SE, U.K.
	Telephone:	(0494) 442121
	Telex:	83651 GSTINTG
SYNTHAVISION	*Contact:*	MAGI - Mathematical Applications Group Inc., CAD/CAM Division, 3 Westchester Plaza, Elmsford, New York 10523, U.S.A.
	Telephone:	(915) 592-4646
TIPS	*Contact:*	Professor N. Okino, Faculty of Engineering, Hokkaido University, Sapporo, 060 Japan.
	Telephone:	711-2111

UNIGRAPHICS II/
UNISOLIDS

Contact:	Mr A.G. Haffender, McDonnell Douglas Information Systems Limited, Meirion House, Guildford Road, Woking, Surrey, GU22 7QH, U.K.
Telephone:	(04862) 26761
Telex:	859521

INTRODUCTION TO CAE SYSTEMS

1. Introduction

Over the last few years the engineering industry - and in particular mechanical engineering - has accelerated the implementation of Computer Aided Engineering Codes. Companies have been acquiring analysis, graphics and geometric modelling packages, each of them with their own hardware and software requirements. This tendency is to continue within the foreseeable future and is dictated by consideration of efficiency and productivity.

The design of mechanical components using computers commences with the description of the particular piece or structure under consideration applying a geometric modelling system. Once the piece is defined it can be displayed and different perspectives, cross-sections, juxtaposition with other parts, etc. can be studied on a graphics computer terminal.

The next stage is the analysis of the component under the type of force, thermal state, etc. under consideration. This is done using analysis codes such as Finite Elements or Boundary Elements. A pre-processing code is here needed to link the geometric module to the analysis package. These codes are of great practical importance in the design process and require specialised training.

Once the analysis has been completed the results need to be presented in a form which is easy to interpret. This is usually achieved by using a post-processing graphics package and special emphasis is nowadays laid on the use of interactive colour graphics.

The next stage is - or should be - an interactive process, during which the designer makes certain modifications to the computer model until the desired stress or temperature profiles are obtained. Finally the data file obtained can be plotted to obtain the blueprints required in the manufacturing process, or it can be used to operate a CIM or robotics facility. This process is diagramatically shown in figure 1.

This scheme may change in the foreseeable future if Artificial Intelligence is applied to CAE. Although Artificial Intelligence is associated with esoteric applications, the discipline is simply concerned with making computers more useful. It will affect CAE in so far as the code will be able to let the user know if the answers are reasonable or the results meaningful. To achieve this the programmer will be able to learn from experience and hence Artificial Intelligence incorporates data base management, optimization techniques and empirical information, most of which are not used in present data codes. This field of research is now very active although there are not yet major design codes which utilize these concepts.

2. Geometric Modelling

Geometric modelling deals with the formal description of an object in the computer. Two important aspects need to be taken into consideration when designing a geometric modelling system. The first aspect, the core of the system, is to define the fundamental components of the modeller, ie lines, edges, forms, surfaces, solid parts and how to operate with them in order to build up the desired shapes. The second aspect relates to general facilities of the system, such as the graphical pre and post-processing which are required in the interactive computer aided design process. These facilities include scaling, perspectives, geometric transformations such as rotations and translations, windowing, sectioning, colouring, dimensioning, library of predefined elements etc.

The proper geometric definition of the solid is the essential and basic step of the design process. After this, one can proceed with the analysis and impose the original design through a series of trials and iterations.

Geometric modelling codes can be classified in accordance with the techniques used, ie i) Wire framing; ii) Curve and surface modelling; iii) Solid modelling. Once the representation technique is chosen, it is desirable for the scheme to have some formal or informal properties. Among the formal, unambiguity is important, because it guarantees that only one object corresponds to a given representation. Other informal properties are computational efficiency and ease in the creation of the model.

Wire framing is the simplest of the modelling techniques and it was the most wide-spread technology before the development of the current solid modellers. It simply consists of modelling the objects by means of discrete points joined by straight or curved segments. This representation has the drawback of being ambiguous and it is not very precise. It has the advantage however, that it can be easily constructed and modified by the operator in an interactive way. Some of its formal deficiencies can b an obstacle in computer modelling and because of this, wire frames tend to be used nowadays as useful auxiliary tools to define geometries rather than as a basic technique.

Interpolation and approximation by means of curves are classical problems in mathematics. One can use several methods to fit a continuous curve to a given set of points in the plane or in space. Among these techniques are the use of cubic splines which guarantee curvature continuity and the application of parabolic blending, which

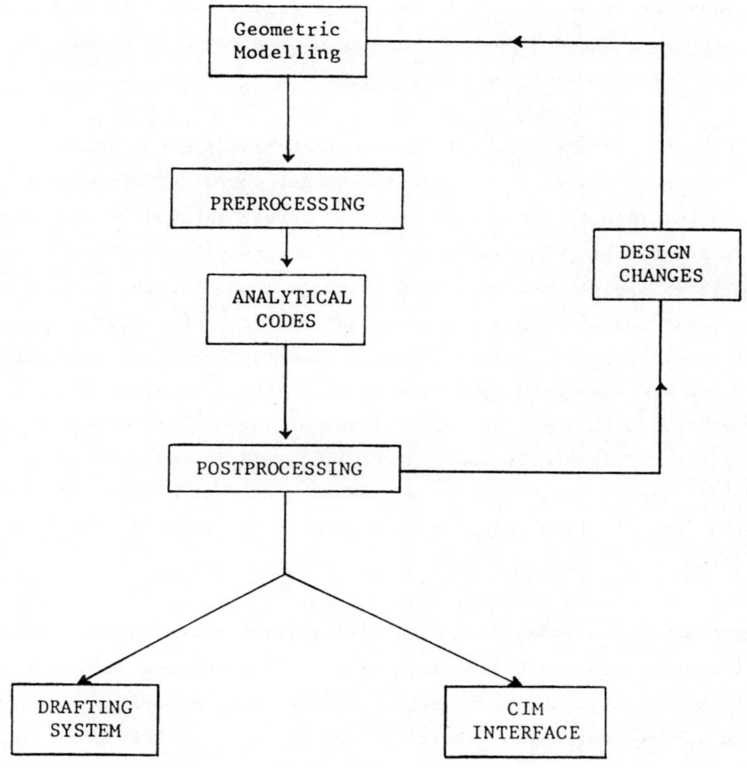

Figure 1 The Design Process

sets continuity of tangents only. Other methods exist that are designed to represent curves which are not required to pass through given points, but rather to adopt certain shapes which are controlled with the help of a special set of points named control points, such as the Bézier and B-spline curves, both of them polynomials. One important characteristic of a curve or family of curves is its local or global nature. By local it is meant that it is not necessary to recalculate the whole curve if a basic point is changed. On the other hand if a curve is global altering one point will modify the definition of the whole curve.

The construction of surfaces has some common features with the development of curves. Besides the classical translational and rotational surfaces, different surface models exist based on the idea of a tensor product of curves defined on the projection planes. Such products are the bi-cubic splines, Bézier and B-spline surfaces. In all these cases the surfaces are defined over a rectangular mesh. Surfaces can also be modelled as rectangular patches with some local characteristics, which gives more flexibility to the model. This property is particularly important when designing sculptured surfaces. There are also other models similar to the ones discussed but defined over triangular meshes. Coon's patches with different degrees of continuity are another family of surface models widely used in practice. It is interesting to point out that many of the families of basic functions used to construct curves and surfaces are identical with those families used to approximate the field functions studied in the analysis modules.

The most important CAE systems have progressively incorporated solid modelling facilities into their software. Working with solid modellers allows for formal properties to be taken into account better and permits to perform more advanced designs The most used schemes for solid modelling are: i) Cellular Decomposition; ii) Sweeping; iii) Boundary Representation (B-Rep) and iv) Constructive Solid Geometry (CSG).

Cellular Decomposition - In this case the solid is generated by fitting together disjointed small pieces, all of them without holes. Generally these pieces are simple cubes and they are chosen using the so-called 'octree decomposition'. This process consists of decomposing the solid into cubes with edges whose sizes are always proportional to a power of two of the minimal size. This minimal size is said to be the resolution of the representation. During the octree representation those cubes that belong to the solid are selected, improving the fitting between solid and representatio by decreasing the resolution. Octree decomposition is a systematic and comparatively simple process which is computationally very efficient.

Sweeping - This representation is based on a set of points creating an area by moving through the space along a certain line and sweeping a certain volume. The basic sweeping movements are rotation and translation. This method may also be used to generate surfaces when the initial set of points constitutes a line.

Boundary Representation (B-Rep) - The solid is represented by its boundaries, which are divided into no-overlapping faces or patches, joined at their edges. This representation is completed by associating to each face (planar or curved) the edges and any additional data required (such as the equation of the surface on which it lies). The method has been frequently used in computer graphics because it guarantees formal properties.

Constructive Solid Geometry (CSG) - This technique consists of describing complex structures by performing special version of the Boolean set operators (intersection, union and difference). Several simple solids named 'primitives' are used as initial generators, amongst them cuboids, spheres, cylinders, cones, etc. A CSG representative of a solid is based on a tree structure where non-terminal nodes represent operators and the leaves are the 'primitives'.

The above described methods are all non-ambigious and each of them is suitable for a certain range of applications. Hence solid modellers usually work with several of these schemes and the most appropriate can be used for a given task. For instance, B-Rep is adequate for handling graphics, but is not suitable for input data or to analyse interferences, for the latter, it being better to use CSG. Cell decomposition could be more appropriate to study problems with mass properties and for eventual finite element meshing. Because of all this, conversion algorithms are needed to pass from one scheme to the other. Unfortunately these algorithms are not always available or when they are they may be computationally inefficient.

Most of the systems based on solid modelling allow for complete automation in generating graphics, including facilities such as hidden line removal, perspectives, colour shading, etc. Other important facilities also included are integral properties calculation and static interference analysis.

These particular kinds of analyses are often included as a part of the solid modelling module, because they depend strongly on the nature of the modeller. Integral properties are surface, volume, mass, centre of gravity and inertial properties.

By static interference the following is meant. If one has a collection of solids, to check for static interference is to test for nullity, a solid defined as the union of all distinct pairwise regularized intersections of the solids in the initial collection. Dynamic interference checking, on the other hand, not only deals with the previous problem, but also checks faults for the possibility of the solid components to sweep through spatial trajectories. This problem is more difficult, but very important in fields like robotics or machines with moving parts, where collision problems may occur and must be prevented.

3. Pre-Processing

Pre-processing codes interface the solid modeller results to the actual analysis codes. During this stage the data to run the problem is prepared. Typically the solid will be discretized into surface - Boundary Elements (BE) - or volume - Finite Elements (FE) - elements, the loads and boundary conditions defined, material properties prescribed, etc. The pre-processor will prepare the necessary data file and should also check for consistency.

Most analysis programs - finite or boundary elements - have some form of pre-processing. Many solid modelling systems include also some mesh generation capability and, in these cases, interfaces can be built directly between the solid modellers and the FE/BE codes.

The complete automation of the mesh generation process for BE/FE codes starting from a general geometric model, has not yet been achieved. Hence the interfacing between solid modeller and meshing codes in the pre-processor usually requires manual intervention by the user in order to generate appropriate finite or boundary element meshes. This is done interactively using the results of the solid modeller which have been dumped into a data file.

Proper mesh generation facilities are an integral part of any well written finite or boundary element package and the types of interactive facilities offered by the codes are of fundamental importance to the designer. (For instance rotation, scaling, mirrore removal or addition of elements or nodes, hidden line removal, etc.) Many analysis programs have their own pre-processing facilities to generate discrete meshes.

4. Analysis

In this part we discuss the analysis of structural and field problems within the CAD process. The two most widely used numerical techniques are the Finite Element Method (FEM) and the Boundary Element Method (BEM). The choice of one technique over the other is usually dependent upon the type of problem under consideration as both present certain advantages or disadvantages as shown in Table 1. In many design applications, for which the problem can be considered linear, the BEM techniques offers a much more efficient solution in terms of man-time. Not only are meshes easily generated but, what is perhaps more important, design changes can easily be introduced as they do not involve a complete remeshing.

Other advantages of boundary elements are that it usually gives more accurate results in regions of stress or flux concentration and that the method is ideally suited to treat problems with infinite domains. The method can however, be cumbersome for certain non-linear applications for which internal points will be required. It is also difficult in many cases to vary the material parameters within the domain or to consider certain orthotropic material properties.

FEM, on the other hand, is difficult to use for problems extending to infinity for which special conditions are required at an outer edge. The method may give very poor results for certain problems with high gradient regions. The technique is attractive however if the material properties vary considerably in the domain or the problem is highly non-linear.

In spite of the substantial mathematical differences between the two techniques, the ideal analysis code should combine both methods. But in spite of many papers on this interesting topic, only a few operational special purpose codes exist which can carry out some form of BE/FE combination.

	ADVANTAGES	DISADVANTAGES
BEM	* Mesh required only on the boundary * High accuracy for concentration problems * Ideally suited for domains extending to infinity * It is simple to alter mesh in the design process	* Requires internal points for non-linear applications * Material parameters may be difficult to vary within the domains * Orthotropic material may not be easy to solve * Theory is mathematically more complex
FEM	* Same type of work for linear and non-linear problems * Material parameters are element dependent and easy to vary in the domain * Simple theory	* Requires special boundary conditions for domains extending to infinity * Surface and domain meshes are always needed * Meshes are difficult to alter once they are produced

TABLE 1 COMPARISON OF BEM AND FEM CODES

The user should be aware that BEM codes are mathematically more complex and consequently difficult to alter than FEM programs. This complexity which somewhat contributes to give more accurate results in well written BE codes, can easily produce poorly written programs as the BE method is very susceptible to errors when not using the right numerical technique. The recommendation, valid for FE as well as BE codes is to check your analysis programs before acceptance, using rigid body, constant strain and other simple tests. Do not take accuracy for granted!

The designer has nowadays a wide choice of finite element codes from those which can be used in powerful supercomputers down to others for user dedicated micros. Unfortunately, in spite of the importance of FE codes, few evaluations or comparisons of results have been published up to now. The few attempts to do this have largely failed. The problem is compounded by the difficulty of devising truly impartial tests as some codes perform better than others for specific cases. In addition, old versions of a code may behave badly and compare unfavourably with new ones.

The greatest advantage of boundary elements lies in its surface rather than volume representation. Contrary to finite elements, one only needs to discretize the surface of the solid under consideration. This greatly simplifies the data required to run a problem and the best property of the BEM from the designer's point of view. With computing costs still declining and engineers time becoming more expensive, the savings in engineer's time is far more significant than savings in machine time. Also, engineers welcome any advance that relieves them of the dreary task of data preparation and leaves them free to concentrate on more important tasks. Even more important is the fact that analysis invariably lies on the "critical path" in the design and production process and any tool which can shorten the "turn around" time through the design office, can bring forward the date of completion of the project. Although it is frequently stated that FEM generators can make FEM data as easy to prepare as BEM data, in the editor's opinion, mesh generation is still a problem. Industrial designers welcome the reduction in the order of mesh generation complexity associated with BEM and appreciate the flexibility offered by the non-continuous elements present in the code*.

5. Post-Processing

The presentation of analysis data in a form that is easy to interpret and of relevance to the designer is the function of post-processors. Although some programs have their own post-processors, the tendency in recent years has been to use more general codes. Normally the same software house offers a pre and a post-processing package. Practically all modern post-processing codes offer colour graphics capabilities. Colour is nowadays an important tool in engineering design, as it allows for an easy interpretation of the results and consequently shortens the time needed to complete the design. In addition to more complex codes, graphics packages also exist, which can be easily implemented within existing analysis modules.

---

* The interested reader is referred to BREBBIA, C. A. "Finite Element Systems Handbook" 3rd Edition, Springer-Verlag, Berlin and NY, 1985

Graphics are the main capabilities needed during post-processing but there are other aspects that can also be relevant. One is the capability to compare the latest designs with the tolerances affecting the final product. These tolerances will have great importance not only for the design but also during manufacture. Some systems also offer the facility to interface the design with numerical control machines. It is then possible to perform a simulation of the machining process, representing in the graphics system, the trajectory of tools and their effects in the solids to be manufactured. This representation may result in some changes in the design and permit to choose the best sequence for the production process.

Database systems are always underlying the CAE process. They are used to store during the whole process, the permanent information which completely defines the objects under design. It is desirable that their data adjust to a standard. IGES (Initial Graphics Exchange Specification) is an attempt to CAE standardization and supported by public and private institutions in the USA. IGES is a standard data format to design products as well as a format for the necessary information for their production. The data can then be created and stored in a CAE/CIM system but be independent of that particular system. This would allow a given design to be implemented on different CAE/CIM systems.

It is also important to mention the Graphical Kernel System (CGS) which is the first international standard system for programming computer graphics applications. This is presently a 2D graphics standard but its extension to 3D is being studied.

Some CAE systems offer drafting facilities as part of their post-processing. This may only allow the drafting of the mechanical or structural component developed by the geometric modeller or in certain cases includes the plotting of analytical results.

Many independent drafting packages are available for mechanical, civil and other engineering disciplines. They vary in degree of complexity and generality of use, but few of them present proper interfaces to the rest of the CAE codes. Here again the necessity of some type of standard is imperative.

6. Future Trends

The most marked trend in CAE is the integration of the different packages through interfaces and common databases. This is happening with a wide variety of codes and in a range of machines, ranging from supercomputers to single users micros. Current developments in communications and robotics may accelerate this process even further and help to integrate Design with Computer Manufacturing in a completely automatic process. The availability of powerful interactive graphics packages has improved the efficiency and productivity of the design engineer. Systems with these capabilities will continue to increase in popularity within the foreseeable future.

Artificial Intelligence is a topic usually associated with the more esoteric applications of computer science, but has numerous applications in engineering design. Future CAE codes should investigate topics such as; "Are the answers reasonable?", "Is the solution meaningful?", "Is the model a fair representation of the system?" etc. It is easy to envisage that in the next few years some of these AI capabilities will be incorporated in future CAE codes.

The Editors

ANSYS®

Swanson Analysis Systems Inc., U.S.A

ANSYS® is a general purpose, finite element computer program for engineering analysis which is developed, marketed, and supported by Swanson Analysis Systems, Inc. in Houston, PA, USA. ANSYS has the ability to solve a wide range of structural electro-magentic, and heat transfer problems.

ANSYS AND CAD

The ANSYS program contains preprocessing, solution, and postprocessing phases for model preparation, solution, and results evaluation. During the preprocessing phase, the analyst creates the finite element model and specifies components needed for the subsequent analysis. The ANSYS preprocessor contains extensive solid modeling capabilities. To facilitate model generation, the program separates the functions of geometry and boundary condition definition and the creation of the finite element mesh. Model geometry is first described to the program by the user. The resulting model is then meshed by the ANSYS program by calculating node locations and element connectivity. Meshing features such as splines, intersecting lines or areas, fillets between intersecting lines, and automatic meshing using 6-node triangles for areas and 10-node tetrahedra for volumes is available. As the analyst inputs data which defines the model, a database is created. Information describing nodes, elements, and loads, for example, is stored and can be manipulated as required.

ANSYS is also able to accept a finite element model from many CAD systems and allow modification of it, if necessary. A translator utility converts a coded ouput file from various well-known CAD/CAM programs into an input file for the ANSYS preprocessor, PREP7. Once the converted file is read into PREP7, all PREP7 capabilities, including additional model generation, data modification, and plotting, are available. The ability of ANSYS to interface with different CAD systems makes it a powerful analysis tool. ANSYS interfaces with these CAD systems: ANVIL-5000, Auto-trol, CADDS FEM, FEMAS, GRAFTEX, IGES 2.0. INTERGRAPH, PATRAN, SUPERTAB, PRIME MEDUSA, UNIGRAPHICS, and COMPUTERVISION. Some systems not listed here have their own translators to ANSYS, in which case the individual software developers should be contacted for further information. The ANSYS program also contains an additional command which causes certain geometric data to be written to a coded file in the IGES format. This is an important feature for CAD interfaces.

INDUSTRIES AND APPLICATIONS

ANSYS has been used worldwide for over 10 years in a wide variety of industries:

* Power - nuclear, transmission towers, turbines

* Transportation - automotive components (brakes, door, suspension systems), aircraft vibration
* Farm equipment - tractor design
* Consumer products - diswasher, stereo speaker
* Computer Manufacturing - disk drive, electronic packaging
* Leisure/sports - skis, football helmet
* Medical - artificial heart valve
* Civil construction - buildings, bridges, tunnels
* Aerospace - Gyro packaging design, turbine blade, jet engine
* Electronics - Electromechanical components, chip carrier, ceramic DIP with chip

HARDWARE REQUIREMENTS

The minimal hardware configuration typically includes:

Floating point in hardware
2 MB Main Memory (more is desirable)
150 MB Disc (more is desirable)
Tape drive (or distribution media)
Printer
Graphic terminal

ANSYS currently supports over 20 types of computer hardware, including mainframes, minis, workstations and microcomputers. In the near future, ANSYS will support additional computers - some of which will be micros. A wide variety of plotters and graphics devices are also supported. A 1-2 page FORTRAN source program to link with plotters is available. ANSYS is distributed on either floppy disk or magnetic tape, depending on the computer hardware.

ANSYS DESCRIPTION

ANSYS employs the finite element analysis (FEA) method for the solutions. The FEA method is a mathematical technique for constructing approximate solutions to boundary value problems. The method involves dividing the solution domain into a finite number of subdomains, or elements, and constructing an approximate solution over the collection of elements. The elements connect at points called nodes, at which continuity of the approximating functions between elements is maintained. FEA programs are general purpose in that they apply the technique to a wide variety of scientific and engineering boundary value problems. Most major civil and mechanical engineering design firms use FEA programs as a design tool since they are very accurate and cost-effective. An engineer can analyze an object and make predictions about its performance before the first model is manufactured.

The ANSYS element library contains over 70 distinct elements. Each element may simulate several different theories as special element options.

Structural:

* 2- and 3-D beams and pipes
* axisymmetric with axisymmetric loading
* axisymmetric with nonaxisymmetric loading
* shells and plates
* 2- and 3-D solids
* interface/gaps
* immersed pipe with wave loading
* 3-D reinforced composite/concrete
* crack tip
* nonlinear spring
* composite shells
* 2- and 3-D hyperelastic (rubber) solids

Heat Transfer:

* compatible structural elements for thermal-stress analyses
* conducting bars, areas, and volumes
* convection links
* radiation links
* surface effect element

Electromagnetic:

* 3-D scalar potential with nonlinear BH curves
* 2-D vector potential with nonlinear B-μ curves

Fluid:

* contained fluid, 2-D and 3-D
* incompressible fluid flow

Because ANSYS is one integrated package, users have access to easy-to-use pre and postprocessors, as well as many analytic capabilities. Routines are available for facilitating data input, including model generation. A complete set of graphics provides geometry and loading verification in addition to results interpretation. ANSYS can be used in interactive and batch modes of operation. These features, many of which result in cost savings, are discussed in further detail in the following paragraphs.

The input data for the ANSYS program has been designed to make it as easy as possible to define the analysis to the computer. A preprocessor contains powerful mesh generation capability as well as being able to define all other analysis data (real constants, material properties, constraints, loads, etc.). Geometry plotting is available for all elements in the ANSYS library, including isometric, perspective, section, edge and hidden-line plots of three-dimensional structures. ANSYS also generates substructures (or superelements). These substructures may be stored in a library file for use in other analyses. Substructuring portions of a model can result in considerable computer-time savings for nonlinear analyses.

ANSYS data may include parametric input. By varying some data items, while holding others constant, the user can conveniently input a series of repeating commands. This may be used to create models for design studies. Anticipated variations of the geometry are defined as parameters. Each solution then requires changing only one or two items instead or dozens.

ANSYS uses the wave-front (or "frontal"), direct solution method for the system of simultaneous linear equations developed by the matrix displacement method, and gives results of high accuracy in a minimum of computer time. The program has the ability to solve large structures. There is no "band width" limitation in the analysis definition; however, there is a "wave-front" restriction. The "wave-front" restriction depends on the amount of memory available for a given problem. Up to 3000 degrees of freedom on the wave-front can be handled in a large core. With virtual memory machines and a virtual equation solver in ANSYS, very large analyses can be solved. There is no limit to the number of elements used in an analysis.

Postprocessing routines are available for algebraic modification, differentiation, and integration of calculated results. Root-sum-square operations may be performed on seismic modal results. Response spectra may be generated from dynamic analysis results. Results from various loading modes may be combined for harmonically loaded axisymmetric structures. Post routines also plot distorted geometries, stress contours, safety factor contours, temperature contours, mode shapes, time history graphs, and stress-strain curves.

Graphics capabilities provide many options for verification of model geometry and loads. Windowing on a model can be done by limiting included nodes, included elements, or included geometric distances. The geometry may be limited in any defined coordinate system. Surfaces and defined coordinate systems may be plotted. All boundary conditions (displacements, forces, moments, pressures, and master degrees of freedom) may be displayed on element or node plots. Shrinking elements helps the user to verify that no elements are missing. Element, node, material, type, or member property numbering can be shown on plots of the model. Section views through three dimensional structures, plots of model edges, and hidden line plots are all available for further checking of model geometry and for presentation in reports. ANSYS graphics also provide many plot display options such as multiple windows on one screen, choice of focus point, varying distance from object, perspective, and zoom. Color graphics is available in pre and postprocessing. These color plots help interpret both model geometry and results.

All portions of ANSYS can be operated in either an interactive or a batch mode. When running interactively, the user can take advantage of on-line documentation which provides an explanation for each command at the terminal as well as immediate graphic displays to verify the model and correct input errors. Analyses can be done efficiently by creating the model interactively, obtaining the solutions in a batch mode, and interpreting the results interactively.

The following analysis types are available in ANSYS:
Static - used to solve for displacements, strains, stresses, and forces in structures under applied loads. Elastic, plastic, creep, and swelling material behaviors are available. Stress stiffening and large deflection effects may be included. Bilinear elements such as interfaces (with or without friction) and cables can be used.

Eigenvalue Buckling - used to calculate critical loads and buckling mode shapes for linear bifurcation buckling based on the stress state from a previous static analysis.

Mode Frequency - used to solve for natural frequencies and mode shapes of a structure. Stresses and displacements may be obtained by using the displacement, velocity, acceleration, or force spectrum analysis or modal PSD options. A spectrum may represent a seismic loading.

Nonlinear Transient Dynamic - used to determine the time history solution of the response of a structure to a known force, pressure, and/or displacement forcing function. Stiffness, mass and damping matrices vary with time and may be functions of the displacements. Friction, plasticity, large deflection, and other nonlinearities may be included. An automatic time step procedure is available.

Linear Transient Dynamic - used to determine the time hisotry solution of the response of a linear elastic structure to a known forcing function. A quasi-linear option includes interfaces (gaps) within the structure or to ground.

Harmonic Response - used to determine the steady-state response of a linear elastic structure to a set of harmonic loads of known frequency and amplitude. Complex displacements of amplitudes and phase angles can be input and calculated for output. Stresses may be calculated at specified frequencies and phase angles.

Heat Transfer - used to solve for the steady-state or transient temperature distribution in a body. Conduction, convection, radiation, and internal heat generation may be included. The calculated temperature distribution may then be used as input to a structural analysis. Other options include phase change, nonlinear flow in porous media, thermal-electric and thermal-fluid flow. The heat transfer analysis can also be used to solve many classes of analogous field equation problems such as torsion of shafts, ideal fluid circulation, pressurized membranes, and electrostatics.

Magnetics - used to determine steady-state electromagnetic fields and magnetic forces with either the 2-D vector potential or the 3-D scalar potential method. Linear permanent magnets can be modeled and coil, bar, and arc current sources can be specified. Electric-magentic field coupling is available so that other current-carrying members of arbitrary geometry can be modeled. Nonlinear materials can be modeled.

Substructures - used to assemble a group of linear elements into one "element" (a superelement) to be used to another ANSYS analysis. It is advantageous to use substructures to isolate the linear portion of a structure within an iterative solution.

ANSYS is an integral part of the overall CAD environment. It can provide information about physical structures - information which is essential to proper design decisions. Engineers may select optimum materials and construction designs which are indicated by the analysis results and incorporate these modifications early in the design cycle. ANSYS users can simulate two- and three-dimensional mdoels including surfaces, shells, springs, beams, and others. These models can be subjected to proposed loading and the resulting stress effects are then available for detailed study.

ANVIL-5000®

Manufacturing and Consulting Services Inc.,
U.S.A.

1. INTRODUCTION

ANVIL-5000™ is a 3-D computer-aided design and drafting/manufacturing system for mechanical engineering that integrates drafting, wireframe, surface and solids modeling, finite-element mesh, and numerical-control (both 3- and 5-axis) using the same data structure and interactive interfaces for all functions.

Features

* Flexible Graphic Interaction, either interactive or written
* Geometry Generation, from which part designs are created
* Geometry Manipulation and Analysis, used in building complex designs
* View and Scale Manipulation, through graphic CRTs
* Families-of-Parts support
* Drafting functions, automatic tools for the CRT user
* Numerical Control functions, to generate NC tapes
* File Management, tailored to CAD/CAM user needs
* Ongoing Enhancements, based on user input

2. FLEXIBLE GRAPHIC INTERACTION

ANVIL-5000 users may communicate with the workstation or host computer in either of two ways:

* Interactive graphics - through procedures that turn CRT screens into drawing boards. Automatic graphic functions include scaling, zoom mirroring, translation, duplication and rotation.
* Graphics programming - through GRAPL, the ANVIL-5000 graphic definition language. GRAPL lets engineers code geometric definitions offline from the computer, then input them for display and processing. So, design engineering teams can carry on simultaneous inter-active-CRT and manual design activities - all supported by the same CAD/CAM software.

3. GEOMETRY GENERATION

ANVIL-5000 users begin the design process with a full arsenal of geometric elements, including:

* Points
* Lines
* Chamfers
* Arcs
* Fillets
* Conics
* Planar splines
* Offset curves
* N-gons
* Triangles
* Rectangles
* Hexagons
* Strings
* Composite curves
* Surface of revolution
* Tabulated cylinder

* Ruled Surface
* Developable surface
* Curve mesh surface
* Curve driven surface
* Improved Coon's patch surface
* Normal offset surface
* Composite surface
* 3-D splines
* Analytic solids
* Sweeps solids
* Surface-based solids

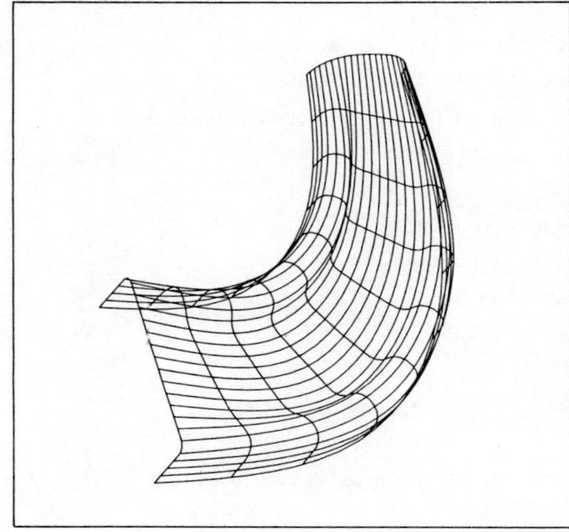

The extended geometric elements of ANVIL-5000 include curves, surfaces and solids. This is a curve mesh surface, a surface composed of an intersecting family of curves.

4. GEOMETRY MANIPULATION AND ANALYSIS

From these elements, ANVIL-5000 builds complex designs with manipulation and grouping options, including:

* 2-D and 3-D translation
* 2-D and 3-D rotation
* Scaling
* Duplication
* Grouping
* Patterns
* Mirroring

Part designs may be verified, or studied, through:

* Parameter verification
* 2-D section analysis
* 3-D part analysis
* Curve analysis

Parameters analyzed include perimeters, areas, moments of inertia, centers of gravity, radii of gyration, polar radii and polar inertia.

Since no single design automation package can hope to meet all application needs, ANVIL-5000 includes two interfaces for outside software:

* Pre-packages software interfaces for popular finite-element analysis programs. These analysis packages tend to have broad application across a large number of industries.
* Also, there is an ANVIL universal file format with sufficient documentation to allow the users to format the output as needed.

5. VIEW AND SCALE MANIPULATION

Since ANVIL-5000 provides many view and scale options, no restrictions exist on a work's dimensions and any part may be scaled to fit the display screen. Zoom and windowing capabilities let the user magnify any desired area, to interactively add or modify design details.

To provide a powerful "What - if" design capability, ANVIL-5000 can display up to 32 simultaneous 3-D views of a construct, where changes to one view automatically update the others. This can be turned off, so that each view is treated as a separate entity.

Other view and scale manipulation features include:

* Automatic scaling
* Controllable view placement and size
* Zoom (entire screen on selected field)
* Isometric and true perspective
* Local coordinate systems

6. FAMILIES-OF-PARTS

ANVIL-5000 supports creation and use of part libraries based on:

* GRAPL programs
* Stored patterns and templates
* Parts merged from existing parts

7. DRAFTING

Automated drafting functions include:

* True 3-D drafting
* Modal control (text size, arrow size, text angle, decimals, etc)
* Cross hatching
* Horizontal dimensions
* Vertical dimensions
* Parallel dimensions
* Angular dimensions
* Circular dimensions
* Diameter dimensions
* Thickness dimensions
* Automatic redimensioning
* Notes
* Labels
* Centerline marking
* Entity modification
* Balloon callouts
* User-defined symbols
* User-created curve fonts
* True position tolerance symbols
* User-generated drafting standards

ANVIL-5000 lets users create their own drafting standards and push-button-select any of eight national and international notation conventions including ANSI, BSI, ISO and JIS.

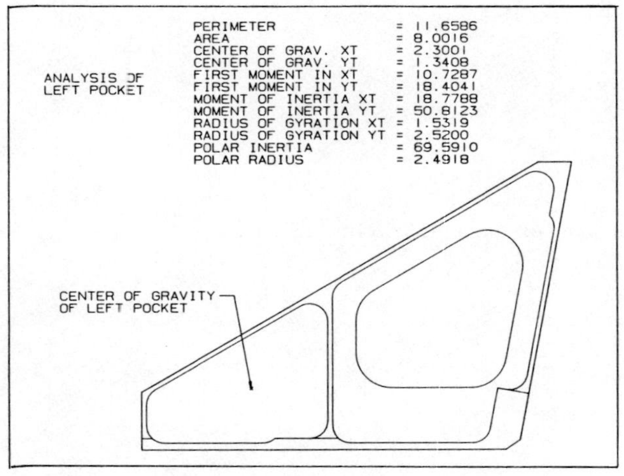

After the initial design has been created, 2-D section analysis calculates such properties as areas, perimeters, moments of inertia, and other values as necessary for a complete analysis of the region.

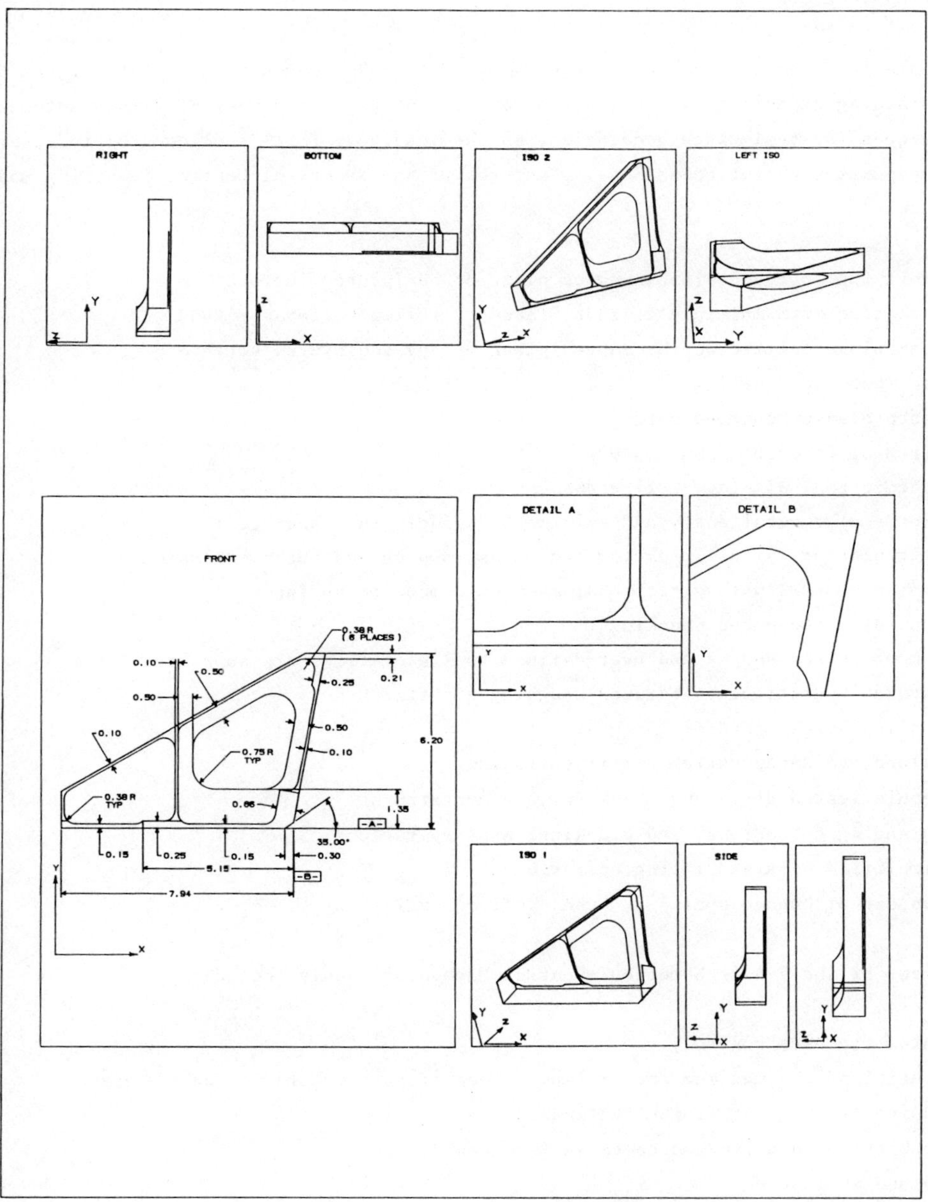

Powerful viewing and scaling functions help the designer by presenting different views simulataneously on the screen and in an orderly manner. Here each view has been given its own border, coordinate axes and identifying titles.

8. NUMERICAL CONTROL

The numerical-control machining modules of ANVIL-5000 represent the state of the art in machining capabilities. Users can take advantage of a number of highly automated techniques for tool-patch generation, or they can have total tool control in interactive point-to-point operations. Features of the Numerical-Control Machining module include:

* Profiling to fixed plane, canted plane or sculptured surface
* Pocketing with multiple islands, laced or follow collapse method
* Pocketing to fixed depth, canted plane or any sculptured surface
* Lace/Non-Lace cutting
* Postprocessor command entry
* Circular interpolation support
* Dynamic tool display - all views
* Choice of several entry and exit methods including tangential (circular or spiral), angular including ramping and curve extension
* Choice of tool path directions, even on composite surfaces
* Sophisticated gouge checking
* Common cutter shapes and user-defined tool geometries are supported
* Automatic distinction between roughing and finish cuts
* Scallop height control
* Island avoidance during 3-axis surfacing
* Sophisticated drive and check surface containment
* Threading, contouring, and blanking lathe operations
* Simplified 5-axis drilling operations
* Support of canned cycles and user-defined cycles

Features of the 5-Axis Numerical-Control Machining module include:

* Automatic bite control
* Control of the maximum and minimum number of cut vectors per path segment
* Choice of rough or finish cutting
* Sophisticated drive and check surface containment
* Island avoidance
* ZT constraints
* 5-axis swarf cutting
* 5-axis end cutting
* 5-axis grooving on a sculptured surface

9. FILE MANAGEMENT

ANVIL-5000 appears to the user as a pictorial graphic system, but the heart of the system is its mathematical database. The database includes libraries and files which are accessed for information storage and retrieval of entire parts, patterns, templates, configuration information and similar data. These may be stored on a system-wide basis or may be associated with individual users in the User Technology library. Items within these user libraries can be saved, restored, listed and deleted. When a work session is initiated, data stored in these different files can be combined, modified and manipulated to develop new parts.

10. ONGOING ENHANCEMENTS

The MCS Software Users Group feeds the company users' own requests for ANVIL-5000 enhancements. Much of ANVIL-5000's present capabilities have stemmed from the ideas of design engineer/users.

Users Group subcommittees determine the direction of future ANVIL enhancements, based on members' day-to-day user experience.

11. SERVICE/SUPPORT/RELIABILITY

ANVIL-5000 is sold and supported by Manufacturing and Consulting Services, Inc. (MCS). The company was founded in 1971 by Dr. Patrick J. Hanratty, a veteran of 15 years in CAD/CAM system design. A leading worldwide supplier of integrated CAD/CAM systems, MCS employes a staff of experts in design, drafting and manufacturing disciplines... from aerospace, automotive, heavy equipment, computer and electronics industries.

For its ANVIL-5000 software, the MCS Customer Service Organisation provides both normal and critical "hotline" maintenance services. MCS also aids customers with emergency software enhancements to meet CAD/CAM production schedules.

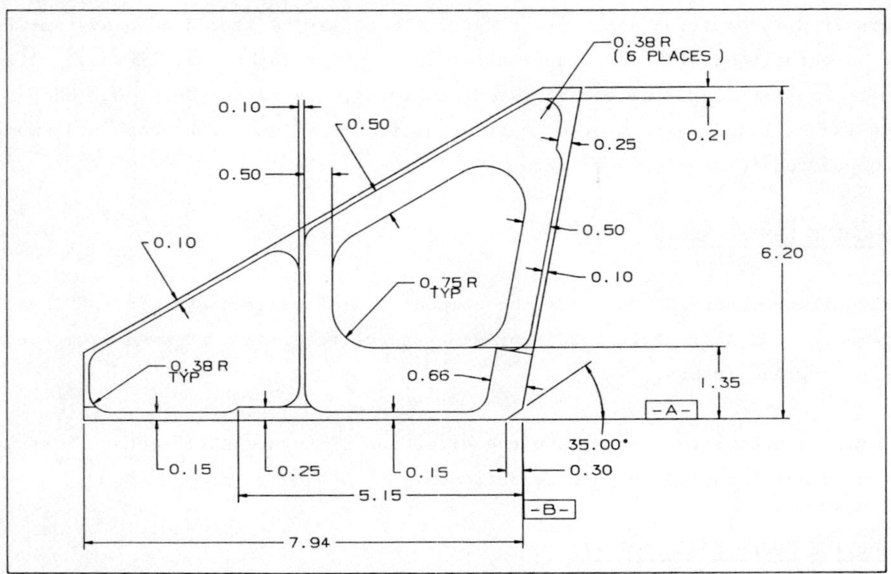

ANVIL-5000 provide an extensive array of drafting functions to generate any desired annotation.

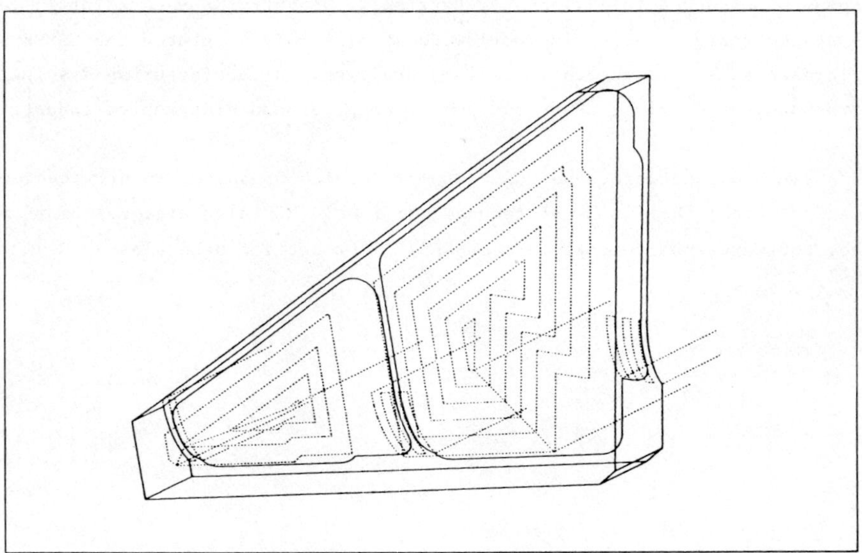

The final step is to produce the numerical control tool paths for producing the part. Here the dotted-lines represent the center of a pocket tool path, and the tool paths for the three contoured surfaces of the aircraft rib.

AUTO-TROL® SERIES 7000/5000

Auto-Trol Technology Ltd., U.S.A.

GENERAL INTRODUCTION

Auto-trol has been a developer and manufacturer of computer graphics systems for twenty years. More recently, CAD/CAM software and hardware have been included in Auto-trol's product line.

Auto-trol® software can be used to solve problems related to the architectural, construction, mechanical design and manufacturing industries. It is possible to transform an idea into a three-dimensional design, analyze it, re-work it, and then produce it as a finished part. The model of the product is built within the data base. Added to this modelling capacity are various engineering and analysis application packages, including finite element analysis and discretization, flat pattern development, nesting and numerical control programming. There are also comprehensive application packages. Facility managers can forecast space requirements, perform space planning and manage personnel and physical resources. Architects and designers can create floor plans, ceiling plans, and preliminary mechanical, electrical and plumbing layouts; plant designers can generate electrical schematics, P&IDs, and dimensioned drawings for isometric and orthographic piping as well as complete material take-offs. Structural engineers can build, analyze and code check structural models, and graphics artists can generate multiple view technical illustrations automatically.

Auto-trol offers a wide selection of CAD/CAM hardware products. Centralized and decentralized processing, highly advanced workstations with colour and monochromatic displays, and a wide range of peripherals are available to fit the needs, from an independent architect to a large manufacturer.

The Advanced Graphics Workstation (AGW) is a low cost, stand alone 32-bit system, with its own dedicated CPU allowing work alone or linked to high speed local area network, exchanging data and sharing resources. Auto-trol's hardware and software also runs on the GPX and VAXstation 2000 family of 32-bit processors.

THE SOFTWARE

Auto-trol's CAD/CAM software is classified in two series, named 7000 and 5000. In both series, there is an "Advanced Graphics Software" and a set of applications software packages.

A description of series 7000 and 5000 software will be given here.

SERIES 7000

Advanced Graphics Software

Introduction

Auto-trol's Series 7000 Advanced Graphics Software is a geometric modelling system which provides a set of tools for the graphic development of 2 or 3-dimensional product models. These models can be used to conduct design studies, generate documentation and prepare numerical control (NC) programs. By using 32-bit computers, Series 7000 provides complete, easy-to-use CAD/CAM capabilities for product fabrication.

Beginning with the first rough sketches, engineers and designers build a product model within the data base. The model can be displayed in multiple views, rotated, mirrored, and examined from all angles with the touch of a few buttons.

Once the product has been designed, Series 7000 can be interfaced with numerous third party software programs for engineering analyses such as solids modelling and finite element modelling and analysis. And Series 7000 allows the design data base to be tied directly to the manufacturing cycle. Manufacturing engineers can design machinery, tooling, piece parts, and assemblies; and by using Auto-trol's application packages they can develop flat patterns, nest parts, and generate numerical control parts programs. All personnel can be confident they are working with information that is current and accurate, because any changes made in the design are immediately incorporated as part of the product model within the data base.

These capabilities add up to dramatic increases in productivity and design accuracy. While the quality of the product is being improved, the time required to bring that product to market is greatly reduced.

Operator/System Communcation

Designers, analysts, drafters and manufacturing engineers can interact with Series 7000 using their knowledge of design principles. Although no computer programming experience is needed, the system can be manipulated at a very sophisticated level.

- For a casual user, menus and user prompts that appear on the screen guide the operator through the design process.
- For an experienced user who is familiar with the sequence of menus, the menu display can be turned off so the operator can immediately activate the particular menu needed.

- Design productivity is enhanced by Eagle, a powerful graphics language that provides versatillity in the command structure to accommodate various engineering design and documentation requirements.
- A keystroke logging feature allows the user to record all keystrokes used to design, draft, analyze or machine parts. The logs can be replayed using different parameters, thus providing an effective tool for family of parts programming.
- The menu function buttons on the workstation can be easily defined or modified by the user, which allows Series 7000 capabilities to be adapted to special requirements.
- FORTRAN programs can be integrated with the graphics software through an Applications Interface that allows users to develop their own application programs and to integrate third party software.

Common Data Base

The first step in developing a truly integrated engineering and manufacturing environment with Series 7000 is to build a comprehensive parts data base. As parts are designed on the system, they are stored in a common data base in exact mathematical form. From this data base, design information can be extracted and passed to all departments in the company. The data base can also be protected by security features so individual users need authorization to access part and/or design information.

The part is the basic element of the data base. Once a part has been fully defined and described, it can be combined with other parts into subassemblies. These subassemblies can then be combined into products.

The part definition includes the wire frame geometry and/or surface geometry that make up the graphic, 3-D representation of the part. Also, the part definition can include information such as drafting and dimensioning, attributes for bill of material extraction, etc.

Communications

Parts data base information can be distributed to all areas of a manufacturing company via various communications networks provided by Auto-trol.

- The workstations can be directly connected to a host computer (shared processor).
- The stations can communicate remotely with the host computer via telecommunications.
- Distributed, stand-alone workstations can communicate with one another through a high speed local area network or to a remote facility via remote communications

MODEL VISUALIZATION

In addition to providing flexible capabilities for geometric construction and manipulation, Series 7000 offers several features which aid users in visualizing the model.

Automatic Scaling

If the user desires, all information is scaled automatically to fit the display screen as design geometry is defined.

Single and Multi-View Windowing

A selected area of a drawing may be magnified so that details can be easily created, modified, and viewed. The display becomes a window providing access to an essentially unbounded work area. All data outside of this window is excluded automatically.

Up to 32 views may be displayed simultaneously, allowing the operator to monitor work in progress from multiple perspectives. Graphic data entered or edited manually in the work view is projected automatically into all other views being displayed. The user has control over the types of views and their arrangement on the screen. The system creates eight standard views (front, bottom, left side, etc.) and enables the user to create an additional 1016 views by utilizing an auxiliary view creation process. This allows the user's viewpoint of the object to be repositioned around any axis or line of sight.

Blanking

As model construction becomes larger or congested, it is often advantageous to suppress (blank) the display of entities not currently needed.

Drawing Layout

To create a final production drawing from the 3-D model, Series 7000 gives users the powerful ability to define selected views and position them relative to each other. The entire screen is then like a 2-D acetate overlay on which the user can perform all drafting functions, even across the window boundaries of the views that have been defined. After a drawing has been created, any changes to the model are automatically reflected in each of the views contained in the drawing. Additionally, any dimensions which were changed may be automatically regenerated to display the correct values in the new location.

SYSTEMS INTERFACES

Eagle

Eagle is a high-level programming language which allows the user to access all capabilities within Series 7000. Eagle programs may be edited to prompt and accept user input while they are being executed. Eagle output may be a geometric model created parametrically, a solution to calculations or design rules, or an output to a formatted text file.

Eagle provides total versatility to accommodate various engineering design and documentation requirements. One customer may use Eagle to graphically study kinematics and dynamics in machine design. Another may use Eagle for vibration and heat transfer analysis.

Based on PASCAL format, Eagle allows Series 7000 users to:

- Develop their own application programs
- Utilize existing PASCAL programs
- Create family of parts programming
- Program within Series 7000 software
- Employ flexibility in entity construction
- Utilize the system debugging capability

Keystroke Logging

Keystroke logging allows the user to record and play back all the graphics commands that have been entered during a session with Series 7000. The resulting file can then be used to automatically reenter the command strings during later sessions. The file can be called up through the operating system and edited with the standard text edit commands.

The logging capability is used to facilitate any repetitive operation such as pattern creation and insertion, attribute creation, bill of material extraction, drafting, or numerical control macro creation. It can also be used as a journal file or an audit trail.

Keystroke logging is especially useful when combined with the data capture and on-line variable storage and calculation features. These functions allow the user to capture values and assign them to names which can be used as variables during geometric construction.

Applications Interface

With the Applications Interface, Series 7000 offers a powerful link to any existing FORTRAN program and gives the user access to callable routines within the graphics software. This enables users to access third party software, offers flexibility for custom tailoring applications software and protects the user's software investment by allowing the use of existing FORTRAN programs. CAD/CAM programming is simplified because the interface eliminates the need to have knowledge of the internal graphics software structure.

IGES

IGES (Initial Graphics Exchange Specification) is a neutral file format that allows the exchange of data between CAD/CAM systems from different manufacturers. Auto-trol supplies IGES pre and post processors which support the exchange of numerous geometric and non-geometric entities.

ATTRIBUTE MANAGEMENT

Attributes within Series 7000 are nongraphic information attached to specific geometric entities, i.e. part number, weight, cost, material, etc. There are no limits to the number of attributes that may be assigned, nor to the number of entities within a graphics file.

Series 7000 Attribute Management Sub-System allows the user to produce assembly lists, indented bills of material (BOM), and exploded bills of material easily from the same graphic files. The Attribute Sub-System produces an ASCII file containing the bill of materials information as well as graphic representation within the graphics file. BOM data is then available for transfer to material requirements planning, process planning, and data processing systems.

The interrogate mode of attribute management lets the user look at any selected subset of all the attributes on a drawing. Factors, such as "less than", "greater than or equal to", "equal to", etc. are available for defining subsets of attributes. In addition, the interrogate mode can identify minimum or maximum values of attributes, and will display the total number of all common attributes.

GEOMETRIC CONSTRUCTION AND MANIPULATION

Geometric Entity Types

Series 7000 offers a complete set of tools for the construction and modification of points, lines, curves, and surfaces. Included are fourteen methods of point definition, twelve methods of line definition, and eleven methods of arc, circle, and fillet definition. The user can quickly define and construct the following entities:

Simple Constructions

- Splines
- Offset Splines
- Strings
- Polygons
- Ellipses
- Hyperbolas
- Parabolas
- General Conics
- Loft Conics
- Rho Conics

Curve Types

- 3D-Splines
- Surface Edge Curves
- Surface Intersection Curves
- Draft or Machine Curves
- Composite Curves
- Vectors

Surface Types

- Planes
- Composite Surfaces
- Surfaces of Revolution
- Tabulated Cylinders
- Curve Driven Surfaces
- Offset Surfaces
- Ruled Surfaces
- Developable Surfaces
- Curve Mesh Surfaces
- Fillet Surfaces
- Projected Surfaces

3-D Surfaced Figures

- Spheres
- Cylinders
- Toroids
- Cones
- Hexahedrons
- Ellipsoids

Special features permit modification of designs through trimming, stretching, and compression of lines and figures.

Levels

Designers have long been aware of the advantages of maintaining drawing information on different levels, much as a drafter might use different sheets of clear mylar paper to segregate parts of a drawing. This allows the drawing to be viewed as a whole or individually by sheet(s). Series 7000 not only allows the user to assign and manipulate various drawing components on up to 1024 different levels but it also enables the user to maintain auxiliary information on selected levels. Auxiliary information could include things such as drafting, machine tool paths, engineering analysis results or bills of material.

User Selection Techniques

Series 7000 gives the user a choice of eight methods to use when selecting graphic entities for manipulation such as mirroring, grouping or patterns:

- Single Entity
- Chain of Contiguous Entities
- All Entities Inside a User-Defined Region
- All Entities Outside a User-Defined Region
- All Entities Displayed
- All Entities on a Range of Levels
- All Entities in a Range of Colours
- All Entities in a Range of Fonts

These selection techniques give users the flexibility they need to manipulate design elements in the fastest, most efficient way possible.

Mirroring

A mirroring technique in Series 7000 aids designers in constructing symmetrical figures. Geometric entities may be reflected about a line as an axis. Thus, half of a figure can be created, and by mirroring that half the whole figure can be generated.

Arrays

Series 7000 allows mass generation of geometric entities in either rectangular or circular arrays. Arrays handle numerous geometric entity types including groups and other arrays. After an array has been generated, it is possible to modify the resulting entity. The user can explode elements from arrays so they may be modified individually.

Translation, Rotation, and Duplication

If a designer needs to move a set of entities within a drawing, the three-dimensional translate feature may be employed. Rotation capabilities facilitate manipulation of planar and nonplanar entities about a vertical, horizontal or normal axis. Both translation and rotation allow scaling as an automatic procedure. The duplication capability eliminates redundant effort in generating a large number of entities. The designer may have components produced in mass by initializing a combination of "step and repeat" or "do n times" operations. In addition, Series 7000's dynamic shape dragging allows the user to visualize the placement of figures before entering them into the model.

Grouping

Since a single entity can be manipulated much faster and easier than numerous individual entities, a special grouping feature allows geometric entities to be gathered together for treatment as a single entity. The grouped entities will retain their geometric properties (line definition, dimensioning etc.) as well as their relative position within the group.

Drafting

The drafting capability provides vertical, horizontal, parallel, angular and circular dimensioning, complete with semiautomatic functions such as text justification and angle control, dimension calculation from single entity selection, and datum line dimensioning. The system allows drafting in both English and/or metric units, and also provides a complete set of units identification in both English and metric dimensioning standards.

Automatic crosshatching can be performed within a main border and outside of any islands, if necessary. There are eight standard crosshatch materials, and the user can define the spacing and angle of the pattern.

The user can also employ geometric tolerancing symbols from a complete ANSI standard library. Notes and labels can be generated, as well as single or split balloons for annotating drawings. The detail magnification capability allows the user to automatically expand a section of the drawing to create a magnified auxiliary view which can be placed on the drawing and dimensioned accordingly. The style with which dimensions are presented is completely user-controllable. Series 7000 causes all dimensions to conform to ANSI Y 14.5. However, the user may easily change styles to conform to other standards.

Patterns

The patterning capability allows 3-D shapes and symbols to be pre-defined and incorporated into new designs with new scaling or rotation. This allows the users to create comprehensive symbol libraries.

Geometric Analysis

With Series 7000's extensive analysis features, a user may easily examine a design or components of a design to determine user-selectable characteristics and relationships. Series 7000's capabilities automatically extract the necessary information from data inherent in design construction and present it to the user in the form requested.

Information which may be obtained from a two-dimensional spline includes slope, curvature, and radius of curvature. Series 7000 permits extended analysis which includes tangent and normal lines at a given 'x,y' point on a spline.

Any closed geometric figure bounded by lines and arcs can be analyzed for area and perimeter information, and for any closed geometric figure the following section analyses are available:

- perimeter
- area
- centre of gravity
- first moment
- moment of inertia
- radius of gyration
- polar moment of inertia
- polar radius of gyration

Data Verification

Information can be captured instantaneously from entities on the screen regarding their location and properties or relation to other entities. This information can be stored as variables in a library, and these variables can be recalled at any time. This improves productivity by allowing the user to use the system to store and retrieve mathematical or geometric information instead of having to write it down or calculate it by hand.

APPLICATIONS SOFTWARE

Auto-trol's applications packages for Series 7000 software assist with the design and manufacture of everything from can openers to turbine assemblies. With these packages users can perform solid modeling, finite element modeling and analysis, develop flat patterns, visualize nesting layouts, and generate numerical control parts programs. In addition, an Applications Interface Package allows users to interface their own or third party application programs with Auto-trol's software.

CONSTRUCTIVE SOLID GEOMETRY (CSG)

Auto-trol's Constructive Solid Geometry (CSG) System is a highly interactive and easy to use software package that provides the design engineer with powerful tools to design, analyze, and visualize three-dimensional models. The package allows complete volume and mass property calculations to be performed on any class of 3-D geometry. Using this software can dramatically improve productivity and streamline production schedules.

Capabilities

A design engineer can rapidly conceptualize and construct an idealized model and can freely translate, rotate, scale, mirror and otherwise manipulate the model in true three-dimensional space. The model can be displayed in orthographic, isometric, and an infinite number of other auxiliary views. For additional visualization, a rapid haloed line and hidden surface display are provided along with parallel, perspective, cutaway and windowed viewing capabilities.

Construction times are minimized by a full set of two and three-dimensional primitives, an extremely powerful two-dimensional sketching mode and complete set operation (Boolean) capabilities. Also, the system has its own complete function menu which provides push-button speed and control in the design and analysis process. Data verification is provided through valuable print and list functions, and a comprehensive tabulation of mass properties is readily available through the user of a single, parameterized command.

The designer can also create complete construction and analysis programs off-line using the unique procedure file sub-system. Furthermore, each step of the design session is automatically recorded for later reference.

Product Highlights

- Easy to use, on-screen menu with graphic icons means that designers do not have to learn complex commands
- Complicated models can be created easier and faster than with wireframe or surface modelers
- Single common database eliminates file transfer for applications
- Consistent user interface with standard Series 7000 software makes the solid modeling system easy to use
- Automatic hidden line removal improves the clarity of models
- Mass properties can be calculated automatically
- Automatic interference detection can eliminate manufacturing delays

Benefits

- Increases ease of product design and analysis
- Aids in product visualization
- Increases productivity

FINITE ELEMENT INTERFACE PACKAGE

The finite element interface package, available on Auto-trol's mechanical design and manufacturing system, allows users to interactively generate nodes and elements for use in finite element modeling and analysis programs. The package provides a means of combining Auto-trol's user-friendly model construction techniques with the powerful capabilities of the finite element method.

Capabilities

Using Auto-trol's graphics system, a part designer first generates a part model. The model provides the basis for design visualization, drawing documentation, two or three dimensional analysis, numerical control machining and bill of materials, as well as finite elements and other applications.

Next, the analysis engineer continues the finite element modeling process using Auto-trol's finite element interface package. Nodes and elements can be interactively generated from the design geometry. This feature eliminates the costly and time consuming job of manually duplicating the model using nodes and elements. The user-friendly menu selections allow the user to automatically generate, display, and edit the finite element model. The user may selectively display the entire model using full node and element editing capabilities.

When the modeling process is completed, the node and element informaion contained in the model is output to a disk file. This file is then entered into a finite element modeling program where the analyst specifies the type of analysis to be done (stress, thermal, etc.) and the model may also be further described. The model is then ready for analysis.

Features

- Menu-driven
- Totally integrated within the graphics software
- Supports conventional node and element types
- Interactive or automatic mesh generation
- Equally spaced or logarithmic node/element fill
- Renumbering of nodes/elements
- Automatic or manual merging of nodes
- Modification facilities for all nodes/elements
- Allows incremental generation of nodes/elements with the option to continue or restart

- Full colour
- Interface to various finite element/analysis programs including ANSYS, NASTRAN, etc.

Benefits

- Improved communication between product designers and analysts
- Increased accuracy and reduced time for finite element model generation
- Easy to learn and use
- Reduced analysis cost
- Greater productivity

AUTOMATIC NESTING SYSTEM

Auto-trol's Automatic Nesting System is an interactive software package that speeds the nesting process of two-dimensional parts for N/C flame cutting and various other manufacturing processes.

It not only solves the problem of efficient material utilization, but reduces the cost of labour and materials, shortens machine cutting time, provides inventory control for both raw materials and finished parts, and allows tighter adherence to production schedules.

Capabilites

There are eight simple steps that comprise Auto-trol's Automatic Nesting System. The order of operation is at the user's discretion. However, if the user attempts to perform operations in an order which is not valid, the system will issue a diagnostic message and disallow the attempt.

1. Entering orders for parts.
2. Performing the automatic nesting.
3. Selecting nest output
4. Defining parts to be nested
5. Defining raw material parameters
6. Defining remnant material parameters
7. Defining cost model parameters
8. Defining N/C machine parameters

The first three functions are used to generate nesting output. The last five define all the user parameters necessary to run the nesting system. Once these parameters are defined, they are changed only when circumstances dictate a revision (e.g. a new part has been designed or the cost of material changes, etc.).

The nesting system receives its input either from a disk file containing the "CLPRNT" file produced in the numerical control machining section of Auto-trol's graphics software, or from a disk file consisting of N/C machine control characters. Output generated by the nesting system consists of nesting data files stored on disk, printed output sent to the printers queue, plot output sent to the appropriate plotter queue, and punched tape output sent to the tape punch queue.

Features

- Nests parts for flame cutting
- Provides coherent menu structure
- Inputs and outputs both English and metric units
- Generates nesting output for plotters, printers and tape punching equipment
- Allows user editing of a finished nest to add, move, delete or modify parts in the nest.
- Provides automatic generation of part cutting order with optional user modification
- Provides an optional material utilization report for each nest produced
- Stores and retrieves data concerning unused material remnants

Benefits

Provides:
- A fast, efficient solution to the entire manufacturing problem of nesting parts
- A customized system to fit a user's particular needs and his environment
- An efficient way to cut costs and conserve material

FLAT PATTERN DEVELOPMENT

In conjunction with Auto-trol's graphics software, the optional flat pattern development package improves the speed and accuracy of transforming 3-D part models into developed flat patterns. The package allows a user to quickly and easily unfold the planes of a 3-D part model on the screen of a graphics workstation.

Capabilities

A product designer first generates a part model. The model can be displayed in several different views, and when a change is made in one view, the change is automatically displayed in all views. This automatic updating enhances the designer's perspective and ability to track model development. It also ensures that the designer can work wit the latest version of the model.

Next, the manufacturing engineer calls up the part image on the screen and initiates the flat pattern development package. Within seconds, the system analyzes the geometry of the model and is ready to unfold the planes on the screen. The operator indicates the necessary parameters (bend radius, material coefficient, material thickness, etc.) or uses standard parameters previously entered.

To unfold a plane, the operator simply indicates one point on the desired plane and specifies a point on the axis of rotation. The system automatically calculates the bend angle and rotates the plane into a flat position. All geometric items (such as drill holes) will be rotated with the plane on which they are located. Because of a unique capability, when two connected planes need to be rotated, the operator just indicates a point on one plane and both will be rotated.

While the unfolding process takes place, the system catalogues the angles, radii, allowances, and length reductions for all bends. This information can be displayed as a separate bend table, and the system can also dimension the finished flat pattern by incorporating the bending data.

To aid in cutting out the flat pattern from sheet metal or other materials, numerical control tapes can be generated automatically from the design data in the data base. The engineer can visualize and verify the optimum tool path on the display screen, and he can obtain the information in APT or COMPACT II output format for use on virtually any machine tool.

Features

- Menu-driven
- Totally integrated within graphics software
- User-definable options and parameters
- Automatic entity coplanarity checking
- Determines connectivity between entities
- Interactive unfolding process
- Automatic bend allowance calculation
- Produces dimensionally correct flat pattern
- Allows automatic duplication of original part
- Produces a catalogue of bending parameters
- Features a geometric analysis of 3-D model
- Automatically computes associativity between previous bends
- Automatic trimming of entities to allow for minor distortions
- Allowance for user-defined neutral axis
- Automatic selection of entities to be folded

NUMERICAL CONTROL

Using Auto-trol's numerical control (NC) software, a manufacturing engineer can generate the NC programs required to machine a part created on an Auto-trol CAD/CAM system, without having to redefine the part's geometry. The system will create the source program in either APT or COMPACT II, and will at the same time display the tool motion on the graphics screen. By reducing programming time and increasing the ability to generate accurate programs the first time, Auto-trol's NC software can reduce the cost of fabricating prototypes or batch production lot sizes. New products can now be brought to market faster and more economically.

Capabilities and Features

Input in APT or COMPACT II

Auto-trol's NC software has the unique capability of allowing input, edits, and post-processor commands to be entered in either APT or COMPACT II. This means that APT and COMPACT II programmers can both work in their own language. Present programmers can easily adapt to the system without training in a new language. Also, a company no longer needs to hire only one type of programmer or to retrain new programmers in another language.

Once the program is complete, it can be output as a source file in either APT or COMPACT II. This protects any investment already made in special NC programs or post-processors.

Wide Variety of Machining Operations

Some of the available operations are:

- Point-to-Point
  Drilling, tapping, boring, reaming, threading, deep hole drilling, layer drilling, spot-facing, counter sinking
- 2-Axis
  Turning, facing, boring, punching, milling, flame cutting, threading, grooving
- 3-Axis
  Milling with full containment, drive curves, check curves, islands, pocketing, lace/non-lace, automatic roughing and finishing
- 5-Axis
  Milling while maintaining the tool normal to part or surfaces, containment and islands, lace/non-lace, automatic roughing and finishing

Look-Ahead

The system looks ahead of its current position to ensure that it will not violate the part. For example, if the tool designer mistakenly selects a 0.5" radius tool to cut around a part with a 0.4" radius in a bend, the Auto-trol system, unlike APT or COMPACT II systems, will avoid cutting into the part. The display screen will show the part, tool path and uncut area.

Modal Control of Set-up Information

Set-up information such as spindle direction and speed, feed rates, tolerances, clearances, retract plans, and coolant use are all under modal control. To enter this information, all the programmer has to do is modify or verify the values in a list displayed on the screen. This greatly reduces programming time, and also guarantees that the programmer will not accidentally overlook some of these key items.

User-Assignable Menu Buttons

240 menu buttons are available to the user. Each button can store any system function or combination of functions, which will be activated when the button is pushed. The functions are assigned to menu buttons by simply entering lines in a text file consisting of the steps to be executed. One of the great advantages of using the menu is that the knowledge and experience of the senior tool designer, for example, becomes available to everyone. The experienced designer can program modals, post-processor commands, and NC macros and can assign these instructions to a menu button. Then whenever these instructions are needed, they can be added to a new program with the touch of a button.

Interactive Editor

One of the most important features of the NC software module is its comprehensive interactive editing capability. The programmer can search both forward and backward through the program by using single steps, giving the number of lines forward or backward, specifying a line, or indicating a check surface. The programmer can then insert APT or COMPACT II commands, new tool positions, or NC macros. When NC macros are inserted, all the text is displayed so the macros can be reviewed and/or edited. The tool path can also be modified by indicating a screen position for the tool. When any modification is made, both graphics and text are immediately updated to show the changes. No reprocessing of the tool path is required.

There are many advantages to seeing the results of edits without re-processing the modified program after each change. First, the chance of making small but costly errors is greatly reduced. Secondly, the cost of taking the NC machine out of production so that the tool designer can try and re-try his program is avoided. And, by receiving instant feedback on every change, the tool designer becomes much more productive.

Tool Path Entity Manipulation

Each tool path is handled as a separate entity in the graphic data base, and as such it can be rotated, duplicated, translated, and mirrored. For example, if a part has four identical pockets, the programmer can have the system create the tool path for the first, then duplicate and translate or rotate that path to generate the others. The position and text of the new paths can be reviewed on the screen.

Composite Tool Paths

Tool paths can be combined in any order, which allows the tool designer to plan the program better. For example, an efficient way of using the system is to create the profile cut first. This shows the designer how much material was missed by this cut so he can set up roughing cuts based on this information. Then, when all the tool paths have been completed, they can be combined in the proper order for machining.

Postprocessors

Auto-trol has a large number of post-processors available. If one is required that we have not already developed, we have a team of programmers dedicated to writing customer requested software.

SERIES 5000

Advanced Graphics Software

Auto-trol's Series 5000 Advanced Graphics Software provides 32-bit computer power to speed complex design and drafting functions. Running on Auto-trol's Advanced Graphics Workstation (AGW) or on the GPX and VAXstation 2000 family of 32-bit processors from Digital Equipment Corporation, Series 5000 improves productivity and reduces costs - ensuring that projects are completed on time and budget.

Series 5000 provides these benefits of its ease of use, versatility, high performance, and powerful data base.

Data Base

The powerful Series 5000 data base provides true 3-D geometry, random access with an inplace updating capability, user-definable units, and single or double precision data representation.

Because Series 5000 is a true 3-D geometry system, the X, Y and Z coordinates are specified for all locational data. Even text is three-dimensional. This provides complete freedom to rotate and manipulate objects in 3-D space.

The random access structure of the data base provides fast information retrieval and allows drawing modifications to be done in place without re-copying the entire drawing.

Design and Performance Tools

Quick Actions and Menus

A Quick Action consists of any two or more functions efficiently combined under one command. This one command can be assigned to a menu and executed with the push of a button, thus giving users the entire scope of system power at fingertip control.

Quick Actions

The Quick Action capability aids the user not only because it significantly decreases drawing input time compared both to manual methods and step-by-step computer methods, but also because of the many special advantages it provides.

- Quick Actions can evaluate internal, calculated and user-supplied values and can selectively perform (branch to) user-specified functions.

- Several Quick Actions can be nested (layered so that one triggers another) within a single Quick Action. This enables the user to recall a particular operation within a sequence for use or modification.
- Quick Action parameters may be pre-defined or entered at the time of execution

Quick Action capabilities are greatly enhanced through the calculator feature. The calculator may be used within a Quick Action to perform various arithmetic, algebraic, and trigonometric functions. Results obtained through the use of the calculator can be directly incorporated into a drawing.

Menus

A menu contains 240 "buttons", and each button can store up to 50 user-defined characters. When a menu button is pushed, the characters stored behind that button are executed, thus activitating a Quick Action, inserting a symbol into a drawing, or initiating any system function or combination of functions.

A standard menu is supplied with each system. It contains most of the system commands and may be used as a prototype for creating new Quick Actions and symbols for specialized menus.

Associate Group

Series 5000 Advanced Graphics Software has a fully associative data base. With a unique set of associate group (AG) commands, the user can assemble related graphic and text data into a single structure which can be manipulated as one entity.

For example, a user can associate information with figures representing furniture in an office suite. The user can then modify colours, styles, or fabrics simultaneously without the need to alter each item one step at a time.

The user can select associate groups for manipulation by specifying a location, a region, text within a group, or any combination of these criteria.

Fortran Interface

Series 5000 can interface with FORTRAN programs, providing the ability to access independent software and data. This allows the concurrent execution of a FORTRAN program which communicates with Series 5000 and with the rest of the computer system. The FORTRAN program can get information to and from a Series 5000 user, can get information internal to Series 5000, and can have Series 5000 execute any of its commands. A set of FORTRAN support routines makes it simple to read and/or write external graphic files. Standard FORTRAN provides many tools to manipulate external data and devices. All of these facilities provide a method to access corporate or project data management systems, to get information to and from specialized analysis programs, and to interface user-developed applications directly to Series 5000. Also, the user has access to a broad range of third party FORTRAN application programs.

The Tools of Drawing Creation

Lines

Series 5000 produces solid lines, dashed lines, and double lines, all in variable widths. Lengths and spacing of dashes in dashed lines are user-definable, which allows the creation of lines conforming to individual requirements.

With the line terminator command, a symbol may be inserted automatically at either or both ends of a line segment. Commonly used line terminators such as slashes, arrowheads and dots can be entered quickly.

Regular Geometric Figures

Series 5000 facilitates all planar geometric figures - circles, polygons, rectangles, and ellipses. Any geometric figure may be generated with a centre cross of user-defined size.

Irregular Curves

Series 5000 provides an electronic "French curve" which will form an irregular curve through points entered via a digitizer or graphic CRT.

Symbol Creation

With Series 5000, a symbol can be created once, saved, and inserted in a drawing as often as necessary. Any drawing component may be saved as a symbol: lines, figures, text - even an entire drawing. Scale and rotation of the symbol are user-definable.

Display

Series 5000 enables the operator to see and manipulate a drawing from whichever view-point is most advantageous. An operator can zoom in on a section of a drawing for a close-up or zoom out for a long-range view. A drawing can be moved a specified distance in the x or y axis or moved about a point or vector. And up to 10 images can be displayed as ghosts (background figures) behind the primary drawing.

Drawing Manipulation

Mirror, 2-D or 3-D rotation, and scale functions are features which provide the ability to manipulate a graphic entity without having to redraw it.

Text and Text Manipulation

Auto-trol furnishes approximately two dozen standard text fonts with every system, and an unlimited number of styles and sizes can be created to suit individual needs. Fonts contain 96 characters, including upper and lower case and many special symbols. Fixed or proportional spacing can be user-defined during font creation.

Text may be tailored by the user for each job requirement. Right, left or centre justification can be specified. Heights of letters, horizontal and vertical spacing between characters and slant of characters may also be user-defined. Exact placement of text can be specified by keyboard input of Cartesian coordinates or by using the graphics cursor.

Crosshatching

Crosshatching is accomplished by simply entering the appropriate command and defining the boundary of the area to be crosshatched.

Dimensioning

Series 5000 offers the ability to automatically enter dimension lines with arrowheads, extension lines (boundary lines perpendicular to dimension lines) and text annotation quickly and easily in a drawing.

Editing

Series 5000 provides two unique features in the edit capability. The backspace command permits removal of newly entered graphic data one segment at a time, beginning with the last entity entered and continuing with each preceding entity. And the selective erase feature allows edits to be performed without repainting the entire drawing.

Layering

Various parts of a drawing can be created on up to 250 graphic layers which may be treated as regular drafting overlays. And each layer can be a different colour to help differentiate among disciplines.

Interactive Feedback

Series 5000 provides several forms of feedback to assist the user with drawing creation. User-definable prompts alert the operator that certain action is required.

The look-up feature enables the user to view parameters detailing the status of the system.

The system directory can assist the user in keeping track of drawings and drawing revisions.

Error-related messages are available to notify the user to take corrective action when incorrect information is entered.

Applications Software

For designing everything from an office building to an oil refinery, Auto-trol offers comprehensive applications software packages that help make your work faster and easier. Our architecture/engineering/construction series of applications includes packages to assist with architectural drafting and documentation, spatial programming, process plant design and drafting, cartography and technical publishing.

PLAN: Architectural Drafting and Documentation System

PLAN provides a comprehensive architectural drafting capability for users with a minimum amount of graphics system experience.

Capabilities:

- Architectural floor plans.
- Other plan view drawings: reflected plan capabilities for grid, lighting fixture, and HVAC grille and diffuser layouts.
- 3-D studies: 3-D studies can be automatically generated from 2-D plan views. In addition, these 3-D studies can easily be rendered for presentation drawings by using ILLUSTRATOR, Auto-trol's Architectural Rendering Design System.
- Schedules: Door and room finish schedules can be automatically generated by PLAN.
- Flexibility: The operating menu for PLAN is modular.

The package layout provides architects, interior designers and facility managers with a system to simplify and enhance the facility layout function, after the architectural plan has been created with PLAN.

RAPID-DRAFT Applications

- RAP-PID: A package for process and instruments diagrams (P&IDs).
- RAP-EL: To generate electrical schematics drawings.
- RAP-ISO: For isometric piping diagrams with bill of materials

Orthographic to Axonometric Package (OTAP)

OTAP is an optional software that enables illustrators to enter engineering data into their Auto-trol computer data base and generate drawings at the desired projection.

The illustrator digitizes the geometry of the engineering drawing in two or three views , using a menu to speed input process. On the graphics display screen, the image produced is a true axonometric drawing of the input

Spatial Programming Design System (SPDS)

SPDS allows space allocation problems to be solved by visualizing solutions on a graphics display screen. After initial data gathering, SPDS can be used to facilitate the space allocations and initial layout functions. In a four stage process, the designer interactively or automatically produces relationship charts, cluster diagrams, bubble diagrams and initial floor plans. Editing and data manipulation features are incorporated in each section. Any number of possible layouts can be generated and stored for comparison.

Plant Facilities Design System (PFDS)

PFDS is a comprehensive, easy-to-use set of drafting application programs for process plant orthographic design and drafting.

When designing process plants, it is critical to ensure that piping backgrounds are created accurately to scale and dimensions. PFDS provides features and techniques for accomplishing this task with a high level of productivity.

Once the background is established, a designer uses the menu to build a piping design from the background graphics and associated captured data such as nozzle locations, pump outlets and inlets, column reference points, etc. The piping portion of the menu is as design orientated as possible, allowing piping designers and drafters to input the information in a normal format rather than making additional calculations or decisions. The system's automatic design rule checking and referencing to industry standards will save countless hours of look-up time during the design process.

BASE MAP GENERATION AND LOCATIONAL CONVERSION SYSTEM (BASIS)

Designed as a generic map-making tool for all geoscience and engineering disciplines, BASIS is comprised of two modules: Base Map Generation and Locational Conversion.

The Base Map Generation Module facilitates the production of base maps and allows rapid insertion of geographically referenced data into those maps.

The Locational Conversion Module provides those basic cartographic tools needed to aid in the placement of locationally referenced data (e.g. X, Y, (Z); latitude/longitude; distance/bearing) into the map bases created with the Base Map Generation Module.

Exploration Base Mapping System (EBMS)

Auto-trol's Exploration Base Mapping System (EMBS) provides the energy exploration industry with unique solutions to the problems inherent in the updating and re-drafting of geophysical base data. EBMS also offers transaction file processing if the user needs to interface with existing data bases.

EBMS consists of two interrelated modules: well spotting/annotation and seismic spotting/annotation. These modules work in tandem with the Auto-trol BASIS package, which facilitates base map generation. Both EBMS modules are push-button orientated and designed to provide the user with maximum control over symbol selection/placement and associated text over-write problems.

Automated Technical Illustration Production System (ATIPS)

The Auto-trol Technical Illustration Production System (ATIPS) is optional software that aids in producing both simple and complex line drawings in any desired projection, including perspective drawings. Designed by technical illustrators who have dealt firsthand with manual production problems, ATIPS provides computer aided tools that solve those problems and make production flow more expedient.

THE HARDWARE

ADVANCED GRAPHICS WORKSTATION (AGW)

Description

The Advanced Graphics Workstation (AGW22 - Apollo DN3000) is a standalone CAD/CAM system that provides 32-bit power independent of a mainframe. Each AGW contains its own full function processor, thus providing a dedicated computer for every user. Hundreds of AGW's can be tied together to form a high speed local area network which allows users to share data, programs and peripherals. In addition, the AGW22 can communicate with mini or mainframe host computers, allowing it to become an integral part of a corporate data base.

VAXSTATION II GPX

The VAXstation II GPX is based upon the MicroVAX II Supermicro and is an interactive workstation for technical applications.

The VAXstation II GPX has a powerful VLSI coprocessor for increased speed and high performance graphics, to offload text and graphics computation from the MicroVAX II CPU, together with VMS Operating System. It provides full 32-bits VAX compatibility enabling integration with other Vax systems and the newly released VAXstation 2000.

The system is available in either colour or monochrome, and is complete with VMS to enable windowing operations to take place.

Support is also provided for the latest VAXstation 2000, recently announced by Digital Equipment Corporation.

FINITE ELEMENT INTERACTIVE PACKAGE

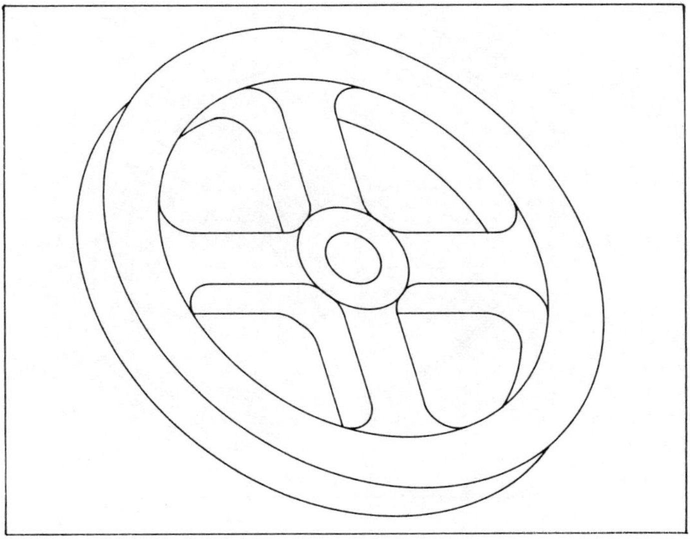

A finite element mode is constructed from
a part design stored in the data base (in this case, a wheel).

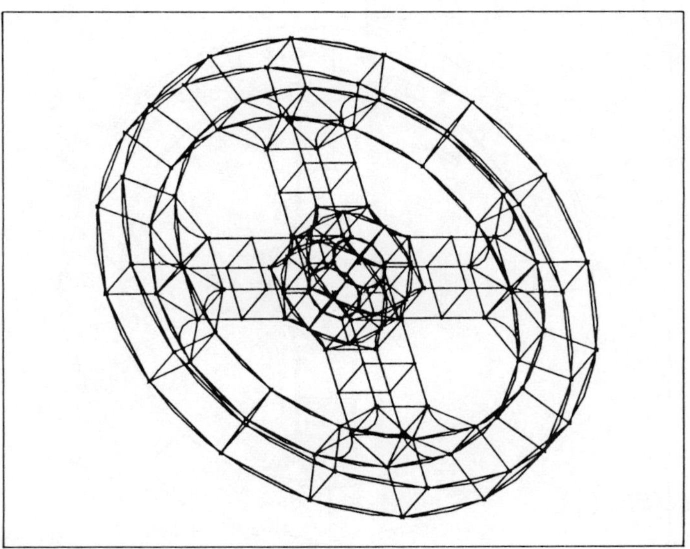

The nodes and elements are interactively
constructed from the part design geometry.

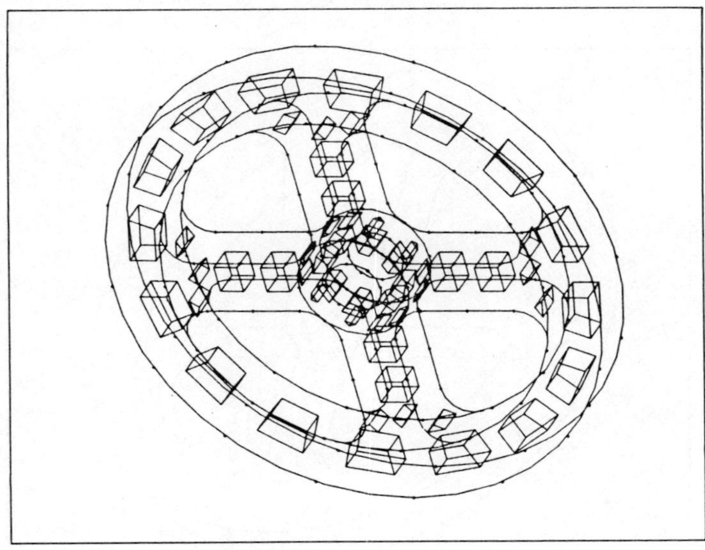

The 3-D wedge and brick elements are displayed using a 50% "shrink factor." This is just one of the numerous features which contribute to productive model building.

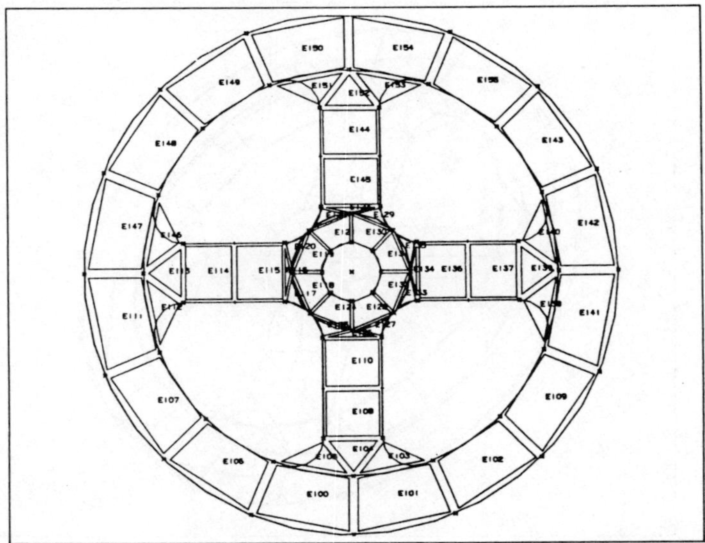

This is a front view of the finite element model with nodes, elements and element numbers.

CADVANCE™/SOLID VISION™/ SYSTEM 25/PRISMA™

ISICAD Inc., U.S.A.

ISICAD presents two CAD systems at the level of personal computers. They are CADVANCE and SOLID VISION. Also discussed are ISICAD's SYSTEM 25 and PRISMA^{TM}.

1. CADVANCE^{TM}

General Description

CADVANCE is a two-dimensional CAD software package for the IBM XT, AT personal computers and true board compatibles designed to create productivity among users in the AEC marketplace. CADVANCE is a powerful and user-friendly package that allows architects, engineers, facilities planners, and designers to create high quality professional drawings and designs.

For increased versatility and productivity, application data files can be used in popular database programs, such as DBASE II or LOTUS, for project data management, time accouting and other analyses. Compatability is also possible with IGES 2.0.

With CADVANCE, nested commands can be invoked while another command is active. Thus, users can pan, zoom, display a grid, or run a macro while still in the DRAW command. This dramatically speeds the design process by reducing switching between menu selections, which eliminates extra steps.

Intelligent Macros are a CADVANCE feature that can save many hours in repetitive design. The user simply defines a design element once, saving it as a macro. The macro may then be inserted in the present or future design with a single keystroke. It's a particularly valuable feature in repetitive designs or designs which utilize standard elements.

Powerful design features such as automatic dimensioning, automatic symbol insertion within walls, automatic wall creation and intersection clean-up demonstrate the power of CADVANCE. Other advanced features include the ability to stretch entire walls and rooms with one command, or real time dragging, scaling and text editing.

CADVANCE incorporates interactive features such as on-screen menus for choosing commands and sub-commands which make this package easy to use. Prompts which appear at the bottom of the screen guide the user through operation of the commands.
The 3D Projections task allows the user to produce oblique, isometric and perspective views of his/her designs, ready for rendering or approval processes.

Flexibility

CADVANCE presents no limitations in drawing size, which facilitates managing major projects. Large files overflow to disk. CADVANCE uses plotter buffers to reduce the time the computer is tied up. The plot file may also be written to disk file, then the standard MS-DOS print spooler can be used to plot the drawing in the background while design work continues on the computer.

A system of modularly designed device drivers ensures that a wide variety of peripheral options may be utilized with the CADVANCE system. Optional DXF and IGES packages allow compatibility with other popular CAD systems.
For additional applications, drawings can also be transferred to a ISICAD's SYSTEM 25 without modification.

CADVANCE offers features that previously could only be found in a high-end CAD system. Yet, the CADVANCE, PC-based system is easily affordable. And today CADVANCE is the clear leader in PC-based CAD systems for the AEC market.

System Features

- 127 layers with no fixed size per layer
* intelligent (programmable) macros
* multiple vertex move will stretch walls
- data entry in user units
- multiple view/edit recall windows
* text: fonts, slant, justify, rotate height and width factors
- viewing text: box, actual font
- user defined line textures
- nested symbols (up to 3 levels)
- independent x and y scaling
- absolute vs. relative coordinate input
- polar and polar-absolute input
- cursor snap to grid, node, vertex, intersection or nearest line point
* nested "display" commands
* database extration
- "/" + a letter" (i.e. "/D" menu selection from keyboard
- special keys - to invoke macros plus function keys implemented
* nested status line option
- definable grid locations
- mouse, digitizer or keyboard input
- dynamic menu & prompt, line select
- mirroring
* automatic symbol insertion within lines
- trim line
- filleting
- object dragging, rubberbanding
- user definable prompts and error messages
- automatic dimensioning
* on-line help files
- no-wait while plotting
- plot to disk file and "spool" plot
- symbol libraries using MS-DOS sub-directory plotting
- run-time loadable device drivers
- users definable communications part set-up
- extensive macros and symbol libraries
* automatic wall creation and intersection clean-up
* full-screen text editor
- rotation to 1 degree increments
- far and near pan views

---

* Advanced features unique to CADVANCE

Minimum System Requirements

- IBM AT or XT (or true board compatible)
- one floppy disk drive and one 10mb hard disk
- one RS-232 serial port
- IBM colour/graphics card
- parallel port
- 512K RAM
- DOS 2.0+
- input device (mouse or digitizer)

Supported Devices

Plotters

CalComp M84, 1043, 1073

HP 7470, 7475, 7550, 7580 A/B, 7585 A/B

Houston Instruments DMP-29, -40, -41, -42, -51, -52, -51MP, -52MP

IBM XY749

Alpha Merics AlphaPlot II

Sweet P "6" Shooter

Zeta 824, 836

Mice

Mouse Systems mouse

Logitech Logimouse

Torrington Mouse

Printers

Epson FX-80

Epson FX-100

Epson MX-80 (with GRAPHTRAX PLUS)

Epson MX-100 (with GRAPHTRAX PLUS)

IBM graphics printer

Okidata 84 (with plug and play)

Okidata 92 (with plug and play)

Okidata 93 (with plug and play)

Digitizers

CalComp 2000, 2100

GTCO Digi-Pad

H.I. HI-PAD

KURTA SERIES TWO

Hitachi Tiger Tablet 2

HI Resolution Boards

IBM colour/graphics card

Conographics cono-colour

IBM professional graphics adapter

Plotter Buffers

Quadram microfazer

Practical peripherals microbuffer

2. SOLID VISION™

General Description

SOLID VISION is a PC-based solid modeling system. SOLID VISION provides the power and flexibility of solid modeling on mainframe systems, but at the microcomputer level.

SOLID VISION uses Boundary Representation and Boolean technology. All coordinate data is stored in floating point format providing a full six digits of numerical accuracy. As a solids design tool, this package allows you to model the design in any view, generate wire frames, perform hidden line removals and produce shaded images at the selection of a menu command. You can even "walk around" the shaded model in real time to show all sides of the project.

Designing in 3D means that you can spend more time on the details of the design instead of on the process of modeling. This package gives you all the tools you need to complement the design process.

The menu-driven structure allows a new user to begin designing in 3D quickly, while the experienced user can key in the commands for even higher levels of productivity. Of course for that custom appeal, any command or series of commands can be accessed from a digitizer template menu. Dimensioning is both automatic and associative so that when a design is modified, dimensions are automatically updated.

Switching between plan, elevation and axonometric views of any drawing is at the touch of a single key. Rotating the model is as simple as specifying the axis of rotation and the angle. Marketing quality images are as fast and as easy as a menu selection. For dynamic presentations, hard copy output then can be generated.

Screen and tablet menus are completely user definable as are the keyboard and the text fonts. New menu commands can be user defined by way of a powerful macro language. An intelligent database allows the user to attach and extract non-graphical information from any object in the drawing.

Completely DXF compatible, SOLID VISION allows 2D drawings to be transferred to and from other popular PC CAD systems.

System Features

CAD For The Next Generation:

- True 3D designing
- Work in 2D or 3D
- Boundary Representation & Boolean Technology
- Mainframe power on a Microcomputer
- Floating - Point Arithmetic
- Design Front - End to CalComp Continuum

Designing in 3D:

- Generates Wire Frames, Sections & Perspectives
- Auto Hidden Line Removal
- 256 Color Shaded Images
- Work in Plan, Elevation or Axonometric

Open Architecture:

- DXF Compatible
- User Defined Tablet Menus
- User Defined Screen Menus
- User Defined Keyboard
- User Defined Commands

Fast & Easy:

- Menu Driven
- Dynamic "Walk Arounds" of Shaded Image
- Automatic & Associative Dimensioning
- Instance Attributes

System Requirements

- IBM PC/AT (or true board compatible)
- One floppy disk drive and a 20mb hard disk
- Two RS-232 ports
- VDI supported graphics board
- 80287 co-processor
- 512K RAM
- DOS 3.0 or higher
- Input Device (digitizer or mouse)

Supported Devices

Plotters:

- CalComp
- Hewlett-Packard
- Houston Instruments
- Roland
- Gould
- HPGL Supported Plotters

Digitizers:

- CalComp 2000, 9000
- Kurta
- Oscon
- Summagraphics

Mice:

- Logitech
- Mouse Systems
- Summa Mouse

High Resolution Boards:

- VDI supporting boards

3. SYSTEM 25

General Description

The ISICAD SYSTEM 25 uses a building block approach to allow users to configure a single user system or a multi-user system from the same basic components. The basic building block consists of a general purpose processor and a graphic design station. A second design station may be added to the processor, and, in turn, multiple processors may be networked together to configure large multi-user systems. Major system components are:

Interactive Applications Processor Subsystem (IAP) - The IAP contains the central processing unit, one megabyte of memory, a Winchester disk unit, and one megabyte floppy disk backup. Operating under the UNIX™ operating system the IAP stores and executes all basic and application software, controls peripherals, handles user interactions and stores in-process drawings. IAP disk storage and peripherals can be expanded to service an entire network of users. Note: The required Winchester disk of user selected capacity, which is priced separately, is a part of the IAP subsystem.

Interactive Design Station (IDS) - The IDS is the user's window into the system. There are three types of IDSs to meet the users' individual needs. These IDSs are:

100 Series - An IBM AT or compatible system which ISICAD does not provide. A 100 Series IDS does not require and IAP.

300 Series - An interactive graphics workstation which uses the IAP for display manipulation tasks to provide an interactive design environment.

600 Series - An interactive graphics workstation which uses the ISICAD picture processing to offload the IAP from display manipulation to provide a highly interactive design environment.

Interactive Design Center (IDC) - An IDC joins an IAP and a 300 Series and/or 600 Series IDS together into a turnkey interactive graphics system. An IDC can be configured with one or two Interactive Design Stations along with desired peripherals to complete the system. A large, multi-station system is achieved by networking many IDCs together. In this type of environment, the independent IDCs provide a high level of interactivity while sharing common data and peripherals.

Shared Function Manager (SFM) - A SFM is an Interactive Design Center which is used as the system dedicated to peripherals and database management in large configurations.

Local Area Network (LAN) - The LAN Ethernet is used to network Interactive Design Systems together to configure large multiuser systems. Using Ethernet, the user can distribute the peripherals and workload over all of the IDCs in the network.

Features

Interactive Application Processor - The IAP runs one or two 300 Series and/or 600 Series Interactive Design Stations as well as controlling a full complement of peripherals (disks, tape, plotter, printer, terminals). The IAP also processes basic and application software, handling all user interactions. The Interactive Applications Processors (IAP) consists of:

* 32-bit dual 10 MHz Motorola 68000 central processing unit
* One Megabyte ECC Memory
* One Megabyte Floppy Disk Subsystem
* Three RS-232-C Serial-Line Ports

Central Processing Unit

Number of Microprocessors	-	2
Type of Microprocessors	-	68000 (10 MHz)
CPU Cycle	-	600 nanoseconds
Physical Memory	-	1 Megabyte, expandable to 6 Megabytes
Virtual Memory	-	16 Megabyte
Cache	-	4K bytes
Memory Cycle	-	500 nanoseconds
Memory Type	-	ECC
RS-232 Ports	-	3
MULTIBUS™ Slots	-	7
MULTIBUS™ Transfer Mode	-	32-bit
MULTIBUS™ band-width	-	6 megabyte/second

Memory

Capacity	-	1 Megabyte
Word Size	-	32 bits
Error Correction	-	Single bit correction, Multiple bit detection
Read Cycle Time	-	500 ns 8/16 - bit or 32 bit Read
Write Cycle Time	-	600 ns 8/16 - bit Write, 500 ns 32 - bit Write

4. PRIMSA™

General Description

PRISMA is a system of multi-discipline software and high-performance hardware. Designed for the architectural, engineering and facilities management company, PRISMA has built-in expansion capacity.

PRISMA is for the creative designer. The system is simple to understand and master, allowing exceptional flexibility and speed. It is designed to support the intuitive manner in which a designer works. One can quickly draw and revise as the design develops. One can instantly pan across any aspect of the design with an exclusive real-time joystick.

PRISMA offers a comprehensive array of in-depth applications software. Extra modules can be added at any time to meet growing project needs or expanding services. Choose from any member of an integrated software family:

* Architectural Design
* Architectural Production
* Facilities Design and Management
* Electrical Design
* Civil Design
* Mechanical Ductwork
* Solid Modeling
* Report Generation
* Database Management
* IGES Translators

PRISMA inspires creativity with its elegant, high quality resolution and choice of 256 colors. Projects can be viewed in changing lighting environments, or one can create design models that represent true solid forms.

Many PRISMA workstations can operate together with a single host computer acting as central storage. Each workstation is connected with the host unit via Ethernet™. All workstations are fully networked to allow maximum flexibility in project coordination.

PRISMA is cost-effective. With its power and performance capabilities one can increase design productivity, cut costs, and each host computer can support multiple workstations, so a reduction in investment in hardware can be made.

DIAD/DGM/C-DATA/C-PLAN/GNC/C-TAPE

CADCentre Ltd., U.K.

A Complete Computer Aided Package

CADCentre offers CAD/CAM power for every stage in the manufacturing process ...
- for design
- for drafting
- for planning and estimating
- for the part programming of NC machine tools.

All our systems can interlink. Each product can be used independently or with others in the range, building into a flexible CAD/CAM system suitable for the largest manufacturing operation.

This independent capability means that CADCentre systems are relevant at any scale of manufacture. Small manufacturing companies, sub-contract machine shops, design consultancies or individual engineering departments can acquire a system specific to their requirements, and as business develops, so can the system.

In the drawing office - Our 2D drafting system is designed to produce mechanical layouts, detail drawings and electrical schematic drawings quickly and accurately.

In the production engineering department - CADCentre's flexible planning and estimating system caters for all production processes, including manufacture, assembly and test.

In the part programming area - We offer a fully interactive graphical part programming system, covering a comprehensive range of machine tool types and including 2, 2½, 3 and 5 axis machining.

Drafting and design

DIAD is a general-purpose 2D drafting system for mechanical and schematic design. You do not need any previous experience of computers to operate it because the system uses construction methods similar to conventional drafting. DIAD instructions are selected from menus displayed on the graphics screen, which avoids extensive typing.

The system offers a complete range of geometric construction and drawing facilities, including:
- curve fitting
- auto-hatching
- dimensioning/tolerancing to BS308, ANSI or AFNOR
- extensive geometry manipulation
- grids
- calculations
- parts and symbol libraries
- parameterisation

Modelling

2D profiles constructed using DIAD can be converted into 3D models using the DGM program. These models can be displayed from any viewpoint using orthographic or perspective projection. Selected views can then be dimensioned and annotated.

Engineering records

C-DATA is an engineering records management system which holds information about drawings and parts and the relationships between them.

C-DATA can reflect the organisation and procedures currently in use. The user has complete control over the content and format of reports produced by the system, which can include:

- searches for specific drawings or parts
- where-used lists
- lists of parts.

Information can be transferred automatically from DIAD to C-DATA where it can be checked, approved, modified or retrieved.

Planning and estimating

C-PLAN helps the process planner to construct plans, estimates, routing instructions and tooling lists for component manufacture and assembly operations.

The C-PLAN system stores your company's own standard definitions for manufacturing methods, material stock selection and tooling, with expressions for calculating planning data such as manufacturing times.

The planner constructs plans combining design data with the stored information. Menus and prompts simplify the entry of information.

Complete process plans can be stored for later retrieval and modification.

Direct interfaces to production control systems can be provided.

NC part programming

GNC interactively generates NC toolpaths from parts designed either by DIAD or by GNC's own component geometry definition facilities.

The engineer can ensure that the machining sequence is correct before creating the NC tape by actually watching the tool move around the workpiece on a graphics display.

Machining modules

GNC's machining modules support the major NC machine tool operations including:

- milling/drilling/boring
- turning
- punching/nibbling
- flame cutting
- wire erosion
- shape nesting.

During part programming the full machining environment of workpiece, tooling, clamps, jaws and turret can be displayed to ensure no collision.

Operators lists showing tooling, feed-rates and machining times can be produced automatically. For repetitive sequences, such as machining families of parts, a simple programming language is provided.

3-axis and 5-axis

For machining double-curved surfaces, such as turbine blades, impellers or complex die-and-mould work, GNC offers a full range of facilities.. .

- 3D surface modelling
- 3-axis milling, including powerful area clearance and maximum and minimum level commands
- 5-axis milling, including swarf and surface normal cutting, and vertical or axial descent/retract.

Post processing

A post processor for virtually any machine tool and controller can be prepared by using the C-TAPE program.

C-TAPE can be integrated into the machining modules of GNC. Alternatively, conventional cutter line data can be produced for subsequent post processing.

A COMPLETE COMPUTER AIDED PACKAGE

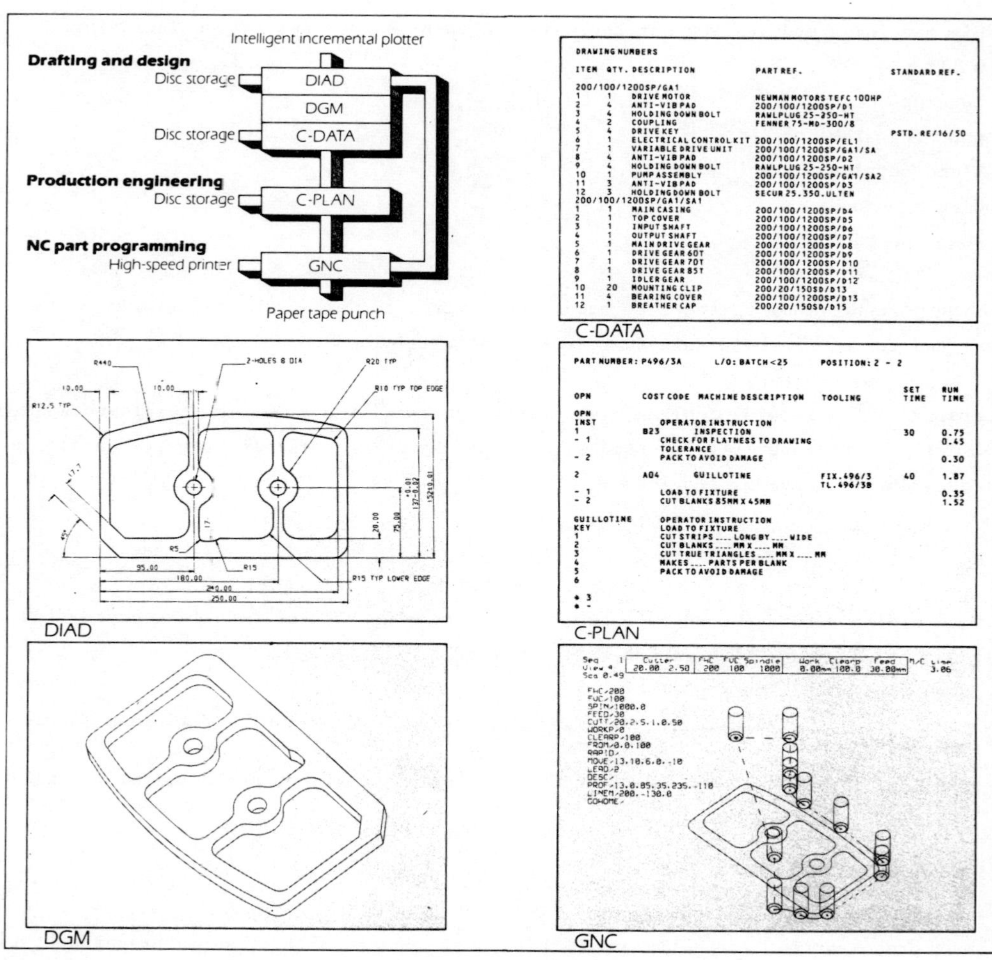

IDEAS™GEOMOD™/SUPERTAB®/ SYSTAN™/GEODRAW™

Structural Dynamics Research Corp., U.K.

1. SDRC I-DEAS^{TM}

Introduction

SDRC I-DEAS (Integrated Design Engineering Analysis Software) includes the full array of capabilities found in SDRC's mechanical computer aided engineering (MCAE) software programs:

I-DEAS Geomod^{TM} - Solid Modelling
I-DEAS Supertab^{R} - Finite Elements Modelling and Analysis
I-DEAS Geodraw^{TM} - 2D Drafting and Design
I-DEAS Systan - System Dynamic Analysis
* I-DEAS Tdas - Test Data Analysis System

Developed by Structural Dynamics Research Corporation (SDRC), I-DEAS integrates these programs into one package with consistent user interface and shared common database. This enables the integration of design, analysis and test into each phase of product development. Design interations can be performed in the computer until the most viable solution is found before the data is transferred to CadCam systems for detailed design, drafting and manufacturing.

* Not discussed in this paper

I-DEAS for Design

The I-DEAS DESIGN System includes the following sections:

I-DEAS Geomod for designing with solid modeling. A complete geometric description allows the user to package the design and check for interferences.

I-DEAS Supertab for engineering analysis. Here one can quickly accomplish finite element analysis with the I-DEAS mesh generation, on-line solver and extensive results display.

I-DEAS Geodraw for drafting. When the design is complete, dynamic dimensioning capabilities allow the user to rapidly arrive at production drawings to ANSI and ISO standards.

Modularity

Each module in I-DEAS is, in fact, wholly functioning and standalone.

I-DEAS runs on the major computer processors and graphics devices

The Common User Interface

With I-DEAS, the menus are consistent throughout the system. The same menu that lets you access the power of solid modeling lets the user create a mesh for finite element analysis. On-line help is available for every command.

The Common Database

The ready exchange of I-DEAS — getting the data from one application to another — is automatic with the common database that underpins the entire system.

One can access the solid model for the creation of the mesh or evaluate the analysis results for modification of the solid model.

I-DEAS Interfaces

I-DEAS can work with present CAD/CAM systems through IGES. Data can be transmitted for manufacturing, to and from any system that supports IGES. I-DEAS also supports direct interfaces to leading CAD/CAM systems and engineering analysis codes.

The Open Architecture of I-DEAS

In the open architecture of I-DEAS, the Project Relational Database (Pearl) is the window. Through Pearl, one has access to data across project applications. Interactive access to the data, through the I-DEAS menu system, allows one to sort, tabulate, plot and analyze the data. Subroutine access allows one to couple the project database with ones own in-house application programs.

Perhaps the most important integratability tool in I-DEAS is the I-DEAS Languages, (Ideal). With it, one can customize the application of I-DEAS with little knowledge of programming. Ideal supports macros, variables, math expressions, cursor interaction, user-defined menus and logic and looping control.

2. I-DEAS GEOMOD™

I-DEAS Geomod is a true solid modeller built on a shared database with other SDRC products as a module of I-DEAS. This provides links to finite element, system dynamic, fatigue and frame analysis. The hybrid geometrical approach to solid modeling gives the speed and flexibility to create objects, and the precision demanded for accurate displays, mass/inertia property calculations and data transfer to CAD systems. The system assembly and kinematics capability allows the assembly of total mechanical systems for interference, packaging, animation of motion, structural reliability and maintainability investigations early in the design cycle.

A unique programmability feature allows customisation of Geomod for specific applications: program files to automate repetitive command sequences, family-of-parts construction, addition of features, or formulation of own menus. Virtually any display option is available including shaded imaging, hidden line removal, multiple and exploded views, zooming, light source control, animation and translucent displays.

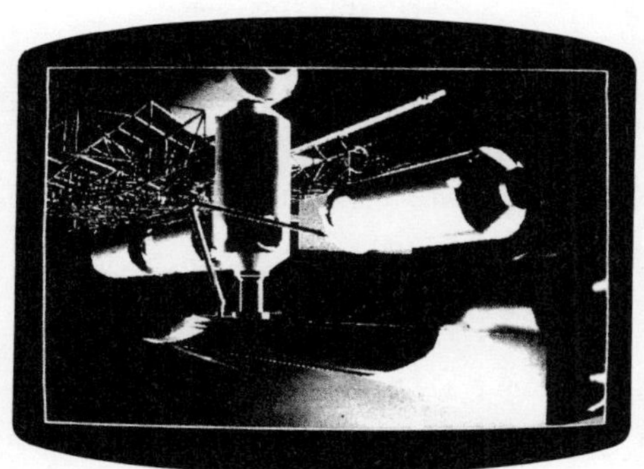

Using I-DEAS Geomod, engineers at the Martin Marietta Aerospace Corporation were able to visualize various space station concept alternatives and evaluate the functionality of the docking mechanism.

I-DEAS Geomod operates on simple logic. First-time users will find it easy to learn and begin to design in just a few short sessions. An intuitive menu structure presents the user with an easily understood progression of functions. Familiar commands, written in plain English, speed the operator through each step, reducing the learning curve of both new and occasional users.

I-DEAS Geomod's unique dual data structure lets you design and build a conceptual model with the speed of faceted geometry. Precision is available on demand, allowing display and manipulation of accurate surface intersections automatically - without retracing your modeling steps.

Rough concepts are thus shaped rapidly and easily. Reducing initial design time to a minimum. At any given point, the operator can throttle back to precise geometry, allowing the computer and I-DEAS Geomod to automatically calculate the true and accurate surface intersections. Without having to back up and repeat any of the design steps already completed.

Most modelers give the design engineer a finite set of tools with which to work. Flat planes. Cylinders. Cones. Spheres. And often the operators necessary to intersect and join these shapes into faceted approximations of a realistic model.

With I-DEAS Geomod, a design engineer simulates reality. With all its free form shapes and movement. Not limited to a finite set of geometric figures, he is free to model virtually any surface imaginable, in any shape or form.

This is made possible by the use of real world tools. In addition to primitive shapes, Geomod allows the creation of complex, sculptured surfaces using an exclusive Skinning operator. With the operator, creating a true sculptured surface is as easy as placing two or more cross sections along an arbitrary path.

Skinning and Shaping operators allow the design engineer to fully manipulate any given object as a sculptor would a lump of clay. Bend, blend, tweak, stretch, thick and warp operations can be enacted to quickly mold and shape an object into its desired form.

The Boolean operator enables the design engineer to cut and intersect shapes to form more complex objects. Or use the Joining operator to "weld" objects together with automatic removal of coincident points and coplanar faces. A Sectioning operator may be used to pass an arbitrary plane through the model to allow viewing of cross sections, or to review modeling of internal details.

An Assembly of Unlimited Components

One of I-DEAS Geomod's most important design applications is in the "packaging" of components with I-DEAS Geomod's top down design approach that includes instancing, flexible assembly hierarchy definition and modification, interactive positioning and manipulation of objects and assemblies, multiple body interference checks, proximity checking, system level mass property calculations and automatic exploded views.

I-DEAS Mechanism Design lets you analyze kinematic behavior, including determination of internal loads, velocities and accelerations. Animated displays to show how the mechanism moves can also be created.

I-DEAS Geomod can not only help visualize a design but communicate it, in all its complexity, to others. With Geomod displays, design is an interactive process. One can go from rapid wireframe to hidden line displays to shaded images. One can show a number of views simultaneously on the same screen with multiple viewports. As a result, manufacturing engineers can visually inspect design details, often avoiding manufacturing problems.

In presenting a design concept, the user can create a "studio quality" image using multiple color light sources of varying concentration, ambient lighting, surface brightness and flossiness and Phong or Gouraud shading algorithms. Finally, with I-DEAS Geomod support of advanced 3D graphics terminals, the user can interactively manipulate models from within the terminal.

Program for Design Engineering

The I-DEAS Language (Ideal) allows the designer to easily and quickly adapt it to fit the precise requirements of his applications.

With Ideal, one can automate commonly used command sequences or tailor menus.

The designer can access Pearl, the I-DEAS Project Relational Database, to sort, archive and organize solid models, develop family of parts libraries and file cost and feature data with their solid models.

Pearl is the ideal data manager for design because it can be accessed from any module in I-DEAS, using a common command syntax and user interface, making it available to everyone on the project team.

Interfacing

Designs modeled in I-DEAS Geomod interface directly with a wide variety of analytical software contained within the I-DEAS system.

With I-DEAS Geodraw, the drafting module of the I-DEAS system, solid models are completely dimensioned, annotated and cross-hatched to ANSI or ISO standards, creating complete, detailed production drawings.

One can use the solid model directly in I-DEAS Supertab to study linear static or dynamic behavior. Most analysis can be performed right in I-DEAS with Supertab's internal solver. However, I-DEAS Supertab will also automatically access industry standard codes such as ANSYS and NASTRAN.

Integratability

I-DEAS Geomod is designed to interface with the leading CAD/CAM systems. Thus, it not only integrates with other modules within I-DEAS, but is also integratable with many present CAD/CAM system.

Thus, 2D wireframe data from a CAD system can be read into I-DEAS Geomod, and used to extrude or revolve solid objects, or to create sculptured surfaces with the Skinning operator. Precise surfaces, 3D wireframes and 2D "snapshots" of solid models can all be transferred to CAD and CAM systems via Universal file or IGES interfaces.

3. I-DEAS SUPERTAB®

I-DEAS Supertab, SDRC's finite element pre and post-processor, frees designers and analysts from many of the time consuming demands of model preparation and results interpretation.

Geometry data can be acquired through interfaces to CAD/CAM systems by digitising from drawings, by generation within the program and through a shared database with I-DEAS Geomod.

A unique enhanced mesh generation feature, Triquamesh, provides tremendous savings over traditional mesh generation techniques. Restraints, loads, couples, multi-point constraints, physical and material properties are quickly created to produce the input required to several FE codes including NASTRAN and ANSYS, or, alternatively model solution capabilities within Supertab.

Post-processing of stress, strain energy and temperature as color contour plots, criterion and x-y plots, tabular data, deformed geometry, mode-shape display and animation is possible.

In addition, results (stress displacement, modes, strain energy reaction force, flow velocity and pressure) can be reviewed in the post-processing task. Interactive mass checks and error interrogation are also available.

Supertab Optimization provides the ability to automatically minimize mass and recommend structural modifications to improve structure performance for given stress and displacement design criteria.

The finite element modeling program is easy to use, capable of generating a variety of complex models quickly, and able to communicate its findings clearly. I-DEAS Supertab has the power to handle a wide variety of problems.

I-DEAS Supertab has been designed to bring all its power through on-screen menus that let the user access standard functions quickly and easily. One can proceed through the menu system or move around tasks by directly entering commands. In fact, one can mix menu and command entry and program many routine tasks, stringing operations together.

I-DEAS Supertab has been a leading finite element modeling program for over a decade.

Model Criterion

Acess to geometry is the first important set in building a finite element model. I-DEAS Supertab provides a wide variety of methods of creating the manipulating geometry. One way is with a digitizing tablet, allowing the user to create a model directly off a designer's drawings.

One can also build geometry directly with curvers, surfaces and volumes, representing both surface and solid geometry. One can build geometry with the same speed and precision found in the industry-leading I-DEAS Geomod Solid modeling program. Because Supertab Object Modeling is based on Geomod one can also get geometry from a CAD/CAM system using IGES or neutral file interfaces.

Mesh Generation

I-DEAS Supertab gives the user three ways to generate a mesh; manually; semi-automatically with conventional mapping techniques; and with TRIQUAMESH, a fully automatic meshing method unique to I-DEAS Supertab. A simple model can often be best generated in the manual mode. Here the user is in complete control, digitizing, copying and reflecting nodes and elements and making use of local coordinate systems.

The semi-automatic method uses a mapped meshing technique to generate nodes and elements on regular geometry regions — three or four edged surfaces and five or six faced volumes. The user segments the geometry into regular regions and defines the node pattern on each edge. Multiple curves can make up each edge, reducing the need to carve geometry into small regions. Bias control allows one to specifiy varying mesh density along each edge of a region. Compatibility across geometry regions is automatically assured, eliminating the need to track and merge masses of unwanted coincident nodes.

TRIQUAMESH creates quadrilateral or triangular meshes on regions with an unlimited number of edges and tetrahedral meshes within volumes bounded by an unlimited number of faces. One merely defines bounding areas or volumes, overall mesh density and desired local densities.

This fully automatic, free mesh generation method practically eliminates the need to segment the geometry into small, regular regions. TRIQUAMESH has achieved time savings of up to 75% in meshing complex geometries.

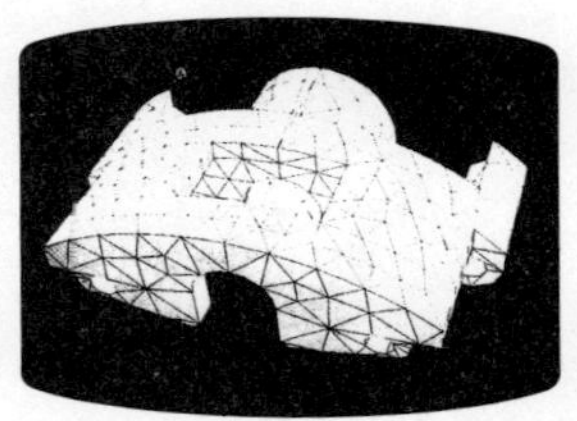

Solid TRIQUAMESH can significantly simplify the process of generating solid element models - especially for complex geometries.

Loads and Restraints

With I-DEAS Supertab, one can create all loads and restraints interactively with graphic feedback. The loads and restraints are directly associated with nodes and elements, maintaining their associativity with the finite element model through all operations.

For loads, one can specify nodal forces, element pressures or temperatures. For restraints, input displacements, kinematic or coupled degrees-of-freedom, and multi-point constraints. The graphical display will show all loads and restraints with color coding.

Completing the Model

I-DEAS Supertab provides for automatic nodal band-width or element wavefront minimization in order to reduce solution time. It has an extensive library of over 30 elements so that one can choose the element type, physical and material characteristics best suited for the analysis. Isotropic and orthotropic material properties may be specified. And I-DEAS Supertab's cross-sectional analysis capability for beam properties automates a tedious manual process for complex section

Model Check

Analyzing a model with errors is both costly and time consuming. Before one submits a model for analysis, I-DEAS Supertab runs it through a number of steps to check it for completeness and accuracy.

Free edge and surface checks verify that all elements are connected and oriented correctly. There's coincident node and element checking, warping and distortion checking, and a shrink element display to verify that elements exist where desired. Errors can be easily corrected, working directly with nodes and elements.

Model Solution

Model Solution is the I-DEAS's on-line solver for linear, static, dynamic and potential flow analysis. By eliminating the need for file translation and interfacing, it greatly simplified and speeds the analysis process.

A wide selection of elements is available, including shells, solids, beams and scalars, such as masses, springs and frictionless gaps. Loads and restraints, like all data, are accessed directly from the I-DEAS Supertab database.

Specific features have been designed for dynamic analysis, including residual flexibility calculation. Dynamic stress calculations are available through a close coupling to I-DEAS Systan.

Optimization

Design is an interative process.

Manual redesign relies totally on the intuition and experience of the engineer to deal with a multitude of interacting variables. Hunt-and-try approaches to solving problems require large amounts of time.

I-DEAS Optimization automates this redesign task and helps you to get better end results.

Through an interactive session, one sets up the redesign process. Optimization then minimizes structural mass, given a set of loads and design constraints on stress, displacement and material geometry such as minimum or maximum thickness. One is totally in control as redesign proceeds. One can review results at any step to understand how the structure is being modified.

Data is accessed directly from the I-DEAS database and results are returned to it. Advanced "hill climbing' algorithms further capitalize on I-DEAS integration to reach an optimum design in the shortest possible time. Usually, significant improvements are seen in only 3 or 4 design iterations.

Optimization gives the engineer new insight into how a design really performs, which areas are most sensitive to change and how variables interact.

4. I-DEAS SYSTAN™

I-DEAS Systan is an interactive, graphically oriented program for analysis of mechanical system dynamics. It allows the designer or analyst to evaluate the performance of a total system from assembled component information.

The database maintains complete project information on components, connectors, sub systems, excitations and analysis results.

For input of component data there is an interface to Supertab and NASTRAN.

I-DEAS Systan is a module in I-DEAS, just like Geomod, Geodraw and Supertab. Thus, it has complete access to the I-DEAS database.

To assemble the components and substructures of the users system, I-DEAS Systan has automatic interfaces to MSC/NASTRAN and ANSYS. Direct access is provided to the I-DEAS Supertab-Model Solution and Geomod modules. Systan will also accept test data from I-DEAS Tdas or MODAL-PLUS as well as analysis input, performing its system analysis including both.

System assembly is automated. There is a library of scalar and matrix connectors to define mass, stiffness and damping. System responses and internal loads are computed and graphically displayed.

Graphics are a powerful engineering tool in Systan. Systan's advanced graphics will verify the proper assembly and constraint of the system model. And Systan graphics show the results of the analysis as animated mode shapes and response plots.

Computational efficiency and design study flexibility are achieved by representing a mechanical system as an assembly of components. Model components can be defined from finite element analysis and modal tests with either free-free modes (with residual flexibility) or constraint modes. Substructure components can be defined by reduced matrix representations of finite element models. As a result, complex structures can be efficiently simulated in the computer.

Direct Interfaces

I-DEAS Supertab has supported internal interfaces with ANSYS, MSC/NASTRAN, ABAQUS, MOLDFLOW, and SINDA. Analysis code masks allow the user to create only the data accepted by the program to be used.

I-DEAS Supertab provides access to virtually all analysis programs through the Universal File. With this text file, one can transfer model data to ADINA, BEASY, SAP, MARC, PAFEC or any in-house code. The I-DEAS Supertab user library of interfaces is fully accessible.

In addition, all finite element model and results data are stored in the I-DEAS Project Relational Database (Pearl). The I-DEAS Language (Ideal) can be used to easily reformat model data to meet specific requirements.

Graphic Displays

I-DEAS Supertab is a flexible tool. Whether displaying stresses, strains, temperatures, heat flux, strain energy, displacements, reaction forces or kinetic energy, I-DEAS Supertab shows them all in precisely the form required. All displays can be shown for the entire model or with the subset "groups" that you define.

I-DEAS Supertab stores the raw analysis results. Derived values, such as principal stress are computed on-line. Load cases can be combined directly within I-DEAS Supertab so cumulative effects may be reviewed.

With a simple command, one can call up color contour plots of stress, strain, deflections, temperature or anything else one wishes to analyze.

When one wants to see how a structure will move under loading, use the Deformed Geometry Display. Deformation can be scaled, either in relative or absolute terms, and compared directly to the original underformed model.

Additional insight can be gained by animating the deformation or when doing dynamic analysis with mode shapes.

If one wishes to evaluate results versus design criteria, one can call for Criterion Plotting. Elements meeting certain criteria can be presented either graphically or in a listing. The criteria can be by value, range or percent.

X-Y Function Plots allow one to get at local details within a region or along a path. Results from various loading conditions or contributions of various stress components can be directly compared. Output is available in global or local elemental co-ordinate systems. For beam elements, X-Y plots provide shear and moment diagrams directly.

Arrow Plots display vector information on the model geometry. They can be used to understand load "flow" through a part by viewing principal stress, as well as deformation and velocity.

The I-DEAS Project Relational Database is designed to perform special calculations. All finite element model and results data are automatically stored in Pearl. So one can access it for tabular listings and reports.

Pearl's relational operators allow one to add, subtract, intersect or join columns. Find maximum or minimum values, average and sort. With Pearl and Supertab, one is in complete control of the data.

5. I-DEAS GEODRAW™

A standalone drafting system I-DEAS Geodraw is also an integrated module within I-DEAS.

With Geodraw the design engineer can quickly create fully dimensioned engineering drawings of an I-DEAS Geomod solid model, create concept sketches or use the system as a standalone engineering CAD system.

I-DEAS Geodraw has been designed as a highly productive drafting system incorporating a menu driven user interface.

Specific capabilities include a wide variety of geometry creation and manipulation tools and an on-screen electronic T-square. The dynamic dimensioning capabilities allow dimensions, leader lines, text and symbols to be interactively placed and repositioned giving the best possible drawing layout.

Final production drawings can be quickly produced through the support of leading pen plotters and Geodraw supports complete data transfer through a full IGES read and write capability.

I-DEAS Geodraw has also been designed to be a highly productive system. Dimensions can be dynamically positioned and repositioned wherever, and whenever, you want. When areas of a drawing become cluttered, dimensions can be interactively re-positioned. And all leader lines, dimension lines and arrowheads associated with the repositioning are also automatically moved with the repositioning.

The dynamic positioning capability applies to balloons,labels, notes and symbols as well. And, all dimensions will be to ANSI and ISO standards. A dynamic T-square further enhances productivity. By automatically computing angles, it eliminates volumes of trigonometric calculations.

I-DEAS Geodraw's projection feature allows one to automatically create isometric views complete with silhouette lines.

Unlike many 2D Drafting systems which are limited in the complexity of drawings they can handle, I-DEAS Geodraw, provides the database capacity to develop complete production drawings of the most complex designs.

I-DEAS Geodraw has a library of cross-hatching patterns with built in intelligence that recognizes internal hole islands.

Interfacing

I-DEAS Geodraw provides complete support of data transfer to other CAD and CAM systems through IGES. One can download complete drawings including text and annotations to review and modify drawings created on other systems. Or can transfer design geometry from drawings begun on other systems and use Geodraw's dimensioning capabilities as a highly productive detailing system.

Unlike turnkey systems which are terminal or computer specific, Geodraw runs on a wide variety of processors and displays.

INTERGRAPH

Intergraph GB Ltd., U.K.

INTRODUCTION

The purpose of this section is to provide an overview of networking and hardware at Intergraph. It is not just a listing of the products, but an explanation of the system philosophies which led to the product line.

In particular, this chapter is intended to show that the product offerings reflect how well Intergraph understands interactive computer graphics. This understanding helps to judge which new technologies will, in fact, improve a graphics system's productivity. As a result, they have consistently evolved new products incorporating selected new technologies, yet which are functionally compatible with previous products.

The Network: Communications To Support a Workflow

To understand Integraph's philosophy toward the design and use of graphics workstations and data processing systems, one should first consider their philosphy toward networking.

Their networking philosophy is molded to fit the profile of the customer's everyday work. A simplified workflow model might include the following steps:

(1) Collect data

(2) Edit data:
   - turn concepts into a design model, OR
   - create a basemap from raw geographic data

(3) Generate output:
   - produce product design and documentation, OR
   - provide map database for queries and analysis

Individual Work and Collective Work

Basically, there are two categories of work accomplished using Intergraph systems. On one hand are situations best described as requiring a personal, or individual, database. Here, within a standalone workstation environment, an individual works on small personal projects or subsets of large group projects. Due to the simplicity and limited scope of the work, these users require relatively limited computing power, limited computer memory, and little, if any exchange of information with others. An engineering workstation may ideally suit their needs.

The second type of work is collective, rather than individual, and is characterized by a large database shared by a number of people. Collective databases are typical of disciplines such as plant design, mapping, and facility management. These disciplines require databases that are "living" entities, constantly changing as many contributors add to and revise a major project. The "personal databases" feed this "master database".

Data might come from a person in the user's organization (e.g., original work of a design engineer). Or it might come from an existing source (e.g., the scanning of a map). Data from all sources is combined in the "master database" to form a finished design model, basemap, or other project. This completed information can, in turn, generate various types of output (e.g. reference maps, assembly drawings, user documentation, presentation graphics).

It is significant to note that the "master database" itself is not copied or distributed; it is in one central location. Rather, there is distributed access to this central database. Many people on the network can access the information stored in the database.

As a supplier of computer graphics systems to all types of end-users, Intergraph must meet the needs of both the large, collective database and the personal database. The approach to both tasks should be functionally compatible, because information often is exchanged between personal databases and the master database. Their response to these needs occurs at two levels : (1) the network and (2) devices operating on the network.

A Network For the Graphics Environment

In terms of hardware and software, a network consists of:

- a communications medium connecting two or more devices
- communication processors serving as "gatekeepers" between each device and the network, and
- the software protocols used to route messages from one device to another.

Intergraph has chosen to use the IEEE 802.3 (Ethernet) specification for its local area networks. Their choice of IEEE 802.3 is based on several considerations. It supports high speed data transfer, is very reliable, and is easily maintained. It is expandable: any number of data processing systems, workstations, output devices, and storage devices can be supported through additional network cable. Therefore, existing network facilities are not rendered obsolete as growth occurs.

Furthermore, Intergraph believes the IEEE 802.3 protocol is appropriate for the graphics environment, in which data is transferred on a "random" basis. Much of the time, a graphics device has no need to send messages to other devices on the network. But, when it does, the data being transmitted is often quite lengthy by data processing standards. Under alternative networking specifications, the token bus and token ring technologies (IEEE 802.4 and 802.5, respectively), the sending device has only a predetermined transmission time, and then must wait until all nodes on the network have had an opportunity to transmit before it can resume. These approaches are not as suitable for the transfer of graphics data.

While for its own graphics environment Intergraph is implementing IEEE 802.3, the network interfaces with the IEEE 802.4 protocol. IEEE 802.4 supports the MAP network, a manufacturing-oriented communications system developed by General Motors Corporation.

In a similar vein, Intergraph provides communication links between their system and mainframe computers from other vendors. They view their role as one of supplying the tools to create project databases, which are graphics oriented. As part of their communications philosophy, the graphics network co-exists with other networks, allowing free information exchange between the graphics environment and other non-graphics aspects of a customer's data processing operation. The network also makes possible the economical sharing of resources such as plotters and printers.

VAX-based Intergraph Data Processing Systems

The "devices" found on the network can be grouped into three broad classes: data processing systems (DPSs), workstations, and peripherals.

The role played by the DPS on an Intergraph network is three-fold. First, some of their application software resides on the DPS where it is accessed by individual workstations. Second, the DPS is available as a computing resource. Third, its extensive storage serves as a central repository for master project databases; data from individual workstations pours into this collective database.

The hardware platform used in Intergraph Data Processing Systems since 1981 has been the VAX family of central processors from Digital Equipment Corporation. Often described as the dominant processor among engineers and scientists, the VAX has been the basis of software development by many third-party programmers. Thus, customers can maximize their investment by using their Intergraph system VAX for other applications, when needed.

In particular, their VAX-based DPSs now include:

- Intergraph 785 - a system for large-scale production environments requiring multiuser/multifunction capability and involving extensive computational loads. Based on Digital Equipment's VAX-11/785.

- Intergraph 8650 - provides the same functionality as the Intergraph 785 with increased processing power. Based on Digital Equipment's VAX 8650.

MicroVAX II-based Intergraph Data Processing Systems

In 1985, Intergraph extended their use of the VAX standard by adding Data Processing Systems based on the new MicroVAX II, also from Digital Equipment. This microprocessor is compatible with the VAX minicomputers, yet offers high performance at a lower cost. Intergraph DPSs using the MicroVAX II include:

- Micro II - this suitcase-sized unit, serves as a distributed processing node on a computer graphics network.

- Intergraph 200 - This unit and its counterpart, the Intergraph 250, provide multiuser, multitasking processor support in an economical packages.

- Intergraph 250 - The Intergraph 250 is functionally identical to the Intergraph 200. It simply has a larger tape drive and mounting space for more disk drives.

- Intergraph 252 - This dual-processor system uses two MicroVAX II CPUs for additional throughput capacity (twice that of the Intergraph 250). Built-in system redundancy, gained by dual-porting a portion of the disk storage, assures access to data.

All Intergraph Data Processing Systems, except the Micro II, are configured with both of the following specialized processors. These offload particular functions from the central processor, resulting in improved multiuser and multitasking operations:

- The Interbus File Processor functions as disk controller and data preprocessor.
- The Communications Processor provides access to the IEEE 802.3 (Ethernet) network.

  (The Micro II has only the Communications Processor and not the Interbus File Processor).

In addition, optionally available on all VAX- and MicroVAX-based Intergraph DPSs (except the Micro II) is the Company's Graphics Processor. This 64-bit array processor offloads calculation-intensive functions from the central processor.

The Changing Role of Workstations

The second broad class of devices found on the network is the graphics workstation. The role of the workstation in a computer graphics systems is changing. This is because recent advances in technology have given rise to workstations having minicomputer-level processing power and greater memory than in the past.

Unfortunately, in some circles these beneficial changes have led to confusion about the workstation's role. All too often, the workstation, with its increasing power and functionality, mistakenly is being viewed only as an end in itself. Quite to the contrary, despite its impressive capabilities, the workstation usually is just one link in a chain. In general, the work generated at a computer graphics workstation does not stay within that single device. Rather, it must be shared with other members of a project team. Likewise, the workstation operator often draws on information originating with co-workers.

Thus, reliance on a standalone workstation approach to computer-aided engineering, design and manufacturing can be too confining. A personal computer, for example, cannot support the database, communications, or computation-intense analysis typical of any sizeable project.

In Intergraph's view, the workstation's expanding capabilities are valuable because they allow the user to work independently. His progress is not tied to the availability of a central processing resource. These local "computing centers" process the users' work quickly, maintaining the interactive response speed so critical to productivity. Also, having multiple computing resources is better than relying on a single host processor which, if lost due to technical problems, would halt the work of all users.

Intergraph's aim is to offer state-of-the-art workstations which perform equally well in a standalone mode or as nodes within a network. In so doing, they support both the individual and collective phases of a typical workflow. Initial project activities involving the collection of data or the creation of personal databases are carried out in a "standalone" mode at the workstation. Results of individual work can be sent across the network to a master database on a DPS.

Workstation Family Suits Different Needs

Intergraph entered the workstation design arena in 1974 with innovative dual-screen workstations. Today, the Company continues to be a leading developer of workstations built expressly for use in interactive computer graphics.

Two lines of workstations - the dual-screen InterAct line and the desktop InterPro line - are used most often by Intergraph's customers. These two lines, introduced in 1983, have different primary purposes. The InterAct line is designed for use in "production" environments. Its ergonomic design, local display processing, and dual screens are especially beneficial when performing detailed graphics work for extended periods. The InterPro line, meanwhile, offers a compact desktop design suitable for the professional office environment.

The Advent of 32-bit Intergraph Workstations

In 1985, Intergraph began delivering a second generation of the InterPro line, a newly-designed, 32-bit workstation known as the InterPro 32. In May 1986, the same 32-bit microprocessor used in the InterPro 32 was used in the InterAct 32, a second generation of that workstation line. The microprocessor was the 32032 from National Semiconductor Corporation.

In addition to delivering more local power to the workstation, the 32032 introduced the concept of standalone workstation operation. Where previously the InterAct and InterPro functioned only as terminals which must be connected to a host Intergraph DPS, they now were also capable of running programs internally under the UNIX operating system. As a third option, the "32 generation" of workstations could use IBM's PC-DOS operating system, functioning as personal computers compatible with the IBM-AT. Lastly these workstations can emulate industry-standard terminals and communicate with mainframe computers.

Setting New Industry Standards for Graphics Workstations

In July 1986, Intergraph unveiled a major new dimension in workstation technology: workstations which deliver standalone computing power equal to that of five VAX-11/780 minicomputers. The new units are named InterAct 32C and the InterPro 32C. The "C" suffix refers to the CLIPPER 32-bit microprocessor from Fairchild Semiconductor Corporation, the workstations' new UNIX "engine". This microprocessor executes instructions at an average rate of five million instructions per second (5 MIPS). The InterAct 32C and InterPro 32C each have six megabytes of main memory, an 80 megabyte (formatted) hard disk drive and a 1.2 megabyte (formatted) floppy disk drive. In addition to applying new levels of technology, these workstations have defined new price/performance standards within the engineering workstation market.

In summary, the main Intergraph graphics workstations include:

- InterAct -- The original member of this line of dual-screen graphics workstation.

Ergonomically designed for round-the-clock use in a production environment. Features include dynamics, an extensive colour palette, high-speed repainting of screens, and a built-in digitizing surface. Available in monochromatic, mono/color and color/color combinations.

- InterAct 32 -- A 32-bit color workstation which packages the major multi-function capabilities and UNIX operating system of the InterPro 32 professional workstation within the production-oriented housing of the InterAct. Main processor is National Semiconductor's 32032 microprocessor.

- InterAct 32C -- A substantially more powerful color member of the InterAct line. Offers the same multiple modes of operation as the InterAct 32. Main processor is Fairchild Semiconductor's CLIPPER chip set.

- InterPro -- A desktop workstation for production graphics. Features same electronics as in the InterAct, with a second "virtual" screen available at the touch of a button. In monochromatic and color models.

- InterPro 32 -- A 32-bit multipurpose professional workstation. Functions as an Intergraph graphics workstation, an engineering workstation running under UNIX, a terminal emulator for several industry-standard terminals, and as an IBM PC family-compatible computer under PC-DOS. Operates both standalone and networked to the VAX. Main processor is National Semiconductor's 32032 microprocessor.

- InterPro 32C -- A substantially more powerful member of the InterPro line. Offers the same multiple modes of operation as the InterPro 32. Main processor is Fairchild Semiconductor's CLIPPER chip set.

Other special-purpose Intergraph workstations include:

- InterMap -- A boom-mounted graphics workstation specially designed for mapping applications. Features optional interface to stereoplotters, through-the-lens superimposition, and voice data entry. Monochromatic only.

- InterMap Analytic -- A photogrammetric workstation combining interactive color graphics and advanced stereoplotter technology in an integrated system. Extensive ergonomic and computer-controlled features provide for a high degree of operating efficiency. Available in color only.

- InterView -- Dual-screen display unit for use with large digitizing tables. Features same electronics as in the InterAct. Available in monochromatic and color/mono models.

Peripherals devices are the last major class of devices on the network. Intergraph provides all typical peripherals required by the graphics user, including printers, plotters, disk drives, and tape drives. They also supply special-purpose hardware such as laser photoplotters and scanners used in Electronics Design, Mapping, and Electronic Publishing applications.

Intergraph hardware is modular, permitting the use of a range of DPSs, workstations, and peripheral devices as required by customer applications.

A Look at Standards and "Standard Platforms"

In its hardware, software, and networking developments, Intergraph seeks to follow industry standards. This is done to protect the interests of both themselves and their customers. Standards provide continuity. They are the common link that makes multiple generations of Intergraph products compatible. They also permit compatibility among computer-based products purchased from multiple vendors.

Because Intergraph does not periodically "wipe the slate clean" and start over, their customers know their investment will be enhanced, not outdated, by future Intergraph products. New products do not disrupt data already existing on customers' Intergraph systems and their goal is "planned growth", not "planned obsolescence".

The standards present in Intergraph products include:

- IEEE 802.3 (Ethernet) network.

- VAX and MicroVAX II central processors from Digital Equipment - a favored processor among engineers and scientists; the center of much third-party software development

- VMS Operating System of the VAX - the uniform environment for their traditional IGDS and DMRS graphics and database management software, permitting data exchange among all disciplines using the Intergraph system.

- UNIX System V Operating System from AT&T - a workstation-based complement to VMS. Intergraph believe System V UNIX already is becoming the standard with which most large companies will want to develop their own software; as with VMS, much third-party software has been written under UNIX and is available for their customers' use.

- PC-DOS Operating System - makes available to users of the "32" and "32C" workstations the thousands of software programs written for the IBM PC family and its emulators.

- Graphical Kernal System (GKS) - provides software developers a standard set of tools for building a graphic display on the screen of the "32" and "32C" workstations.

- Initial Graphics Exchange Specification (IGES) - a "neutral format" for transferring graphics files generated on an Intergraph system to systems manufactured by other vendors.

- Electronics Design Interchange Format (EDIF) - for exchanging files in the highly specialized electronics design industry.

Under the "standards" umbrella, Intergraph does not define a "standard platform" as a particular workstation from a particular vendor, but rather as a "set of functions". Those standard functions include: the operating system (UNIX, PC-DOS); networking (IEEE 802.3); graphics (GKS); and compilers (C, Fortran, Pascal). When combined, these functions compose a "standard platform", one to which most of the software developed under UNIX can readily be ported. Because of adherence to these standards, Intergraph believes its new workstations readily meet the definition of a "standard platform".

Intergraph, InterMap, and InterPro are registered trademarks of Intergraph Corporation.

InterAct, Micro II, InterView, and File Processor are trademarks of Intergraph Corporation.

CLIPPER is a trademark of Fairchild Camera and Instrument Corporation.

UNIX is a registered trademark of AT&T.

VAX, MicroVAX, PDP, and VMS are trademarks of Digital Equipment Corporation.

IBM is a registered trademark of International Business Machines Corporation.

Ethernet is a trademark of Xerox Corporation.

Series 32000 is a trademark of National Semiconductor Corporation.

MECHANICAL ADVANTAGE®1000™/ MA1500/GPX

Cognition Inc., U.S.A.

1. INTRODUCTION

Conceptual design is the most important phase in determining ultimate product cost, performance and reliability. Mechanical Computer-Aided Engineering (MCAE) enhances conceptual design by allowing mechanical engineers to create and analyse product concepts rapidly.

Cognition, the Engineering Optimization Company, has created two fully integrated MCAE systems, the Mechanical Advantage 1000™ and Mechanical Advantage 1500/GPX. MA1000 and MA1500/GPX improve engineering productivity by helping engineers optimize designs. Design optimization leads to improved product quality, increased efficiency and lower manufacturing costs. The systems help companies create better products in less time.

With these tools, an engineer can rapidly sketch design concepts, then use appropriate first order analysis tools to reduce costs, maximize performance, and improve product reliability. MA1000 and MA1500/GPX create an integrated engineering model that stores both the geometry of a design concept and the underlying engineering principles. An intelligent electronic notebook captures the history and engineering intent of a design. The systems facilities will extend the engineer's skills, allowing the user to explore design and manufacturing alternatives easily. Engineers can easily explore design alternatives to create a more optimal design, which can then be passed to a CAD/CAM systems, via IGES and specialized translators, for the creation of detailed engineering drawings.

The MA1000 and MA1500/GPX are integrated turnkey systems designed to be the mechanical engineer's personal resource. Each system includes a Cognition Application Engine Plus™ (CAE+™) and several Personal Workstations. Personal Workstations sit on the engineer's desk and are easily accessible for non-design applications, such as word processing and spreadsheets. An advanced visually oriented user interface makes the system easy to learn and easy to use without any knowledge of programming whatsoever. Best of all, it's available at an affordable price. By helping engineers design better products in less time, the MCAE Systems will help revolutionize the practice of mechanical engineering for product design.

2. SYSTEMS ARCHITECTURE

The MA1000 and MA1500/GPX's open system architectures integrate industry standard hardware platforms with specially developed hardware enhancements. Careful selection and integration of advanced technologies with Cognition-specific hardware and software makes MA100 and MA1500/GPX finely tuned, powerful systems that meet the engineers needs.

Hardware

Both Mechanical Advantage 1000 and Mechanical Advantage 1500/GPX include a Cognition Application Engine Plus™ (CAE+™). The basic CAE+ configuration includes a Digital Equipment Corporation MicroVAX™ II with a 5MB of memory, a 95MB streaming cartridge tape and two 71MB hard disks. Options include a laser printer, plotter, additional memory, hard disk storage and other peripherals.

- MA1500/GPX includes either one or two DEC VAX station II/GPX™ Engineering Workstations. Each desktop workstation consists of a 19" high-resolution monitor with tilt/swivel, full function keyboard, and three-button mouse. An extended configuration allows the user to add up to two additional Personal Workstations, based on IBM PC/ATs with High resolution color display.

- MA1000 includes up to five Personal Engineering Workstations. Each desktop Personal Workstation consists of an IBM PC/AT™, 15" or 19" high-resolution color display, expanded memory, math co-processor, full function keyboard, a 1.2MB floppy disk and data tablet with pen. Options include a larger data tablet, two-button mouse, and hard disk storage.

Networking

Individual Personal Workstations are connected to the CAE+ via an Ethernet local area network (LAN). Additional servers and workstations can be added to the LAN as needed. Laser printers and plotters can be connected to the CAE+ and accessed by all workstations on the LAN. MA1000 and MA1500/GPX systems are compatible with existing networks and can communicate with UNIX™ or VAX™ VMS™-based hosts. A special virtual terminal capability allows the Personal Workstation to emulate a DEC VT100™ or Tektronix 4010 terminal via either the LAN or RS232 serial connections.

UNIX and IBM PC Compatibility

The CAE+ uses ULTRIX-32M™, DEC's UNIX operating system for high performance. UNIX-based systems enable the user to easily access popular programming languages such as C or FORTRAN. Personal Workstations, based on the PC/AT, use the MS-DOS™ operating system, allowing the engineer to access thousands of existing software packages for word processing, presentation graphics, electronic mail, forecasting, spreadsheets and other engineering analysis. The high-resolution graphics environment is CGA-compatible for full use of IBM graphics programs.

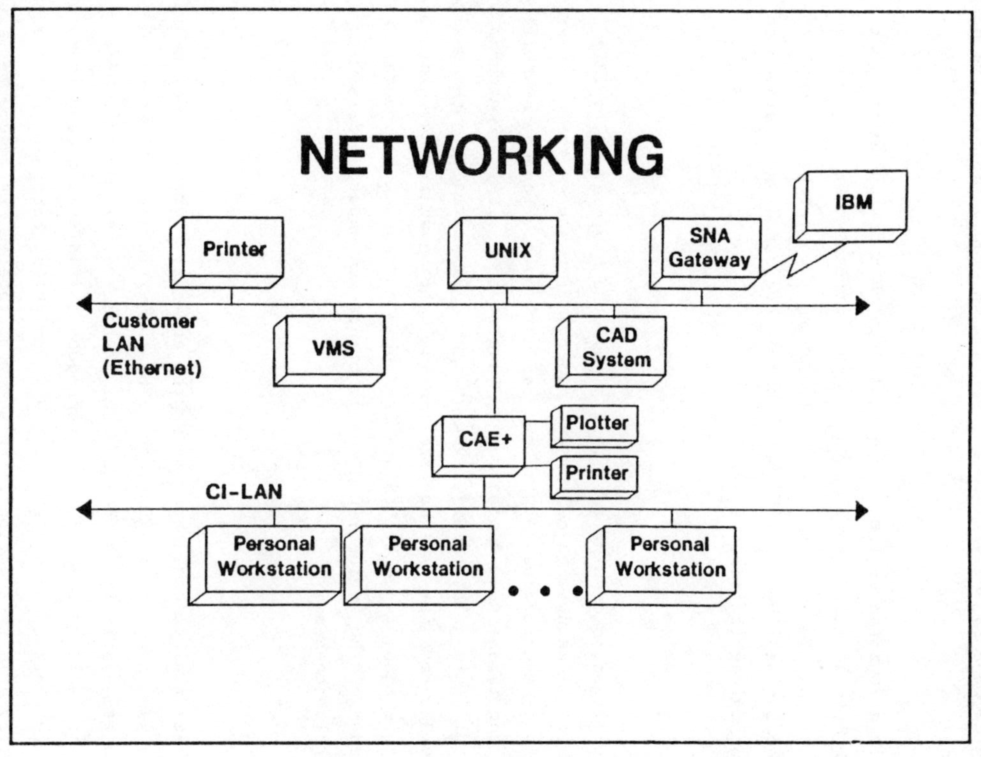

The MA1000 and 1500/GPX are designed to be used with existing customer networks

3. THE OPTIMIZER SOFTWARE

The Optimizer Family of tools is an integral part of the Cognition Mechanical Advantage® series of Mechanical Computer-Aided Engineering (MCAE) systems. The Optimizer Family helps mechanical engineers easily create, analyze, and optimize product concepts. It includes SketchPad™, MathSolve®, Intelligent Notebooks™, on-line engineering handbooks, analysis tools, virtual terminals, interactive help, and text annotation.

The Optimizer Family allows the engineer to quickly sketch a design concept. The engineer can then create sets of equations that represent the underlying engineering principles of the design. These equations are linked to the sketched concept to create an Integrated Engineering Model™, which can be evaluated and iterated to arrive at a more optimal design concept.

SketchPad

SketchPad is an intelligent sketching tool that allows the engineer to rapidly input design concepts as if sketching with pencil and paper. It captures the engineer's intent and preserves geometric constraints, such as horizontal, tangent or collinear. For example, if a line is sketched approximately tangent to a circle, SketchPad will automatically maintain this relationship, even when changes are made to the design. SketchPad also provides immediate feedback to the engineer on what constraints are being applied, in this case, tangency. Since SketchPad automatically updates the sketch after each change, the engineer can easily create and update models with extremely complex relationships.

MathSolve

MathSolve is a mathematical package that allows the engineer to rapidly define and solve sets of linear and non-linear equations. These equations can be used to represent the engineering principles in a design. MathSolve automatically determines whether to use direct or iterative solution techniques. It displays equations in a natural format and includes a summary sheet of all variables contained in the equations It contains most relevant math functions, including arithmetic, trigonometry, exponents and logarithms. Univariate optimization techniques help the engineer arrive at a better solution.

On-Line Engineering Handbooks

The Optimizer provides an on-line version of frequently used sections of standard engineering reference handbooks. These include Marks', Roark's and Shigley's reference books. Engineers can also develop their own handbooks, containing customized equations or design methodology. Equations appear just as they do in the standard book.

Analysis Tools

The Optimizer includes a set of first order, or preliminary, analysis tools. These include capabilities for analyzing physical properties and kinematics. The optimal BEASY Boundary Element Analysis System is available for stress and thermal analysis, and interfaces are provided for other popular third party design and analysis tools.

The Integrated Engineering Model

The Optimizer allows the engineer to link SketchPad geometry with MathSolve equations to create an integrated engineering model. The engineer can then perform "what if" analyses by changing either a variable in a MathSolve equation, or a dimension in the SketchPad geometry. Both the equations and the linked geometry will automatically be updated to maintain all previously specified constraints. This allows the engineer to concentrate on the engineering aspects of the design.

The Intelligent Notebook

The Integrated Engineering Model is stored in the Intelligent Notebook, an automated version of the traditional engineer's notebook. All the components of a design, including sketches, engineering equations, and descriptive notes, are stored together on a notebook page. Alternative design concepts can also be stored in the notebook to preserve the engineer's rationale in choosing the final design concept. This design history can be easily understood by other engineers for future modifications or redesigns and is available to manufacturing engineers as well.

Virtual Terminal

The Virtual Terminal capability allows engineers to access other computing environments and run additional software packages. The Optimizer includes emulation of DEC VT1XX and Tektronix 4010 terminals without leaving the Mechanical Advantage environment.

Text Processing

The Optimizer includes a text processing capability that allows the engineer to annotate sketches, write notes or prepare mail message.

Electronic Mail

The Optimizer's Electronic Mail facility allows the engineer to send and receive electronic mail messages, including sketches, math notes and text. The engineer can also transmit to and receive mail from the corporate computing environment.

4. THIRD PARTY SOFTWARE

The Mechanical Advantage provides tools for engineers to integrate or interface their own design and analysis tools. In addition, the engineer can interface to popular third party software packages, such as PATRAN™. Cognition is continually evaluating various classes of third party software to determine which tools would be most appropriately integrated into the Mechanical Advantage 1000 and 1500/GPX system.

5. THE ENGINEER'S DESKTOP™: AN ADVANCED USER INTERFACE

All of The Optimizer functions are integrated in the engineer's desktop, an easy to learn and use system interface. Familiar engineering concepts are consistently utilized throughout the Optimizer Family. The emphasis is on pointing, using data tablet and pen, rather than typing. All system tools and functions are represented with small graphic symbols or "icons". Together with on-line context-sensitive help, this enables the engineer to become productive in a matter of only hours.

6. COGNITION: A TURNKEY SYSTEM SUPPLIER

Cognition is a full-service system supplier, offering a wide range of post-sales support, hardware and software service, technical training, documentation and consultation. As a pioneer in the field of MCAE, Cognition is committed to providing mechanical engineers with the increased functionality and performance they will need for complex design tasks. Cognition products are available through a direct North American and European sales force and distributors worldwide.

7. MECHANICAL ADVANTAGE 1000 SPECIFICATIONS

SOFTWARE : Standard Software and Analysis Tools

The Optimizer™ Family

* SketchPad
* MathSolve
* Kinematics
* Physical Properties
* Intelligent Notebook
* Univariate Optimization
* Engineering Handbooks (selections from Roark's, Mark's and Shigley's)
* Text Processing

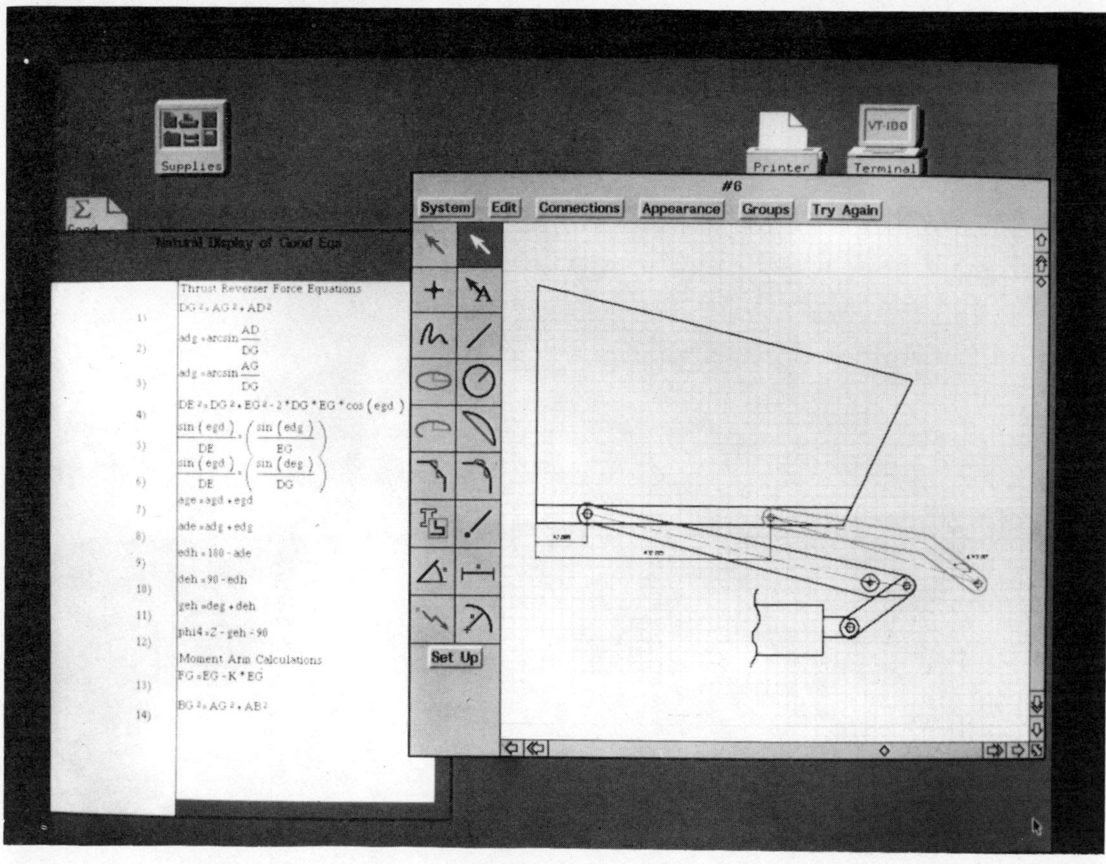

Cognition's Mechanical Advantage MCAE workstation lets the engineer optimize design concepts by creating an Integrated Engineering Model, combining sketched geometry (right) with engineering equations (left).

Ethernet Connection

* Console Terminal with Hardcopy Printer
* Diagnostics

CAE+ Options

* 1200 Baud Modem
* Async Interface (4-RS232 ports)
* 1/2" 1600 bpi Magnetic Tape
* Laser Printer - 300 dpi, 8 copies/minute
* HP7475 Plotter
* Additional 71 MB 5-1/4" Winchester Disks
* Additional Memory (9MB)
* Multiworkstation Interconnect (Required for multiworkstation configuration)

8. MECHANICAL ADVANTAGE 1500/GPX SPECIFICATIONS

SOFTWARE: Standard Software and Analysis Tools

The Optimizer Family:

* SketchPad
* MathSolve
* Kinematics
* Physical Properties
* Intelligent Notebook
* Univariate Optimization
* Engineering Handbooks (selections from Roark's, Mark's, and Shigley's)
* Text Processing
* On-Line Help
* Electronic Mail

ULTRIX-32M (UNIX-Compatible)

Optional Software and Analysis Tools

* Boundary Element Analysis (BEASY™)
* IGES
* DECNET
* Virtual Terminal: Tektronix 4010, DEC VT1XX
* UNIX™ Software Development Environment
* ROMAX

HARDWARE: GPX Personal Engineering Workstation

* 19" Color Graphics Display
  1024 x 864 Resolution
  16 active colors from pallette of 16.7 million
  Tilt/Swivel Base, Non-glare Screen

* On-Line Help
* Electronic Mail

MS-DOS
ULTRIX-32M
(UNIX-compatible)

Optional Software and Analysis Tools

* Boundary Element Analysis (BEASY^{TM})
* IGES
* ASCII Database Extractor
* DECNET
* Virtual Terminal:
  Tektronix 4010, DEC VT1XX
* UNIX^{TM} Software Development Environment
* ROMAX
* MetSel2^{TM}

HARDWARE: Personal Engineering Workstation

* IBM PC/AT
  2.25 MB Expanded Memory
  Full 640KB of IBM PC/AT
  Base Memory for 3rd party software

  1.2 MB Floppy Disk
  Full Function Keyboard
  Numeric Coprocessor
  Data Tablet
  Ethernet Connection
  1024 x 768 Resolution
  16 Colors from pallette of 4096
  CGA compatibility
  Tilt/Swivel Base
* Data Tablet with Pen (6"x 9")
* Hardware Diagnostics
* Additional Disk & Memory Included with Multiple Workstations

Workstation Options

* 19" Color Monitor (1280x1024)
* 30MB 5-1/4" Winchester Disk
* Data Tablet with Pen (12"x12")
* Two Button Mouse (in lieu of tablet)

Cognition Application Engine Plus (CAE+) Minimum Configuration

* Micro VAX II; 5MB RAM
  95 MB Streaming Cartridge Tape
  2-71 MB 5-1/4" Winchester Disks

* Three-Button Mouse
* Full Function Keyboard

Cognition Application Engine Plus (CAE+) Minimum Configuration

* Micro VAXII: 5MB RAM
  95MB Streaming Cartridge Tape
  2-71 MB 5-1/4" Winchester Disks
  Ethernet Interface
* Diagnostics

CAE+ Options

* 1200 Baud Modem
* Async Interface (4-RS232 ports)
* 1/2" 1600 bpi Magnetic Tape
* Laser Printer - 300 dpi, 8 copies/minute
* HP 7475 Plotter
* Additional 71MB 5-1/4" Winchester Disk
* Additional Memory (to 9MB)
* Ethernet Connection

Mechanical Advantage and MathSolve are registered trademarks and MA1000, The Optimizer, SketchPad, Intelligent Notebook, Cognition Application Engine Plus, CAE+ and Engineering Model are trademarks of Cognition Inc.

BEASY is a trademark of Computational Mechanics Inc. MetSel2 is a trademark of the American Society for Metals.

All information subject to change without notice

PADL-2

Cornell Programmable Automation, Cornell
University, U.S.A.

DESCRIPTION OF THE PADL-2 SOLID MODELLING SYSTEM

1.0 INTRODUCTION

PADL is an acronym for Part and Assembly Description Language. More generally, "PADL" has come to designate a family of languages and geometric (solid) modelling systems wherein the primary representational medium is Constructive Solid Geometry [REQU82]. PADL-system research and development was launched in 1974 by the Production Automation Project at the University of Rochester, and continues today under the same technical leadership at Cornell University in the Cornell Programmable Automation group.

1.1 Historical Summary

The PADL-1 system was built at the University of Rochester in 1974-77 to handle objects describable as compositions of orthogonally positioned blocks and cylinders [VOEL78]. PADL-1 was never intended to be an industrially viable modelling system; rather, it was designed to be an elegant "turnkey toy system" that would demonstrate some new principles and algorithms, serve as a teaching and research tool, and provide started-technology for vendors. The first version of PADL-1 was equipped with powerful graphic display and drawing-layout facilities. These were supplemented in 1980 with a color-graphic shader and a mass-property calculator.[<1-1>]

PADL-1 is fulfilling effectively the first two goals -- demonstrating principles and algorithms, and serving as an educational and research tool. Well over 100 copies are in the field at mid-1986, and it is still used effectively in educational settings. However, the vendor community did not elect to extend and commercialize PADL-1 when it first appeared, for reasons summarized in an essay within [BROW82]. This lapse led to the formation of a project called PADL-2, whose major technical objectives were the design and implementation of a more modular and extensible system, with increased geometric coverage, for eventual use in the mechanical industries.

The central premise underlying PADL-2 is this: geometric modelling systems can be used for diverse purposes and can have diverse input and output sybsystems, but most should be able to use,

---

[<1-1>] In early 1982 a version of PADL-1 equipped with a graphic input sybsystem was offered to a dozen Unigraphics<TM> licensees by the McDonnell Douglas Automation Company.

internally, a common core of representational and computational facilities. It is this putative common core that the PADL-2 Project sought to develop. The common-core concept determined PADL-2's constituency:

- users of solid modelling technology having enough in-house expertise to interface core modules to their existing graphics systems, database systems, and application programs;

- vendors of CAD-CAM technology needing core modules for proprietary systems;

- research groups needing powerful modelling facilities for experimental purposes.

The character of the constituency led to the following arrangements for staffing and funding of the PADL-2 Project.

- The Production Automation Project agreed to provide technical leadership and some of the manpower for the Project, and to serve as the public custodian of the Project's results. (The custodial function was transferred to Cornell Programmable Automation in 1986; see below).

- Ten Industrial Sponsors<1-2> agreed to provide about half of the Project's funding and six man-years of engineering effort in return for special rights to the Project's results for a finite period. (These rights are summarized in [BROW79] and reflected in the dissemination policy described below.)

- The National Science Foundation agreed to provide the remaining funding because PADL-2 posed interesting research and system-design issues, and also to secure access to the Project's results for the research and educational communities and for government agencies and contractors.

The PADL-2 Project was launched formally in December of 1978 and was concluded formally on May 19, 1981. An initial version of the core system designated P2/MM was released to the Industrial Sponsors on the latter date [BROW82]. A small P.A.P. team continued to debug and redesign portions of the system in 1981/82 using residual funds from the original project and some NSF continuation funding. This effort produced PP2/1.0 at mid-1982, this being Version 1.0 of a Public PADL-2 core system.

Maintenance and improvement of the core system led to occasional later releases -- PP2/1.1, PP2/1.2, etc. (The current version as of September 1986 is PP2/2.1). In addition, some PADL-2 application modules and core-system extensions (usually called "optional modules" in the sequel) have been developed with independent resources, e.g., by industrial Residents working at the Production Automation Project and/or by P.A.P. personnel funded from private sources. The first such module, a mass-property calculator, was released in 1983. A visualization package has also been released, and other optional modules are in development.

The PADL-2 core has been put to use in diverse ways. Known research applications to date include CNC-machining simulation, verification and programming; simulation of industrial robots; representation of dimensions and tolerances; automatic feature extraction; machining process planning; and automatic adaptive finite-element mesh generation and analysis. Several commercial systems incorporate PP2, including Unisolids (McDonnell Douglas), Cynergy (Westinghouse), Series 7000 (Autotrol), and Engineer

---

<1-2> Boeing Commercial Airplane Co., Calma Co., Deere & Co., Digital Equipment Corp., Eastman Kodak Co., Lawrence Livermore Laboratory, McDonnell Douglas Automation Co., Tektronix, Inc., Sandia National Laboratories, and United Technologies Research Center.

Works (Cadetron). A bilateral translator between PADL-2 and Combinatorial Geometry representations has been built at Sandia National Laboratories to facilitate object definition for radiation transport codes.

On August 29, 1986, by agreement of the University of Rochester, Cornell University, and the National Science Foundation, title to the PADL-2 software systems was transferred from the University of Rochester to Cornell University. The Cornell Programmable Automation group within the Cornell Manufacturing Engineering and Productivitiy Program (COMEPP) assumed the responsibilities and commitments for PADL-2 maintenance, dissemination, and development.

In summary, a "core system" solid modeller dubbed PP2/n.m is available for public dissemination. The system has considerable power and is likely to gain more through improvements and extensions, but it is NOT a turnkey CAD/CAM system for immediate industrial use. Its commissioning, integration with other systems, and in-house extension and maintenance require considerable software sophistication and some knowledge of geometric modelling theory and technology. Those who want a turnkey solid modeller for teaching and general familiarization are encouraged to consider PADL-1 [PEIR80]. Those wanting turnkey systems for mainline industrial use are advised to contact the vendor community.

1.2 Summary of the Dissemination Policy

The main themes of the PP2/n.m dissemination policy are the following.

- The ten Industrial Sponsors of the PADL-2 Project have essentially unrestricted rights to use, modify, and (re-)disseminate PADL-2 systems.

- Non-profit educational institutions and non-profit U.S. domestic research organizations can obtain an internal-use license for PP2/n.m for $800, but they may not redisseminate the system.<1-3>

- U.S. Government agencies and contractors can obtain a license to use PP2/n.m, for governmental purposes only, for $800.<1-3>

- Other organizations can obtain an internal-use license for PP2/n.m for $20,000 but they may not redisseminate the system.<1-4>

- Organizations not having redissemination rights may obtain them on payment of a total license fee of $50,000 (which was the original Industrial Sponsor's fee for the PADL-2 Project).<1-4>

- PP2/n.m is disseminated as outlined above with essentially no commissioning or maintenance support available to individual licensees. Maintenance and improvement of the system at large are handled through the dissemination of updates.

- The dissemination of optional modules developed with independent resources is handled by separate licenses.

<1-3>The $800 fee covers direct dissemination costs. It may be adjusted after January 1, 1987.

<1-4>A portion of the fees from PP2/n.m commercial-use licenses will be used to maintain the system and to do some limited further development. The residual funds, if any, are to be split between the National Science Foundation and Cornell University, with the latter's share tagged for the support of research in programmable automation.

2.0 PADL-2 SOFTWARE

PADL-2 software consists of the core modelling system PP2/n.m, where n.m is a version number, and a set of optional modules which extend and apply the core system. All PADL-2 software is supplied in source-code format.

2.1 The PP2/n.m System -- A Few Key Facts

- PP2/n.m is concerned only with nominal (ideal, untoleranced) geometry; tolerancing facilities are not provided.
- The domain of PP2/n.m is the class of objects representable by bounded compositions of

  - planar halfspaces
  - cylindrical halfspaces
  - conical halfspaces
  - spherical halfspaces
  - toroidal halfspaces<2-1>

  using the (general) regularized set operators

  - union
  - intersection
  - difference

  plus an aggregation operator for "assemble" and (general) rigid motions (translations and rotations). The halfspaces are available through the bounded primitive solids BLOCK, WEDGE, CYLINDER, CONE, and SPHERE, and through a general "metaprimitive" construction facility.

2.1.1 Core Subsystems

Nearly all of the core modules on the right side of Figure 1 are organized as procedurally accessible subsystems. This means that one uses them through subroutine calls rather than by accessing directly their internal data structures. Brief descriptions of the major core modules follow.

The CSG graph manager, **GRAPAK** manages (creates, edits, deletes, etc.) graph representations of constructively defined solids and assemblies, coordinate systems, and real expressions; it also manages generics (parametric library objects) and contexts [BROW82, MARI82]. CSG graphs differ from CSG trees in that entities in graphs may be shared.

POSTFIX is a collection of direct-access Fortran Arrays containing tree representations of solids and assemblies in postfix format. These are constructed by a GRAPAK procedure that 1) instantiates generic (library) objects, 2) creates separate instances of shared entities, and 3) pushes rigid motions onto the leaves of trees.

The boundary subsystem, **BFILE/2** manages a four-level representation scheme whose logical entities are linked collections (graphs) of "assemblies", "solids", "faces", and "edges". The main role of BFILE/2 is to provide a repository for boundary representations of solids and assemblies [REQU82], but it may also be used to store wireframe and other representations of solid and non-solid entities because BFILE/2 imposes no geometrical semantics on its logical entities.

The computational geometry package, **CGPAK** is a collection of procedures that do useful geometrical calculations -- surface/surface intersection, curve/halfspace classification, and so forth [BROW82, TILO82].

<2-1>The torus halfspace is not supported by all computational geometry services.

The boundary evaluator, **BEVAL** converts a CSG-tree into a boundary representation. PP2/2.1 is supplied with an incremental boundary evaluator which handles certain kinds of edit operations efficiently.

RMPAK and **STGPAK** are supporting subsystems for the management and manipulation of rigid motions and character strings. (The two subsystems are independent although shown as one in Figure 1.)

Supporting subsystems drive data-structuring and **storage management** facilities in a Fortran environment.

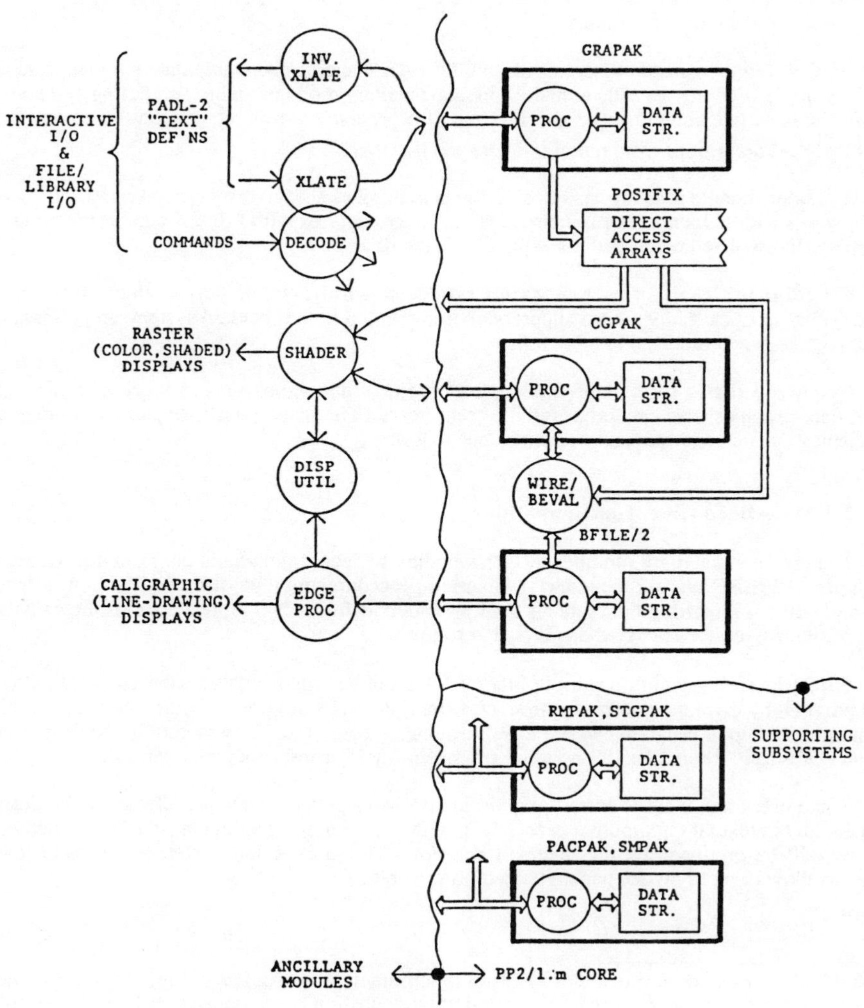

Figure 1.

2.1.2 Ancillary Modules

The modules on the left side of Figure 1 provide some I/O facilities and means for controlling the whole, thereby creating a system from a collection of wholly or partially independent subsystems. Many PP2 users will want to replace some or all of the ancillary modules with others better suited to their needs. Brief descriptions of the supplied modules follow.

The PADL-2 **language translator** contains two kinds of statements [MARI82]:

- definitional statements for solids and assemblies, coordinate systems, symbolic-parameter expressions, attributes, and so forth, and
- commands which evoke actions, e.g. produce displays, store object definitions in a library.

An *interactive definition translator* issues calls to GRAPAK to create and manipulate graph representations, and a *command decoder* issues calls to many core and ancillary modules and to computing system utilities. These two modules interact and serve as a PP2 monitor (system controller). An *inverse-translate module* produces PADL-2 definitions from representations in GRAPAK.<2-2>

A **shader** module uses ray casting algorithms to produce shaded displays and raster representations of line drawings with hidden lines suppressed. The shader supplied with PP2/2.1 can accommodate many raster displays by localized modifications to the device interface.

A **calligraphic display generator** produces wireframe displays which include profile (silhouette) edges. Local-hidden-edge suppression is supported in the standard system; an optional module which suppresses global hidden edges is available.

Display utilities form a graphic support package analogous to, but more compact than, the "standard core graphics" systems proposed in recent years. The display-utilities package allows users to specify display devices, viewpoints, viewports, and so forth.

2.1.3 Alternative Configurations

The core and ancillary modules in PP2/n.m may be reconfigured and controlled in various ways. For example: BFILE/2 and the boundary evaluation procedures may be discarded without affecting the Shader, and without impairing the system's ability to support from CSG representations the calculation of mass properties, ray-caster generated displays, and so forth.

Similarly, the system or a subset of its modules can be organized as a subsystem callable from an external program by invoking the translator/inverse-translator via a program callable interface. In this mode of operation the external program can use PP2 "through the front door" by generating PADL text, or it can issue direct calls to PP2 modules if it assumes responsibility for consistency maintenance.

Some users will want to install graphic-input subsystems for humans. These can be designed to cooperate with the textual input/output procedures, with the assurance that human-readable, archivable text definitions will be produced by the inverse-translator. The graphic-input system may also invoke the translator to allow users to invoke parameterized library objects.

<2-2>Archival (library) definitions in a PP2/2.m environment are PADL-2 string. This has a number of advantages - conciseness, human readability, parameter substitution at invocation (very powerful!) - but entails translation overhead when library objects are invoked.

2.1.4 Core System Improvements

The effort that the Cornell Programmable Automation group can apply to further development of the PP2/n.m core system is limited rather severely by the resources available to fund such work<2.3> , and also by issues of propriety: how far should a university group carry a system when commercial vendors are developing derivative, similar, and competitive systems?

We intend to focus such effort as can be spared from our research activities and funded by commercial licensing revenue on **maintenance** and localized **improvement** of the Figure 1 core. Specifically, we expect to issue some later versions of PP2/n.m which will correct bugs found in earlier versions, and which will provide significantly improved versions of a few specific modules.

2.2 Optional Modules

Certain application modules and core-system enhancements developed with non-federal resources are made publicly available from time to time as "optional modules." Generally these have the character of plug-in components which require very modest modifications to the host PP2/n.m system. At present, only the two modules described below are available, but more will become available in 1987. For example, experimental IGES translators developed by the Ford Motor Company will be made available soon as an optional module.

2.2.1 Mass Property Module PMP/n.m

PMP/n.m designates a PADL-2 Mass Properties module or subsystem. The module computes estimates, using approximation and modified Monte Carlo techniques, of the following properties for any PADL-2 definable solid:

- volume;
- centroid (barycenter);
- moments of inertia about the PP2 LAB coordinate system;
- products of inertia about the PP2 LAB coordinate system;
- standard-deviation estimates for the distribution of the foregoing estimates about their true values;
- principal moments of inertia (derived from the LAB moments and products) and
- principal axes (also derived from the LAB moments and products).

<2.3> We take here a legalistic view of what constitutes PP2/n.m: it is software whose dissemination is governed by the fee and condition schedule set forth in Section 3.2.

Two alternative, user-selectable calculation techniques are available: ray classification (uniform columnar decomposition, which is the default technique), and hierarchical cell decomposition. The accuracies of the estimates produced by either method, and the corresponding computing times, may be increased or decreased through a subdivision-level parameter that the user may set.

Modules which convert PADL-2 CSG representations to octree representations are included with PMP/n.m distributions.

2.2.2 PADL-2 Visualization Package PVP/n.m

PVP/n.m denotes a two-part Visualization Package for PP2/n.m. Part "a" (PVPa/n.m) provides full hidden edge removal facilities for caligraphic display generation, while Part "b" (PVPb/n.m) is an enhanced PADL-2 graphic output package developed at the Ford Motor Company and released by Ford for dissemination as a PADL-2 optional module. PVPb has not been released by Cornell Programmable Automation pending its update from version /1.2 to /2.1.

2.3 Character of PADL-2 Software

Publicly disseminable PADL-2 software is designed to operate in medium-scale 32-bit, virtual memory computing environments. We recommend that PADL-2 software not be commissioned on systems smaller than a DEC MicroVAX II or equivalent unless significant re-engineering of the system is done.

Because portability was an important design goal, PADL-2 software is implemented in Fortran — specifically in FLECS, a structured Fortran pre-processor (FLECS translators are supplied with the software.) PP2/n.m is relatively large and can generate multi-megabyte storage images when handling complex objects. (PP2/2.1 contains about 40K lines of declarations and executable statements and about 40K lines of comments and header information.)

The PADL-2 development system was a VAX-11/780 running the VMS operating system; it is now maintained on a MicroVAX II. The research versions of the software depend on the VMS operating system for conventional run-time support; file handling, and so forth. Two versions of certain supporting systems are supplied — one which is portable and one which is written with VMS dependencies to gain performance advantages in the VMS environment. Users of PP2 software have re-written some supporting systems with system dependencies to gain similar performance improvements in other environments.

2.4 Experimental Software

For the record...

The Cornell Programmable Automation group expects to use PP2/n.m and optional modules as major tools in our research on NC verification, NC code generation and process planning, FEM meshing, and various other topics in CAD, CAM, and robotics. We expect to extend the modelling system in significant ways in the course of such research. .Some initial targets: the provision of feature-naming facilities, support for multiple computing processors, and an efficient null-object detector.

PADL-system extensions developed to support our research will have the character of experimental software... locally useful, sometimes "interesting", but idiosyncratic and not robust enough to export. Sometimes we share experimental software with collaborators at other research institutions, and sometimes experimental software shows enough promise to warrant the very considerable effort needed to convert it into publicly disseminable software. However, at this time, we make no promises that any such conversions will be made.

3. THE DISSEMINATION POLICY

3.1 Dissemination Packages

Software packages traditionally have three components: computer software, documentation, and support (i.e., service). The nature of each component in PADL-2 dissemination packages is discussed below.

3.1.1 Computer Software

PP2 computer software falls into the following four categories.

1) PP2/n.m modules, including supporting subsystems, in source-language format. The source languages are FLECS and Fortran/77. The versions of certain modules are furnished, one with and one without VAX system dependencies.

2) System-building tools, the major items being FLECS translators [BEYE75] and the LR Parser Generator [WETH79].<3-1>

3) Test programs

4) VAX/VMS .com (command) files for building the system in a VAX/VMS environment

Software may be ordered in the magnetic tape formats shown in Table 3.1.

Media:	1600 bpi 9 track DEC TK50 cartridge
Contents:	VAX/VMS Backup format VAX/VMS Copy format Unlabeled Blocked ASCII

Table 3.1

3.1.2 Documentation

PP2 modules are stable and reasonably documented both internally, via comments, and externally, via explanatory text. Table 3.2 provides a list of current system documents.

The PADL-2 Users' Manual has been designed to serve as both a primer for literate and numerate novices and a reference manual for experienced users.

<3-1>The LR system consists of a Parser Generator and an LR(1) Parser, both in Fortran 66. A customized version of the Parser is a component of PP2/n.m's input-statement translator. The Parser Generator need not be used unless a PP2 licensee wishes to generate a new Parser for a locally extended version of the language.

3.1.3 Commissioning Support and Maintenance

The "Commissioning Guide" consists almost entirely of a set of VAX/VMS .com files for building the tools, the supporting subsystems, and the whole system in a VAX/VMS environment. These files are liberally commented, and any moderately experienced system programmer who reads them carefully should be able to devise analogous procedures for different computing environments.

Document	Title	Pages
UM-10	PADL-2 Users' Manual	82
PP2G-02	PADL-2 Commissioning Guide	25
SGM-40	PADL-2 Language Interpreter	9
SGM-41	CSG Data Structure Management	21
SGM-42	PADL-2 Post-fix Representation	7
CGGM-8	RMPAK: FORTRAN Routines for Manipulating Rigid Motions	15
CGGM-12	Representations in the PADL-2 Processor: Low Level Geometric Entities	57
CGGM-13	COMPAK: FORTRAN Subroutines for Comparing Real Numbers, Vectors and Rigid Motions	15
CGGM-17	CGPAK: A Computational Geometry Package	77
CGGM-20	BFILE/2: A Boundary File for PADL-2	34
CRDM-19	PACPAK: FORTRAN Subroutines for Creating and Manipulating Data Structures	25
CRDM-20	SMPAK: FORTRAN Subroutines for Data Management	17
CRDM-21	A Policy for Character Handling in Transportable FORTRAN and Subroutines for Creating and Manipulating Strings	24
CRDM-22	Flecs/77 Users Manual	30
CRDM-24	SDPAK: A Set of FORTRAN Subroutines for Managing a 3-D Spatial Directory	11
IBE-4	PP2/2.n Boundary Evaluation	36
IOG-10	Graphics Output Processor	23
IOG-14	Programmer's Guide to the PADL-2 Shaded Graphics Output System	10
WFE-01	PADL-2 Edge Evaluator	2

Table 3.2

The Cornell Programmable Automation group will provide no commissioning assistance and no on-going support (e.g., to verify, localize, and repair bugs) to individual licensees on a formal basis, and very little on an informal basis. (Again: PADL-2 is not a turnkey CAD/CAM system; it is a system core whose integration with other systems requires considerable software maturity.)

Naturally we would like bugs to be reported to us in as orderly and documented a manner as possible. We may elect to handle serious bugs through repair bulletins issued to all licensees, but our general policy is to install repairs in batches, together with improvements, and create thereby Later Versions of the software which licensees may elect to acquire.

3.2 Licenses for PP2/n.m

Significant portions of PP2/n.m are copyrighted by the Cornell Programmable Automation group; dissemination involves the issuing of licenses to use these copyrighted materials subject to the payment of appropriate fees and the execution of agreements to adhere to certain conditions. Both the fees and the conditions were determined in 1978/79, when formal agreements were made with the Industrial Sponsors and the Public Sponsor (the National Science Foundation) of the the PADL-2 Project.<3.2>

Table 3-3 shows the PP2/n.m license fees by licensee category; the associated conditions are delineated in the cited license agreements, copies of which are attached to this document. (The major conditions are also summarized in Section 1.2.)

PP2/n.m License Fee by Category	PP2/n.m License	License Fee	Update Fee
Category 1 Industrial Sponsors of The PADL-2 Project	Special agreement	0	$800
Category 2 Agencies of and contractors to the U.S. Government	GL-1	$800	$800
Category 3 Non-profit U.S. domestic research organizations and educational orgs.	CL-2	$800	$800
Category 4 Other organizations	CL-2	$20000	$800

Table 3.3

As noted earlier, PP2/n.m is disseminated with virtually no commissioning and maintenance support for individual licensees. Corrections and improvements for the software are handled through occasional updates which usually create new versions of the core system. A licensee's original PP2/n.m license covers use of updates.

Redissemination rights for the copyrighted materials in PP2/n.m, including updates, are governed by the following conditions.

- Redissemination rights became available on June 30, 1984.
- Fee: $50,000; a prior PP2/n.m license fee, but not fees paid for updates or optional modules, is applicable to this fee.
- Mechanism: waiver of Paragraph 3 of the basic license agreement (CL-2 or GL-1).

<3.2>The various requirements imposed by the NSF are delineated in the NSF grant instrument, which is a public document. The "Agreement to Sponsor the PADL-2 Project", which (as amended) is the instrument governing relations with the Industrial Sponsors, is not a public document, but we shall usually honor requests to inspect it for non-prejudicial purposes.

3.3 Licenses for Optional Modules

The term "optional module" refers to software useable with PP2/n.m but developed with private resources beyond those provided by the PADL-2 Project and revenues generated by PP2/n.m licenses. The license and field support policies for optional modules are similar to that for PP2/n.m; details of fees are summarized in Tables 3-4 and 3-5. CPA may offer discounts on certain optional-module fees to organizations which support CPA research.

3.3.1 The PMP/n.m Dissemination Package

PMP/n.m is coded in FLECS/FORTRAN 77, and it calls many subroutines and accesses data structures in the PP2/n.m host system. The following software is supplied.

- PMP/n.m source code, organized into 24 files containing a total of about 5000 lines, of which about 2900 lines are comments.
- VAX/VMS command files which effect the integration of the module with the PP2 host system. These files are heavily commented, and the experienced system programmer should be able to devise, after reading them carefully, analogous integration procedures for other computing environments.
- Text files containing other helpful information
- For VAX/VMS users: an object-code library and a PP2/n.m-cum-PMP/n.m executable module.

3.3.1.1 User Documentation

Document IOG-15, "A Programmer's Guide to the PADL-2 Octree Processor Output System" (9pp) and insert pages for the PADL-2 Users' Manual (Document UM-10) will be supplied.

3.3.1.2 System Documentation

There is no system document devoted specifically to PMP/n.m. The code is well organized and liberally commented, and is easy to understand if one understands

- the PP2 procedures and data structures that PMP uses (these are covered by PP2 documentation), and
- the mathematical and computational principles used in the ray classification and cell decomposition methods.

These latter are described in Document TM-35a and in

"Algorithms for computing the volume and other integral properties of solid objects", by Y. T. Lee and A. A. G. Requicha, Comm. ACM, September 1982.

Copies of these documents will be supplied on request to PMP/n.m licensees.

3.3.1.3 Licenses and Fees for PMP/n.m

PMP/n.m is a PADL-2 "Optional Module", i.e. PP2-compatible code developed with private resources beyond those provided by the PADL-2 Project and revenues generated by PP2 licenses;<3-3> its dissemination is not governed by the PP2/n.m conditions set forth in Section **1.2.**

PMP/n.m will be disseminated via the standard license agreement CL-2, attached to this document, under the fee schedule shown in Table 3.4.

PMP/n.m **License Fee by Category**	PMP/n.m License Fee	Redissemination Fee
Category 3 Non-profit U.S. domestic research organizations and educational orgs.	$1000	$6000
Category 1,2,4 All Other organizations	$2000	$6000

Table 3.4

3.3.2 Availability of PVP/n.m

3.3.2.1 PVPa/n.m

The hidden line processor PVPa/n.m is disseminated via the standard license CL-2, attached to this document, and according to the fee schedule summarized in Table 3.5.

PVPa/n.m **License Fee by Category**	PVPa/n.m License Fee	Redissemination Fee
Category 3 Non-profit U.S. domestic research organizations and educational orgs.	$600	$3600
Category 1,2,4 All Other organizations	$1100	$3600

Table 3.5

Document PVPG-02, "Hidden Edge Removal for PADL-2" (46 pp) is distributed with PVPa/n.m.

3.3.2.2 PVPb/n.m

Largely due to the unavailability of suitable hardware, PVPb/n.m has not been upgraded to be compatible with the current Version of PP2/n.m and *is not distributed by CPA at this time*. CPA plans to upgrade PVPb code to be compatible with PP2/2.1 and later versions.

<3-3>PMP/1.0 was coded by Alan L. Clark, an employee of the Ford Motor Company, during an Industrial Residency at the University of Rochester Production Automation Project. PMP/1.0 draws upon and extends significantly the PADL-1 Mass Property module coded in 1979-80 mainly by Y. T. Lee.

3.4 Eligibility

All domestic and Canadian organizations, and foreign organizations in Country Groups T and V [USDC85], are eligible licensees for PADL-2 software. Organizations in Country Groups Q, S, W, Y, Z, the People's Republic of China and Afghanistan are ineligible unless they (not CPA) obtain appropriate Department of Commerce licenses for the export of PADL-2 software.

References

[BEYE75] T. Beyer, "Users' Guide to Version 22 of the Oregon FLECS/FORTRAN Programming System", October 1975, reprinted as Doc. No. CRDM-11, Production Automation Project, Univ. of Rochester, November 1976.

[BROW79] C. M. Brown and H. B. Voelcker, "The PADL-2 Project", Proc. 7th NSF Conf on Production Research & Technology, Ithaca, N.Y., pp. F-1 to F-6, September 25-27, 1979.

[BROW82] C. M. Brown, "PADL-2A: A technical summary", IEEE Computer Graphics and Applications, vol. 2, no. 2, pp. 69-84, March 1982.

[MARI82] H. A. Marisa and E.E. Hartquist, "PADL-2 Users Manual", Doc. No. UM-10/n.m, Production Automation Project, Univ. of Rochester, December 1985.

[PIER80] H. B. Pierce *et al.*, "Dissemination of the PADL-1.0/2 processor", Doc. No. ADM-01b, Production Automation Project, Univ. of Rochester, December 1980.

[REQU82] A. A. G. Requicha and H. B. Voelcker, "Solid modelling: Historical summary and contemporary assessment", IEEE Computer Graphics & Applications, vol. 2, no. 2, pp. 9-24, March 1982.

[USDC85] "Technical data", Supplement No. 3 to Part 379, Export Administration Regulations. Washington, D.C.: U.S. Department of Commerce, 1985.

[VOEL78] H. B. Voelcker *et al.*, "The PADL-1.0/2 system for defining and displaying solid objects", ACM Computer Graphics, vol. 12, no. 3, pp. 257-263, August 1978.

[WETH79] C. Wetherell and A. Shannon, "LR: Automatic parser generator and LR(1) parser", Preprint UCRL-82926, Univ. of California at Davis, 1979.

PALETTE®

Palette Systems Inc., U.S.A.

INTRODUCTION

PALETTE® is a highly integrated suite of software modules that provide general-purpose interactive graphics, CAD, (Computer-Aided Design) and integrated text, graphics and database solutions to a wide range of technical users including Government, Aerospace and Defense Industries, Manufacturers, Consulting Engineers, Architects, Utilities, Exploration Companies and Educational Establishments.

In the CAD field, PALETTE is particularly strong for high-productivity drafting applications involving one-off drafting (where there is little opportunity to benefit from the computer's incredible efficiency at repetition), very complex drawings (such as those involved in Computer-Aided Facility Engineering), and applications involving many diverse drafting disciplines. PALETTE provides off-the-shelf CAD solutions encompassing two-dimensional drafting, three-dimensional modeling and color-shaded image generation. Interfaces to most other CAD systems are available, and interfacing toolsfacilitate the development of special-purpose interactive interfaces into most major design and analysis programs. The software provides facilities for users to tailor and enhance their own systems using either a built-in command language (macros) or any of the major high-level programming languages. Users operate the system using on-screen pop-up menus, tablet menus, a powerful keyboard-driven command language, or a mixture of all three.

PALETTE's general-purpose interactive graphics system contains a proprietary graphical (spatial) database and interfacing tools that allow the graphical data to be related directly to non-graphical data stored in independent third-party relational databases such as ORACLE, VAX Rdb and even DB2 (via a network).

This makes PALETTE particularly suitable for a very wide range of non-CAD applications such as special - purpose graphics systems for defense purposes, factory floor information systems, (paperless factory) and Facilities Management. PALETTE also produces combined text and graphics documents on laser printers by merging the output from CAD systems, interactive graphics applications, databases and text processing systems, making it suitable for integrated processing and technical documentation applications.

PALETTE MODULES

PALETTE consists of the following software modules:

* Two-Dimensional Drafting
* Three-Dimensional Modeling

* Color-Shaded Imaging
* Manufacturing Instructions
* Spatial Database
* Materials Quantities and Costing
* Text and Graphics Merge
* Independent Program Interface
* Application File Interface
* IGES Interface
* SIF™ Interface
* Intellicap Interface
* Interleaf Interface
* Total Plan Database™

TWO-DIMENSIONAL MODULE

Provides full-functionality drafting including: lines, text, circles, arcs, ellipses, polygons, fillets, chamfers, tangents, french curves, dimensions, symbols, scaling, rotation, reflections, stretching-deletion, relocation, step and repeat, layers, gridding, thickness, texture color, macros and parametric design capabilities; user-defined fonts, textures and area fills, calculation of lengths, areas, centroids and second moments.

THREE-DIMENSIONAL WIREFRAME MODULE

Provides orthographic projection, first and second angel auxiliary projections, isometrics, oblique and perspective, simultaneous operation in up to four views, scaling, rotation, reflection, stretching, symbols, copying, sectioning, walk-throughs, interference checking and two-way interchange of information with the drafting module.

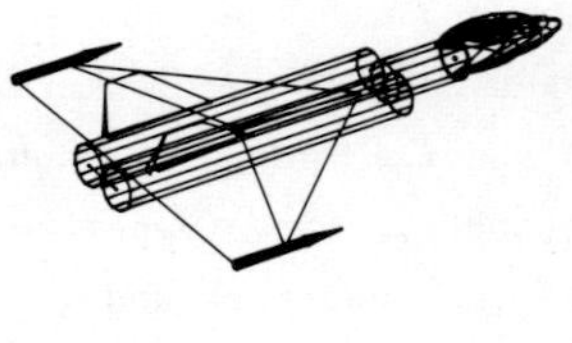

COLOR-SHADED IMAGING MODULE

Provides color-shaded images and hidden-line suppressed drawings of models developed in the Three-Dimensional Wireframe module. Supports multiple light sources, smooth (Gourand) shading, dithering, transparency and fog. Images can share the display screen simultaneously with wireframe images produced by the Three-Dimensional Wireframe Module.

MANUFACTURING INSTRUCTION MODULE

PALETTE is an industry leader in the preparation and delivery to the factory floor of computer-based manufacturing instructions (paperless factory). Instructions are assembled from existing hardcopy material (via scanning), existing CAD-based drawings (via IGES), existing text files (from wordprocessors), and existing databases (via IPI). The combined text and graphics instructions are edited in PALETTE and transmitted to the factory floor in both vector and raster form. Operators select information for display using function keyboards, bar code readers, badge readers, foot switches and continuous-speech recognition.

SPATIAL DATABASE MODULE

Allows the association of arbitrary non-graphic data with the graphical entities of a drawing or map. Queries can be constructed using both graphic (spatial) and non-graphical conditions, and results can be displayed either graphically or in the form of textual reports. For example, a plant engineer can query the database to highlight in red on a plan of the factory floor all electrical distribution boards that are north of a materials conveyor, west of an aisleway and within 53 metres of a given machine that have a surplus capacity in excess of 100 amps. The Spatial Database can also be linked transparently to existing third-party databases such as ORACLE, VAX Rdb and even DB2 (via a network), providing truly integrated graphical/non-graphical database applications.

MATERIALS, QUANTITIES AND COSTING MODULE

Automatically extracts Bills of Materials and Bills of Quantities from database drawings and produces user-defined reports, including costing information. Assemblies include both direct components and other assemblies, and can be nested to any depth.

TEXT AND GRAPHICS MERGE MODULE

Merges text from third-party wordprocessors, document preparation systems, and databases with technical drawings and illustrations produced in PALETTE or third-party CAD systems to produce camera-ready technical documentation on laser printers.

INDEPENDENT PROGRAM INTERFACE™ MODULE

This is a programming tool that uses multiple parallel processes and inter-process communication to allow independent programs written in almost any high-level language including FORTRAN, C, PASCAL and BASIC to be integrated transparently with PALETTE's own integrated suite of interactive modules. The Independent Program Interface allows customers' own programmers to enhance PALETTE in a virtually unrestricted way so as to integrate PALETTE with virtually any third-party design, analysis, text processing, database or communications program.

INTERFACE MODULES

PALETTE provides a number of pre-defined interface modules to third-party CAD, graphics, publishing and manufacturing systems including: Application File Interface (PALETTE's own proprietary ASCII file format), IGES, SIF (Integraph Corporation's CAD format), Interleaf (electronic publishing), and Intellicap (CIMtelligence processing planning system).

TOTAL PLAN DATABASE™ MODULE

This module, which is due for release early in 1988, provides the ability to create a single arbitrarily large and complex drawing or map (graphical database), which multiple users can simulataneously inquire from or update. This module is fully compatible with the Spatial Database module, allowing it to be integrated transparently with third-party databases. It is particularly suitable for Geographic Information Systems applications and Computer-Aided Facilities Engineering.

COMPUTERS AND WORKSTATIONS

PALETTE runs on:

* Digital Equipment Corp: All VAX computers and VAX station workstations with VMS operating system.
* Apollo Computer Inc: All Apollo workstations with AEGIS operating system.

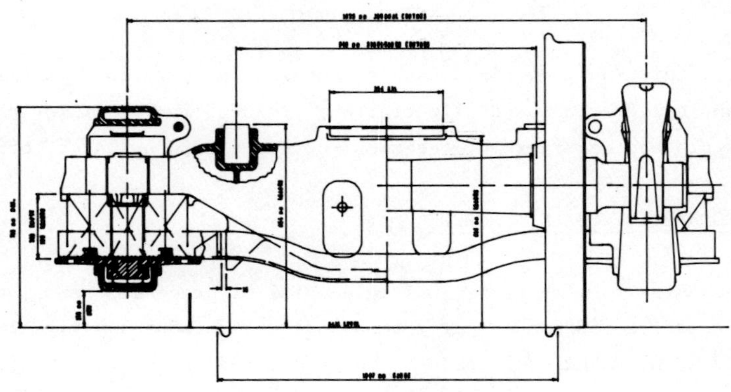

GRAPHIC DISPLAYS

PALETTE supports a wide range of terminals including:

* Tektronix
* Westward
* Pericom
* Digital
* Visual

PLOTTERS

* Hewlett Packard
* Calcomp
* Versatec
* Benson
* Houston Instruments

DIGITIZERS

* Summagraphics
* Tektronix
* Houston Instruments
* Calcomp
* GTCO

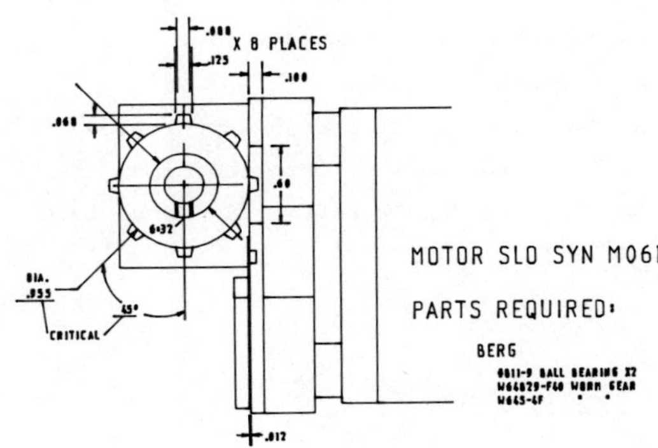

SCANNERS

* Skantek
* Vidar
* Optographic

DISTRIBUTORS

PALETTE software and support is available worldwide through an extensive network of distributors. The principle distributors are:

* USA & Canada

  Palette Systems, Inc.
  Two Burlington Woods Park
  Burlington, MA 01803
  Telephone: (617) 273-5660
  Telex: 948502
  Fax: (617) 272-4660

* Australia

  Palette Systems, Inc.
  Level 1, Silverton Park
  101 Wickham Terrace
  Brisbane 4000, Australia
  Telephone: (07) 832 4955
  Telex: 44407
  Fax: (07) 832 2693

* Europe and Japan

  Digital Equipment Corporation
  (see local phone book)

LICENCES

Licence conditions vary from country to country. In general, there is a one time fee which includes documentation and 90-day warranty. Training is performed at distributor or customer site.

TRADEMARKS

* PALETTE is a Registered Trademark of Palette Systems
* Independent Program Interface and Total Plan Database are trademarks of Palette systems
* VAX, VAX Rdb, VAXstation and VMS are trademarks of Digital Equipment Corporation
* Apollo and AEGIS are trademarks of Apollo Computer Inc
* Oracle is a trademark of Oracle Corporation
* DB2 is a trademark of IBM
* SIF is a trademark of Intergraph Corporation
* Interleaf is a trademark of Interleaf Inc
* Intellicap is a trademark of CIMtelligence Corp.

PATRAN®

PDA Engineering, U.S.A.

PATRAN®: A Computer-Aided Engineering System

ABSTRACT

PDA/PATRAN has been developed to provide engineers with a highly interactive solid modeling and analysis software system based upon an integrated data base. It operates on most advanced computer and graphic display terminal hardware. PATRAN significantly increases the productivity of engineers, accelerates the product design cycle, enables design optimization, and diminishes the need to rely on costly prototypes and tests, all of which result in improved product quality and reduced product cost. This article gives an overview of PATRAN's analytic solid modeling capabilities, finite element modeling features, the STRESS analysis capability for linear statics and eigenvalue analyses, and results evaluation options. Also discussed briefly are interfaces to analysis and CAD software.

MECHANICAL COMPUTER-AIDED ENGINEERING (MCAE)

Mechanical engineering is being revolutionized by the growing use of computers and related software. For the first time, a product such as an aircraft can be designed, analyzed, and tested for performance using a theoretical model represented mathematically with a computer. This process allows for repeated testing of the model to determine where design modifications are necessary or desirable. For example, the process can be used to analyze an aircraft wing in order to identify weaknesses during simulated flight or to highlight modifications that may be made to improve performance. In addition to the new design and analysis capabilities, increases in the power and capacity of computer hardware and reductions in hardware costs have resulted in an increase in both the capability of computer systems and the availability of these systems for use by engineers in their daily work. Recent advances in software technology, including enhancements to PDA's PATRAN software system, have simplified the use of the computer and enabled hardware to be used interactively as an integral part of the design process.

The traditional product design cycle involves the conception of a product by an engineer, the preparation of two-dimensional design drawings by a draftsman, the fabrication of a physical prototype and the testing of the prototype. Analysis and modification of the product design is undertaken only after encountering prototype testing difficulties or unsatisfactory product performance following manufacture. Figure 1 depicts this traditional product design cycle:

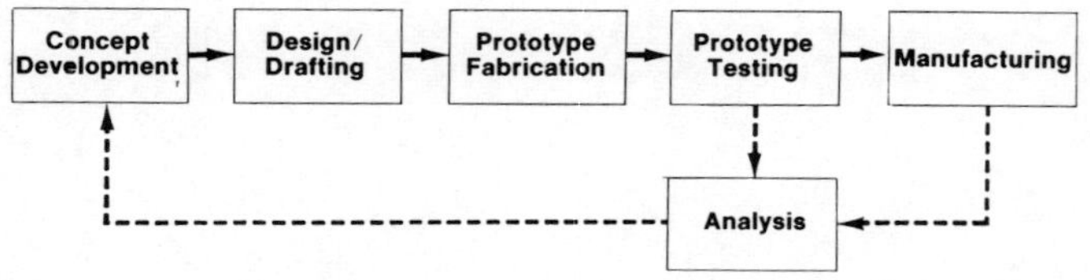

Figure 1 Traditional Product Design Cycle

This traditional process is labor intensive, error prone and time-consuming. It rarely provides sufficient product performance data early enough in the design process to modify the product design prior to the costly prototype stage or commencement of manufacture.

Today, computer software and hardware tools are being integrated into the product design cycle and engineers now are able to use the computer to design and create a computer model of a product, analyze the model, evaluate the results, predict product performance and optimize the design prior to the fabrication of a prototype, as shown in Figure 2:

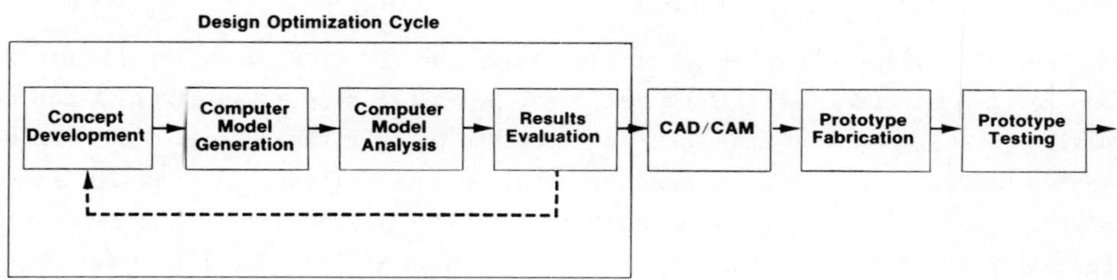

Figure 2 Today's Product Design Cycle

The MCAE process replaces the traditional design/drafting step with the design optimization cycle and provides the link to computer-aided design/drafting and computer-aided manufacturing (CAD/CAM) software.

Until recently, computer-aided analysis involved batch processing on expensive computers and interpretation of the data resulting from the analysis by mechanical engineers with specialized analysis training. Due to the expensive computer hardware and specialized engineering expertise required to accomplish this process, the computer was used for product analysis primarily by separate departments within larger corporations producing complex products. PATRAN is designed to enable the MCAE process to be conducted interactively on significantly less expensive computer hardware by less specialized mechanical engineers as an integral part of the product design process.

Various software programs from many companies and organizations are capable of performing one or more, but not all, of the steps in the design optimization cycle. It is difficult, however, to integrate programs from different suppliers since data generated in one software program must be transformed into an acceptable format for use with a subsequent program. PATRAN is the only software program which uses the same data base to perform each of the steps in the design optimization cycle. Using the same data base dramatically reduces the time involved in the cycle, as well as the possibility for error, by eliminating the need to transform data.

ANALYTIC SOLID MODELING (ASM)

PATRAN uses ASM, a solid modeling technique which is different than the constructive solid geometry (CSG) and boundary representation (B-rep) methods. Lines, surfaces, and solids are defined as continuous parametric cubic functions. The completeness of this mathematical representation assures that: section and mass properties of a solid can be calculated with extraordinary efficiency and accuracy; quantities such as variable density and state variables (e.g., temperature) can be easily represented; 3D geometry construction options are easy to use because they form nested sets; and mesh generation schemes are both flexible and efficient in the finite element model due to the close coupling of the mesh with the geometry model. ASM also allows for the implementation of advanced display and shading algorithms. The mathematical basis of ASM and descriptions of its many varied capabilities and applications (e.g., modeling of composite materials) are described further in [1, 2, 3], and are illustrated in Figures 3 through 9.

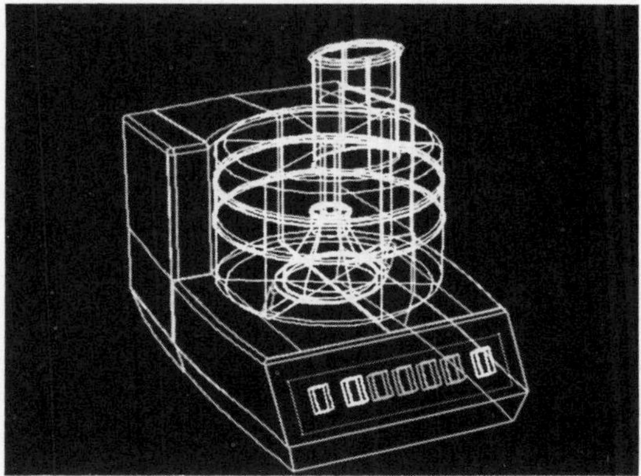

Figure 3 This wire-frame image of a food processor illustrates an early step in model generation and contains the complete mathematical description of the solid for future use in analysis.

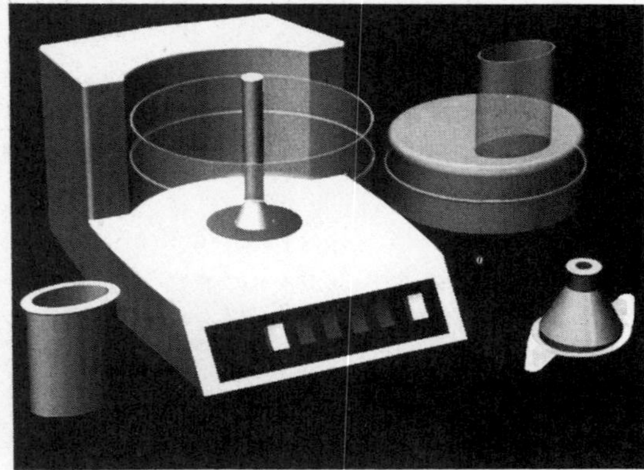

Figure 4 Exploded views permit the examination of interrelationships among components.

Figure 5 For product visualization, a realistic image demonstrates PATRAN's capabilities for transparency, multiple light sources, color ranges, and continuous shading.

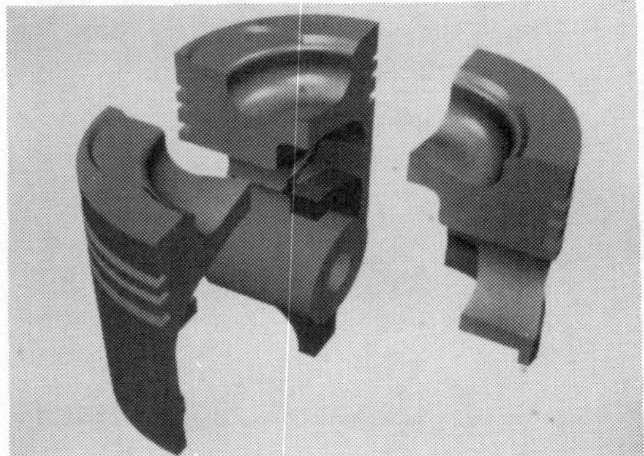

Figure 6 Exploded View of Solid-Shaded Components of a Piston Assembly (Courtesy of John Deere Product Engineering Center, Waterloo, Iowa)

Figure 7 A PATRAN-generated image of a portion of a turbine fan, as exists in any jet aircraft, is typical of a product for which performance analysis is essential.

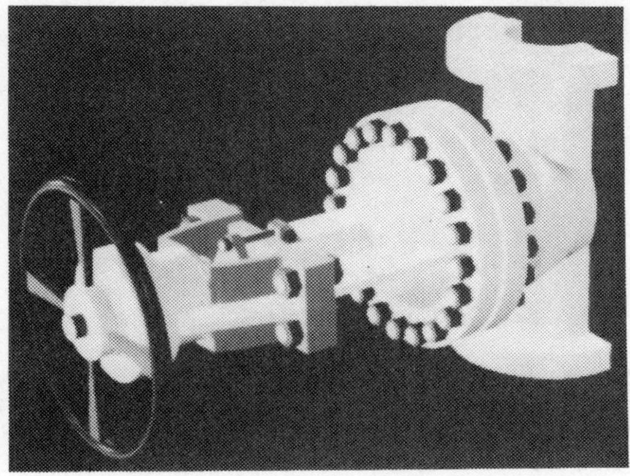

Figure 8 Solid-Shaded Model of a Valve Body (Courtesy of Failure Analysis Associates, Palo Alto, California)

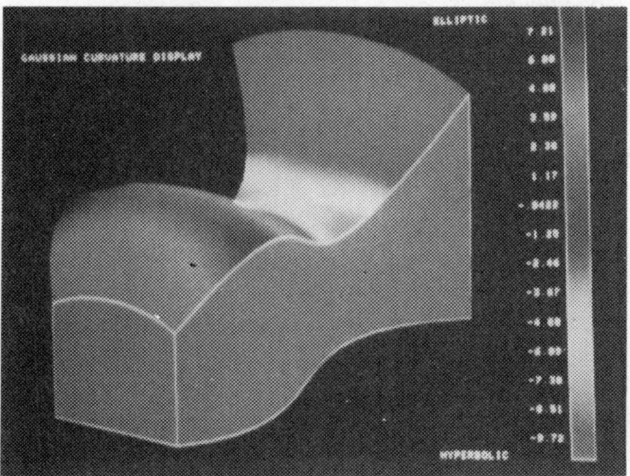

Figure 9 Gaussian Curvature Display for A Solid (Gaussian Curvature is the Product of the Two Principal Curvatures)

ANALYSIS MODELING

Once the geometry model has been generated, PATRAN offers the engineer a large number of options for creating a finite element model. PATRAN has automated uniform and non-uniform mesh generation and transitioning capabilities (Figure 10). It supports the most commonly used linear, quadratic, and cubic finite elements. The material property synthesis capabilities are complete and sophisticated: isotropic, orthotropic, anisotropic materials; as well as laminated and solid composites. Loads and boundary conditions can be concentrated or varying; PATRAN provides instant 3-D graphic feedback to the engineer to verify these are properly applied (Figure 11). Physical properties (such as

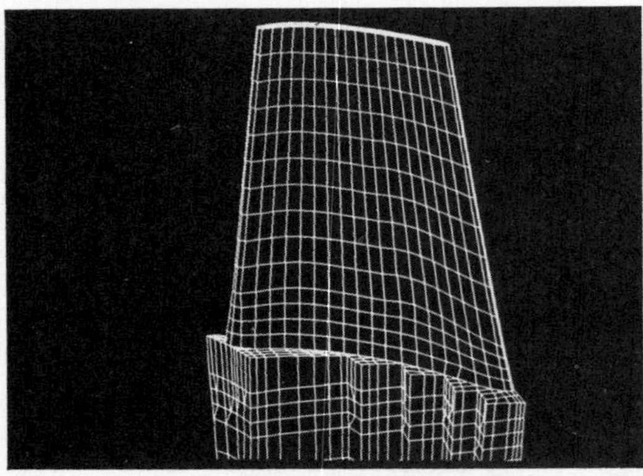

Figure 10 Analysis of the Single Blade Depicted in Figure 7 illustrates the response to the various loads encountered is based upon a finite element model consisting of many discrete elements.

Figure 11 The thermal and structural analyses of the Figure 7 blade show the simulated temperature and pressure conditions of operational use.

thickness) can be constant or varying. To verify the suitability of element shapes in the finite element model, the engineer can access model verification options to check element aspect ratio, skew, taper, and warp. The engineer can also check for free edges, cracks, or reversed surface normals. Before submitting the model for analysis, the engineer can ask PATRAN to minimize the model bandwidth or wavefront in order to reduce analysis costs.

Another example of finite element modeling and analyses is given in Figure 12, which shows a composite rocket nozzle modeled by PATRAN and subjected to thermal and structural analyses.

a. MATHEMATICAL MODEL

As the starting point for analysis, a computer model of the engine nozzle illustrates its geometry and finite elements. The different composite materials are highlighted through color coding.

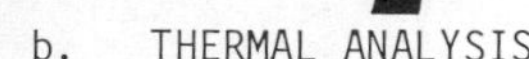

b. THERMAL ANALYSIS

The temperature distribution in the critical throat region of the engine nozzle is the result of the combustion exhaust heating and must be predicted to establish material performance limits.

c. STRUCTURAL ANALYSIS

The survivability of the exit cone component of the engine depends upon its structural response to extreme temperatures and pressure loading and must be accurately predicted to permit maximum strength at minimum weight.

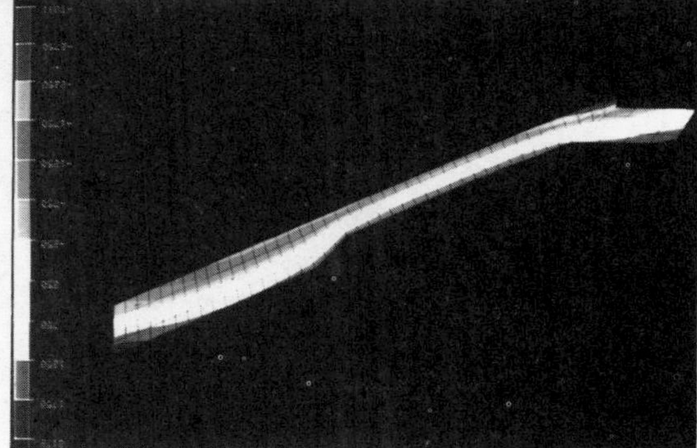

Figure 12 Finite Element Modeling, Thermal and Structural Analyses of A Rocket Nozzle Made of Composite Materials

STRESS Analysis Module

PATRAN offers an optional STRESS analysis module for linear static and eigenvalue analyses. The structural integrity of a design can be quickly assessed by a designer/analyst, without ever leaving the PATRAN system. Modifications to the design can be easily made and evaluated. This interactivity turns the computer into a computational laboratory environment, where the engineer can experiment and gain insight. The user can combine high priority interactive modeling with analysis execution in the background — up to a maximum of five simultaneous jobs can be under his direct control. Figures 13 and 14 show the results of such an interactive analysis session, where the bracket behavior under an end load is ready for results evaluation within minutes.

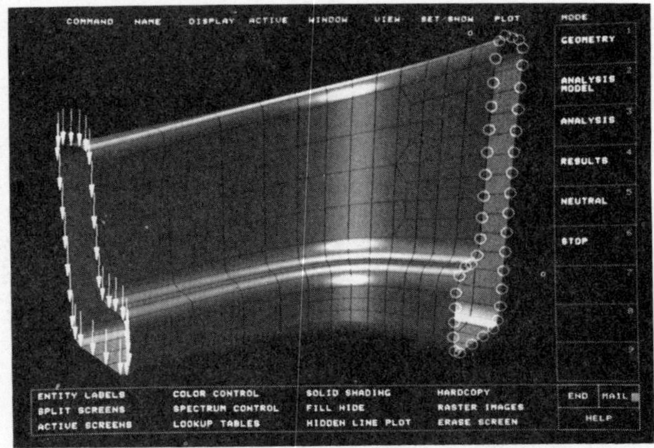

Figure 13 Finite Element Model of A Bracket Superimposed on Light Source Shaded Image — Loaded at Left and Constrained at Right

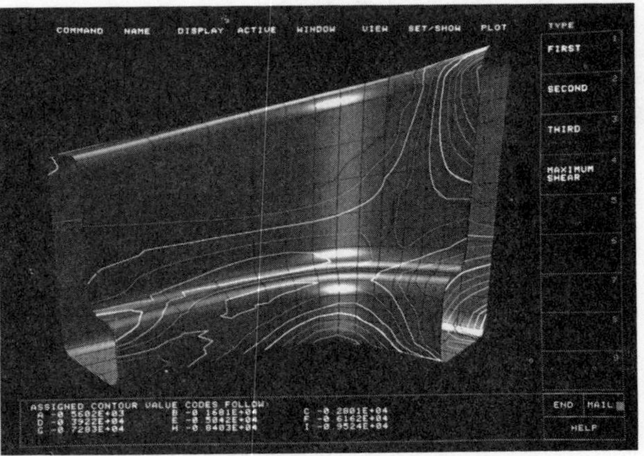

Figure 14 Maximum Principal Stress Contours of Bracket

RESULTS EVALUATION

Post-processing of the analysis results is dramatically enhanced by the use of color. Options to evaluate these results include: deformed geometry plots (with or without hidden lines); color coding of element results (e.g., strain, stress); and contouring. Additional features include: animated mode shapes or deformations, carpet plots of data surfaces, color fringe plots (solid-color contours), scale factor control, superposition of subcase results, and failure criteria display. Figures 15 and 16 are two examples of PATRAN's post-processing capabilities, for the turbine blade (of Figures 7, 10, and 11) and a pipe assembly.

Figure 15 The results of the analysis are displayed in a color-coded image superimposed on the blade itself to highlight the structural or thermal response to the operational loads.

Figure 16 Von Mises Stress Fringe Plot for a Pipe Assembly

COMPOSITE, HEAT TRANSFER, AND KINEMATICS ANALYSIS MODULES

In 1986, PDA Engineering released three additional analysis modules within PATRAN: composite design/analysis for 3D composites with nonlinear material properties; nonlinear thermal analysis (combined mode - conduction, convection, advection, gray or spectral thermal radiation, and arbitrary heat source); and rigid-body mechanism dynamics analysis. Please contact PDA Engineering for details.

INTERFACES

PATRAN communicates to and from analysis codes using a flexible neutral system. A large number of translators are available for finite element, finite difference, and boundary element thermal/structural analysis codes — including the most widely used ones in the world today [4]. PATRAN also interfaces to most CAD systems using: the Initial Graphics Exchange Specification (IGES) format; special-purpose translators such as SDF™, developed by Vought Corporation (to link systems manufacturers Computervision and CADAM® with PATRAN); and one-to-one translators between PATRAN and such CAD systems as ANVIL 4000®, Applicon Corp., Auto-Trol Corp., EUCLID®, and MEDUSA®. This important area of software interfaces is receiving increasing attention; much work remains to be done to improve efficiency and eliminate these "islands of technology" [5].

AVAILABILITY

PATRAN® is a registered trademark of PDA Engineering, 2975 Red Hill Avenue, Costa Mesa, California 92626, USA. (Telephone: 714-540-8900, Telex: 683392.) PATRAN is sold and supported worldwide.

REFERENCES

1. Casale, M. S. and E. L. Stanton, "An Overview of Analytic Solid Modeling", IEEE *Computer Graphics and Applications*, February 1985, pp. 45-56.

2. Ibid, "Advances in Analytic Solid Modeling", *Third Chautauqua on Productivity in Engineering and Design* (ed. by H. G. Schaeffer), Kiawah Island, S. Carolina, Oct. 29-31, 1984, sponsored by Schaeffer Analysis, Inc. (recently acquired by PDA Engineering), pp. 33-50.

3. Stanton, E. L., L. M. Crain, and T. F. Neu, "A Parametric Cubic Modeling System for General Solids of Composite Material", *Int. J. Num. Methods in Eng.*, Vol. 11, 1977, pp. 653-670.

4. Fong, H. H., "Interactive Graphics and Commercial Finite Element Codes", *Mechanical Engineering*, June 1984, pp. 18-25.

5. Hamilton, C. H., "Greasing the Skids — Perspectives on Design Analysis Information Exchange", presented at the Third Chautauqua on Productivity in Engineering and Design, Kiawah Island, S. Carolina, Oct. 29-31, 1984.

PIGS/DOGS/BOXER/PAFEC FE

Pafec Ltd., U.K.

In the mid 1960's a group of research workers at Nottingham University started work on a finite element system. The method was new and the high price of sufficiently powerful computers prevented most potential users from benefiting from the technique. By keeping ahead of finite element trends and by appreciating the requirements for a commercially successful system, this program became one of the most widely used finite element codes in the United Kingdom.

The program was called PAFEC (Program for Automatic Finite Element Calculations).

In the early 1970's the system was being used by a large number of companies, many of which were household names. At this time finite elements were finding wide acceptance in the aerospace and defence industries being used on large mainframe computers often owned by computer bureaux.

In 1976 PAFEC Limited was formed as the natural way of both increasing the business and giving customers a better service. Just seven staff formed the original company.

Today, at the end of the seventh year of profitable trading, nearly 100 staff are employed. With four offices in the United Kingdom, an American subsidiary and agents worldwide the name PAFEC is becoming very well known indeed.

With the arrival of modern minicomputers, customers have appreciated the cost advantages of buying their own in-house computing facilities. As these companies have switched from large mainframe computers and bureaux services they have sought out the most cost-effective programs for their needs.

At the same time smaller companies have realised that they too can justify the purchase of this type of facility. As a result, there are now over 180 in-house users of the PAFEC finite element system.

However, the finite element sales have been considerably overtaken by the rapid growth of the CAD/CAM market and the company has grown to offer a complete range of software.

PAFEC are unusual in having moved from finite element analysis into CAD/CAM . Many of its competitors have tried to move in the other direction and found that the development costs of finite element systems are prohibitive at this late stage. The complexities of finite element theory are such that many companies who are able to write CAD programs find that they are forced to resort to third party software in order to offer finite element analysis.

Why Interactive Graphics

From the earliest days of finite element analysis there has been a continual struggle to reduce the amount of time needed to produce an accurate and compact description of the finite element model. Systems like the PAFEC free format data entry with engineering key words and interactive question and answer sessions represent the simplest and most effective non-graphical modelling techniques.

But there is no way of knowing whether the model that has been created is really what the engineer wanted, and it is usually necessary to run the mesh through sophisticated validation routines and - eventually - the engineer will want to see a drawing of the structure before committing himself to an approval of the analysis.

Similarly, a file of printed output may contain everything the engineer needs to know, but a list of numbers cannot replace a deflected shape or contoured surface in giving meaning to the results.

Interactive Graphics eliminates all these problems. The engineer sees the model taking shape on the screen, correcting errors and remodelling as desired. When finished the user can be sure that the model is exactly as it was envisaged and the analysis can be performed with confidence. Later, the analyst can return to the workstation to analyse the results and discover immediately whether the structure has satisfied its design requirements.

PAFEC's first move into interactive graphics came with PIGS (PAFEC Interactive Graphics System). Initially this was a three dimensional pre and post processor. Finite element meshes could be displayed and simple data corrections made on the screen. Output displays were limited to deformed shapes and mode shapes in 1977 when interactive techniques were relatively new.

Today the position is very different. True mesh generation is an essential part of any finite element pre-processor graphics.

PIGS now provides:-

Digitised input

Creation of a finite element model can take two forms. If detailed information about the structure is available on engineering drawings, then digitised input may be more convenient than interactive modelling.

* Generation of nodal coordinates
* Node numbering
* Element numbering
* Element topologies

* View definitions
* 3-D slicing
* View deletion
* View activation
* Cursor accuracy control

Interactive Modelling

When detailed scale drawings are not available, or where the structural design is only conceptual, the PIGS interactive modelling ability offers the simplest path to the construction of an accurate model. The VIEW menu has options which require the user to define only those nodes which form the basic outline of the structure, a substructure, or even a basic building block which can later be copied and transformed to create additional parts of the model.
Modelling facilities include:

* Key node definition
* Node generation on a straight line
* Node generation on an arc
* 1,2, and 3-D PAFBLOCK definition
* 1,2, and 3-D mesh generation
* Replication of model segments with:
  Rotation
  Translating
  Mirroring
  Scaling
  Dragging
  Combinations of two or more of above
* Removal of redundant nodes (collapsing)
* Hidden line removal

Mesh Modification

PIGS can also be used to correct errors, not only in interactively generated models (where mistakes are rare), but also in meshes created from external data files. Mistakes in node numbering, coordinate input and element topology are easily rectified and a correct data file can then be created or, alternatively, the user can proceed directly to the analysis from the modified data-base created in the current PIGS session.

Mesh modification options are:

* Addition of nodes
* Addition of elements
* Deletion of nodes
* Deletion of elements
* Relocation of nodes
* Correction of element topologies

Results Analysis

In static analyses where displacement is the governing criterion, a view of the deformed shape of the structure can give vital insight into its behaviour. In addition the user may select individual nodes at which he wishes to know the exact value of translations and rotations. The required information is then displayed on the screen.

In 2-D stress analyses, the information normally contained in the nodal stress output file can be displayed in the form of a stress contour plot on the surface of the model. Four types of contour plot allow the user to select the range and type of stresses which are to be contoured.

In 3-D analyses, the SEL DRAW option permits slicing of the model on any plane to allow access to element faces which the user may wish to contour in the same way as in the 2-D analysis.

In 2-D and 3-D heat transfer problems, orientation and slicing of the model will, again, often be required before choosing the option to plot isothermal contours. Individual nodal temperatures can be obtained as well as contour plots from transient analyses.

Post-processing for dynamic analyses may be performed on any structure which has full backsubstituted displacements for all degrees of freedom in a particular loadcase or natural frequency. Deformed shapes are displayed together with any specific nodal information that has been requested.

Post processing capabilities include:

* Static deformed shapes
* Deformed shapes for natural frequencies and selected time steps
* Nodal displacements in statics and dynamics
* Model slicing and orientation
* Stress contouring - 4 types
* Temperature contouring

Other PIGS Options include:

* A number of draw-types (including BOUNDARY, OPTIMISE and SHRINK) and two line-types (SOLID and DASHED) serve to increase the clarity of the plot.
* The model can be manipulated by rotating, windowing, zooming, element, PAFBLOCK, and group selection, returning to the last window and fitting to fill the screen.
* Optional information -element numbers,node numbers and nodal coordinates, loadcase, current rotation, options selected plus other STATUS information. All can be added without redrawing.

INTO CAD

Working on PIGS gave PAFEC staff a wealth of knowledge on interactive graphics programming techniques. Discussions with the users in the mid 1970's frequently highlighted the lack of cost-effective computer aided design systems.

Most of the vendors were still offering 16-bit minicomputers with limited address space. Prices were substantially higher than the total price of individual items of equipment.

PAFEC realised that their existing philosophies which had been successful with finite element systems could be successfully applied to CAD/CAM.
These can be summarised as:-

1. To offer a wide range of software products, wherever practical with interfaces to each other.

2. Design systems for ease-of-use. Minimise computer jargon.

3. Produce general purpose products to span a range of applications.

4. Produce computer (and peripheral) independent software to be easily transportable.

5. Offer software or turnkey systems with the user choosing from a range of different equipment.

6. Keeping prices low and aiming for a high quantity of sales.

DOGS

A two-dimensional draughting system was the natural first step into CAD. DOGS (Design Office Graphics System) was the result. Today there are over 140 users of DOGS, which include mechanical, civil, electrical and structural engineering, public utility mapping and architecture.

DOGS is available on the following computers:-

- Prime
- DEC VAX
- Apollo
- Data General MV Series
- Harris
- Norsk Data
- ICL PERQ
- DEC 20
- UNIVAC
- Hewlett Packard 9000
- Perkin-Elmer

and is sold with a similarly wide range of graphics peripherals.

Why has DOGS been so successful?
DOGS has combined ease-of-use with the sophisticated features usually found only in the most expensive systems. To describe just a few of these facilities:-

PARAMETRIC SYMBOLS may be created using a draughting language to define libraries of components which may be retrieved simply by entering the required parameters. The PARAMETRIC SYMBOL may perform logical checks, consider the validity of data and read or write to or from files.

PROPERTIES _ a flexible non-graphical database which:

* Automatically produces parts lists on drawings
* Allows an unlimited number of user-defined PROPERTY tables
* Allows parts lists to be merged for a series of drawings
* Will compress, sort or total the data in the table
* Outputs any selected columns of data on the drawing, printer or screen
* Gives selective output by searching for any particular type of data

ARCHIVE - the ARCHIVE sub-menu has two functions. First, it provides a cataloguing system for drawing management. It might be used to record information such as the designer's name, the date of producing the drawing, the date the drawing was last modified, the title, and so on. The information can be searched to locate drawings matching certain requirements. The second use of ARCHIVE is to provide an easy to operate system for merging different drawings or maps.

THREE DIMENSIONAL MODELLING
BOXER - is the name of PAFEC's full solid modeller, enabling the user to construct accurate three-dimensional structures that are informationally complete.

BOXER is based upon packages written by staff at the Geometric Modelling Project in the Mechanical Engineering Department at the University of Leeds who have been engaged in the field of solid modelling for ten years.

Complex structures can be produced simply by performing Boolean operations using the primitives: blocks, spheres, cylinders, cones and tori.

Facilities include:-

- Linear and rotational generators
- Object assemblies may be created
- Perspective option

- Volume and inertia calculation
- Optional removal of hidden lines, or show dashed
- Translations and rotations allow new bodies to be formed from existing structures.

For the designer BOXER's parametric design language is its most important aspect.
Any dimensions used in the definition may be given parameter-names and varied at will. This emphasises the fundamental advantage of BOXER: it is an interactive three dimensional modeller rather than a means of producing three dimensional pictures from two dimensional drawings.

BOXER can also claim to be both fast and accurate. By employing double precision arithmetic, BOXER models retain an accuracy of one part in 10^7 even after extensive geometric computation. This was well illustrated in the August 1982 issue of "Finite Element News":-

> The problem required computation of the volume of intersection of two unit radius cylinders that intersect each other at right angles. This was posed to fifteen exhibitors at the 1982 Hannover Fair. Only six of these were able to provide answers. Although not at the Hannover Fair, the problem was easily solved by BOXER producing the correct answer of 5.333.

Being both accurate and informationally complete, BOXER is able to fill the role of a central base for robotics, tolerance checking, tooling design, design check of automatic machining processes etc.

Developments planned by PAFEC Limited centre on improving the ease of use for the engineer

- A menu driven system is now available using a menu similar in layout to that used in DOGS.

- Engineering Primitives will be provided. For example, a tapered pipe is what the engineer wants. He does not adapt readily to considering this as the difference between two cones.

- Cursor input will be allowed. A choice of different keypoints for each primtive may be selected, either by graphics cursor or by typed input. For instance, a block may be located by any combination of any corners, centroid and mid-face points.

- Colour shading

Over the next three years a generally sculptured solid primitive will be produced by Leeds University. In the short term a general "rolling ball" type fillet will be released.

Figure 1 shows PAFEC's current software development plans. In addition to finite element modelling, this includes three other 3-D modellers!
BOXER has already been discussed.

3-D Wireframe Modeller

The three dimensional wireframe modeller is available from January 1984. This allows three dimensional views within a two dimensional DOGS drawing. The draughtsman may interact with up to four views of the object simultaneously. Typically, three of these will be an orthographic projection and the fourth will be a random view, optionally of isometric or perspective projection.

The advantages of wireframe modelling are its high speed and ease of use. In DOGS this has been obtained by offering the two-dimensional draughting features and simply allowing a third dimension to be added. Until recently many potential CAD customers were unaware of the major differences between the types of three-dimensional system. This difficulty was not alleviated by salesmen of vendor companies who only had wireframing modellers, but failed to point out the deficiencies.

PAFEC believe that a wireframe model has definite advantages in some applications. For example, many piping and cabling diagrams can be produced quite adequately as wireframe models. With this in mind the DOGS wireframe system allows pipe angles and/or coordinates to be defined as being fixed with respect to any cartesian plane.

Surface Modelling

Many three dimensional models involve sculptured surfaces which cannot be represented using a library of solid primitives. There can be little doubt that a complete three dimensional modelling facility demands both solids and surface modelling.

PAFEC's current development plans involve two concurrent approaches to surface modelling:

1. The first, due for release in August 1984, will give simple surfaces in conjunction with the wireframe representation. This will offer:

   - Plane surfaces
   - Ruled surfaces (e.g. cylindrical or more complex)
   - Colour shading
   - Hidden line removal

2. Early in 1985 a full sculptured surface modeller will be released. This will allow the user to define any number of two dimensional sections along a spine using any of the powerful DOGS draughting facilities.

Surfaces will be generated using bi-cubic polynomial patches. A reparameterisation technique developed by Dr. Alan Ball of Loughborough University will be used to enable the best possible surface to be fitted.

SOFTWARE INTEGRATION

As figure 1 shows, there are a large number of existing interfaces between the different software products. There are a similar number of additional potential interfaces.

The long term aim is to interface fully all products. Furthermore, it is considered important to ensure as much continuity as possible when moving between these programs. With this aim in mind, the menu system is divided into the following pages:'

PAGE	FACILITIES
1	DOGS - Two dimensional draughting
2	DOGS - PROPERTIES Databases
3	DOGS - 3 dimensional wireframe
4	BOXER - 3-D Solids Modelling
5	Numerical Control
6-10	User defined symbols, parametrics and PROPERTY sets.

Of particular concern to many customers is whether two dimensional drawings should be used to create three dimensional models or vice versa. Three dimensional modelling is a powerful interactive technique giving most advantage to the designer who wishes to design in 3-D. Indeed, it is virtually impossible to interact with a 3-D design by modifying a 2-D drawing and still to obtain acceptable response times. To many draughtsmen the reverse approach is more acceptable. Familiar with laying out orthographic projections, the draughtsman will often prefer to produce pictorial views from his 2-D layout. For many objects this may be an easier way of producing a pictorial view, but the huge advantages of interacting with a 3-D model are lost.

As three dimensional modellers become easier to use, it is likely that the advantages of 3-D input will become more widely accepted. PAFEC offer a BOXER to DOGS interface and are developing a BOXER to wireframe interface. The latter is useful in retaining a three dimensional database and makes the DOGS draughting features available for annotation of views produced by BOXER. For example this allows three-dimensional dimensioning.

In the reverse direction a DOGS to wireframe interface is under development. This will allow two dimensional views to be used automatically to create three dimensional wireframe or surface models.

Of course, to complete the integration of all products, DOGS is already able to produce finite element models and this capability will follow for BOXER.

PAFEC's own numerical control system is designed to operate with DOGS but a much more complex long-term project being undertaken by the staff at Leeds University, and sponsored by PAFEC Limited, will give output from BOXER to produce full five axis numerical control machining.

Also as a long term development, automatic finite element mesh generation from within BOXER is projected.

In conclusion, BOXER can be seen to have justified its claim to be a complete solid modeller capable of forming a central database for output to manufacture, analysis, draughting etc. PAFEC's software development plans show a commitment to build a powerful range of CAD/CAM software. By interfacing these programs and offering the customer the chance to expand painlessly, PAFEC expects to build on its currently prominent position in this market.

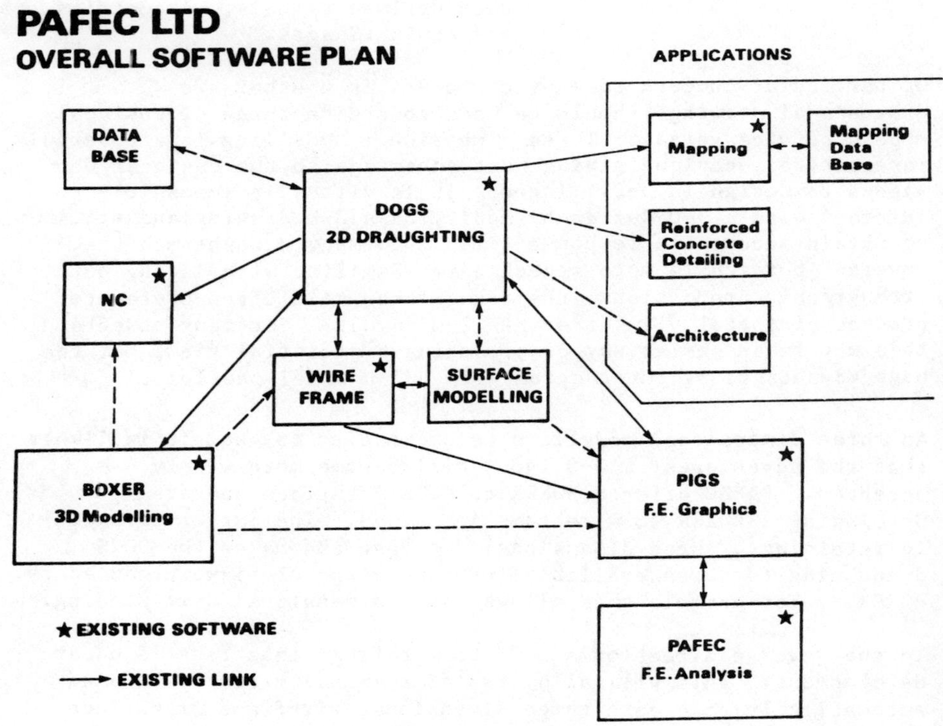

PRIME MEDUSA/GNC/PDGS/ SAMMIE

Prime Computer (UK) Ltd., U.K.

1 PRIME IN CAD/CAM

Prime is a worldwide organization which is a leading supplier of super mini-computer systems and has operations in more than fifty countries.

CAD/CAM is one of the most important and fastest growing business areas for Prime.

PRIME MEDUSA, the company's leading CAD software product, is being employed in over 500 different organizations. GNC, the graphical NC programming system, is running on Prime computers in over 100 manufacturing plants.

Although manufacturing, and particularly mechanical engineering, is the largest area for Prime in CAD/CAM, the company is also well established in the architectural sector through leading UK distributors such as GMWC and ARC; in construction with such packages as PDMS (Plant Design Management System), from CADCentre; in the automotive sector with PDGS (Product Design Graphic System), originally developed by Ford; and in education where Prime systems are widely used for training engineering students in the latest CAD/CAM technologies.

..... and CIM

Computer Integrated Manufacturing is now a real option for progressive organizations.

Although very few manufacturing companies have the resources to introduce a complete CIM system at once, Prime provides the key modules which allows planned implementation and integration.

In addition to a wide range of CAD/CAM products, Prime offers a spectrum of management information systems, both direct and through third party software companies, which address the different functional areas of most organizations.

While there is a wide range of packages to promote information flow between departments, Prime's networking and communications products can be used to link different systems and different organizations, even across national borders.

* Prime mainly distribute software developed by other Companies. Their systems have been included in this chapter in view of their importance in engineering practice. The reader can find more information about CIS MEDUSA in the first volume of this set of books on Computer Aided Engineering Systems.

2 SYSTEMS FEATURES AND APPLICATION SOFTWARE

All Prime CAD/CAM systems are:-

MODULAR

A very broad spectrum of application software programs is available on a totally compatible range of hardware.

EXPANDABLE

All systems are based on Prime 50 Series processors which provide a clear upgrade path using the multi-functional PRIMOS and optional PRIMIX operating systems.

TURNKEY

Systems include hardware, software, on-site implementation, full training, documentation, support and maintenance.

HIGH PERFORMANCE

All software modules have very comprehensive facilities for their particular applications and are designed to operate in multi-user environments.

INTEGRATED

Programs may be interfaced to improve information flow between different departments. Prime processors may be networked to other Prime systems and to many other makes of processor.

EASY TO USE

All systems are interactive and most are menu-driven with prompts to assist new users.

All these features mean that a user can start, for example, with just a 2D drafting system and gradually upgrade to an integrated multi-user CAD/CAM/CIM system with full 3D design, analysis and MRP II facilities, without making redundant any of his original hardware or software.

Prime's core software products for CAD/CAM applications include:-

PRIME MEDUSA

A universal CAD system with modules for:

- Design Drafting (2D)
- Variational Geometry
- Drawing Administration
- Drawing Analysis and Interface
- Design Modelling (3D)
- Model Analysis and Interface
- Shaded Viewer
- Flat Pattern Development

The system can be interfaced to various programs for computer-aided engineering (CA and analysis; to GNC, APT and other NC part programming systems; and to MRP II systems such as PRO III.

GNC (Graphical Numerical Control)

One of the most respected NC part programming systems available, GNC accepts geometry from PRIME MEDUSA and other CAD systems, but also has its own geometry definition capabilities. The system allows users to simulate actual cutting of metal.

Modules include:

- GNC 2/2½D, with programs for:
  Milling and Drilling
  Turning
  Punch/Nibbling
  Flame Cutting
  Spark Erosion
- Post-processing and DNC

PDGS (Product Design Graphic System)

A specialised CAD/CAM system for designing products with complex free form surfaces as typically found in the automotive, aerospace and shipbuilding sectors. Modules include:

- Design (3D) and Drafting (2D)
- Finite Element Modelling
- Numerical Control

SAMMIE (System for Aiding Man/Machine Interaction Evaluation)

A unique system for modelling and analysing environments and products where human interaction is important, such as aircraft cockpits, passenger vehicles, building layouts and robotics. The system includes full 3D visualisation capabilities and a sophisticated man-model.

Other Applications Products

Many different third party software packages are available on Prime computers to complement the above systems, including programs for specialist design (e.g. DUCT), for analysis (e.g. MOLDFLOW, FEMGEN, FEMVIEW, PDA/PATRAN G), and for MRP II (e.g. INFO FLO and MMC) and computer aided process planning (CAPP) which provide the basis for extending CAD/CAM into CIM.

2.1 PRIME MEDUSA

Design Drafting

One of the main advantages of PRIME MEDUSA is that it is easy to learn and use. The whole system is based on the 2D Design Drafting module which uses conventional drawing office terms and techniques. Also, interaction is greatly assisted by comprehensive colour-coded "book" command menus which may be customised to suit individual requirements.

Design Drafting features full geometric construction and editing facilities; automatic dimensioning, sectioning and cross-hatching; comprehensive line and text styles; use of up to 1024 different display layers; parts list generation capabilities; and an on-line graphics programming language, Super Syntax, which allows users to develop customised programs for repetitive operations or parametrically defined parts. It also includes an extensive user-definable symbol library for creating electrical wiring schematics, process flow sheets, and piping and instrumentation diagrams.

The standard system can be substantially enhanced through the addition of modules for:-

Variational Geometry

- facilitates the production of drawings for families of parts and moving mechanisms by inputting sets of pre-defined variables (e.g. dimensions).

Drawing Administration

- incorporates three subsystems which help organize drawings and associated data:

The Reporter sub-system in conjunction with MIDASPLUS, one of Prime's data management systems, allows you to create bills of materials and other reports.

The Retrieval sub-system offers the ability to define and classify hundreds of parts for quick access using simple English-like commands.

The Locator facility helps create and maintain a master directory of drawings, products and associated files.

Drawing Analysis and Interface

- allows users to:

Create and modify information within the drawing data base using Prime's Drawing Access Routines (DARS).

Calculate properties of cross sections.

Interface PRIME MEDUSA with other CAD systems through IGES pre-and post-processing software support.

Shaded Viewer

- enables users to create realistic photographic-quality images automatically. It features controllable dual light sources (direct and ambient), and permits shine and texture characteristics to be varied for each object in the model.

Design Modelling

PRIME MEDUSA Design Modelling is an advanced solid modelling system driven by the Design Drafting module.

With this system, engineers can create three-dimensional wire-frame, shell and solid models by employing familiar 2D drafting techniques and using sweeps, pipes, slides, ruled surfaces, volumes of revolution and surface network generators. They can also use Boolean operations to perform union, intersection and subtraction operations on solids, and can combine models to form assemblies which are automatically checked for interference between parts.

Once created, the solid models can be sectioned in any form; viewed in isometric, orthographic, auxiliary and perspective modes, and be displayed with hidden lines and surfaces removed.

Furthermore, because Design Drafting and Design Modelling are so well integrated, users can easily generate detailed engineering drawings and reports from the 3D models.

PRIME MEDUSA Design Modelling may be supplemented by additional modules which include:

Model Analysis and Interface

- automatically calculates mass properties of solid models, providing information on surface area, volume, moments of inertia, centre of gravity, mass, density, weight, principle radii of gyration and other relevant items.

The module also provides an interface with other CAD systems, allowing 3D data to be exchanged through a standard file format. Thus PRIME MEDUSA models can be passed over to finite element modelling and analysis programs such as PATRAN-G, FEMGEN, FEMVIEW, ANSYS and NASTRAN.

Flat Pattern Development

- contains three subsystems:

The Unfolder, which unfolds an "ideal" model into a flat pattern.

The Bend Allowance Program which automatically adjusts the flat pattern to allow for bends and metal thickness.

The Folder which constructs a 3D model from the adjusted flat pattern and lets you check this against the original model.

2.2 GNC

GNC, Graphical Numerical Control, is an interactive graphical NC part programming system designed to help simulate and verify most NC/CNC machining operations. The system reduces quite dramatically the lead times in producing error-free programs and tapes. It is easy to use with English-like commands entered via keyboard, tablet or screen menus.

Since GNC contains its own geometry definition program for defining shapes and complex surfaces and also accepts geometry from CAD systems, it may be used as a stand-alone system and as part of an integrated CAD/CAM system in conjunction with PRIME MEDUSA.

GNC 2D

Once the shape of a part has been verified in GNC, it is then passed over to the appropriate machining module for interactive prove-out. GNC can be used to simulate most 2/2½ axis operations, including:-

Turning
Milling (2/2½D)
Punch nibbling
Flame/plasma cutting

For most operations, the entire machining environment, including component, tooling, fixtures and tool paths, may be visualised, using colour graphics to assist. Different tools can be selected from user-defined graphics libraries and repetitious sequences can be executed rapidly using macro commands.

GNC 3D

This optional module provides for simultaneous multi-axis machining of full 3D part surfaces as found in dies, injection molds, propellers, engine manifolds and automotive pressings.

It has its own geometry definition system which can be used to define even the most complex sculptured surfaces.

GNC 3D allows the programmer to visualise part and feedrate surfaces and the position of work, feedrate and clear planes. The system contains powerful area clearance routines and many other facilities to aid efficient metal removal.

Post Processing and DNC

When satisfactory machining sequences have been established, GNC command data is post processed into formats suitable for particular machine tools. Prime offers a universal post processor which caters for over 80% of machines, while specific post processors are provided for others.

A DNC (Direct Numerical Control) option is also available from third parties allowing GNC programs to be sent directly to the machine tools, thus removing the necessity for punched tape.

2.3 SPECIALIST SYSTEMS

PDGS

Developed by Ford Motor Company and marketed exclusively by Prime, the Product Design Graphic System is a complete, powerful CAD/CAM product that comprises a set of proven tools for design and development.

PDGS has advanced capabilities for 3D design, as well as drafting and detailing. It is particularly suited to the design of multi-point irregular shapes, complex free-form surfaces and mechanical components.

Created by designers and engineers for their own needs, PDGS is extremely easy to use. It is completely menu-driven, each command being executed on the screen with a light pen.

To improve visualisation and design accuracy, the full display power of PDGS includes infinitely variable dynamic rotation. Its extensive design management facilities ensure that the database reflects all design changes. The system also has optional modules for analysis and NC programming.

Finite Element Modelling

This allows users to perform graphic pre and post processing for design evaluation. It features automatic mesh generation with 16 element types. Analysis may be output for subsequent structural analysis and the results displayed graphically.

Numerical Control

With this module NC part program can be produced rapidly for components designed in PDGS. Output is in the form of ISO standard cutter location data.

SAMMIE

The System for Aiding Man/Machine Interaction Evaluation - SAMMIE - is a unique ergonomic modelling package which simulates man/machine interaction through a computerised man-model with reach and sight capabilities.

An engineer can design a workplace with SAMMIE, then use the man-model to analyse how different body types fit into it. The engineer can even look at the area from the man-model's perspective, as if looking through his eyes.

SAMMIE may also be used to evaluate machine/machine interaction as in robotics applications.

The system can be interfaced to both PDGS and PRIME MEDUSA.

2.4 COMPUTER INTEGRATED MANUFACTURING

For organisations working in a project environment, Prime now offers PSSYSTEM, designed for companies which need to control and progress the production of goods and services being configured to customer requirements and orders.

For the majority of manufacturing companies, MRPII (Manufacturing Resource Planning) systems are the answer. Prime offers several systems written in Prime INFORMATION, our relational-like data management system, which gives management easy access to data. Spreadsheets and decision support graphics can be easily generated from the manufacturing data held in these systems via Prime INFORMATION CONNECTION.

INFOFLO and MMC utilise the latest developments in MRP II systems. They contain the standard features of a closed loop MRP II system, plus many developments reflecting newer manufacturing systems concepts.

With these systems based on Prime INFORMATION, the user is not bound to limitations established when the systems were written, but can set up a system which reflects the requirements specific to his company.

PSSystem, INFLO and MMC can all be integrated into Prime's computer aided design systems, such as PRIME MEDUSA. This link allows the rapid transfer of error-free data from design to manufacturing. In addition to the interface to CAD, these systems can also be linked with project management systems, shop floor operations and office automation products.

For companies which have installed their primary manufacturing system and are now looking for an additional competitive edge, Prime can offer several advanced manufacturing systems.

Developed on Prime, OPT can reduce inventories and improve due date performance to enable a company to meet world class competition.

LOCAM, an expert process planning system, offers companies the opportunity to produce standard quality products while reducing the design to production time.

Prime offers DNC and shop floor control systems for production. In addition to the aforementioned products, Prime offers simulation, project management and facilities layout systems for manufacturing management.

Many thrid party packages are available to complement the above, addressing such areas as project management, shop floor data collection, factory and robotics simulation. Together with Prime's core CAD/CAM and manufacturing systems these provide the building blocks for CIM.

Rather than attempting to integrate all product and manufacturing data into one monolithic database, Prime supplies the tools for linking systems and sharing relevant information. Prime's office automation system (OAS), data management (e.g. Prime INFORMATION), communications and networking products all help to support this process.

5 SYSTEMS HARDWARE

Processors

For CAD/CAM/CIM systems the Prime 50 Series of superminicomputers provides one of the broadest ranges of totally compatible processors. All feature 32-bit architecture for high performance and accuracy, and all have virtual memory with up to 32 million bytes of program space for each user. Proven in both scientific and commerical applications, these processors are well suited to manufacturing organizations.

Operating Systems

From entry-level office environment machines up to mainframe equivalents, all Prime processors run the same multi-user, multi-functional PRIMOS and optional PRIMIX (PRIMOS + UNIX) operating systems. This means that an application package developed on one Prime system will run on all the others without costly modification.

Furthermore, for developing your own programs, PRIMOS supports a wide range of high-level industry-standard languages including FORTRAN, COBOL, Pascal, BASIC/VM, PL/I, RPG II and C.

To complement these languages is a comprehensive set of management facilities, including MIDASPLUS, an indexed sequential file access system, and Prime INFORMATION, a user-orientated relational-like management system.

Peripherals and Accessories

A wide range of system peripherals and accessories is offered to complement the 50 Series including memory boards, disk drives, magnetic tape drives and streamers, printers, cables and consoles.

Workstations

Prime supports a compatible range of workstations for all applications. They fall into two general categories:

- CAD/CAM Workstations and Terminals - for design, drafting and NC programming tasks where interactive graphics is important. These incorporate high resolution rasterscan terminals with screen sizes up to 20". Colour is standard, but monochrome hard copy units.

- Business Workstations - for management information applications. These are designed to handle MRP II, financial and DSS needs. With powerful colour and graphics options, they can also be used as 'views only' CAD terminals.

Plotters

The Prime range of pen and electrostatic plotters provides the breadth of speeds, widths and resolutions necessary to support Prime's extensive CAD/CAM software.

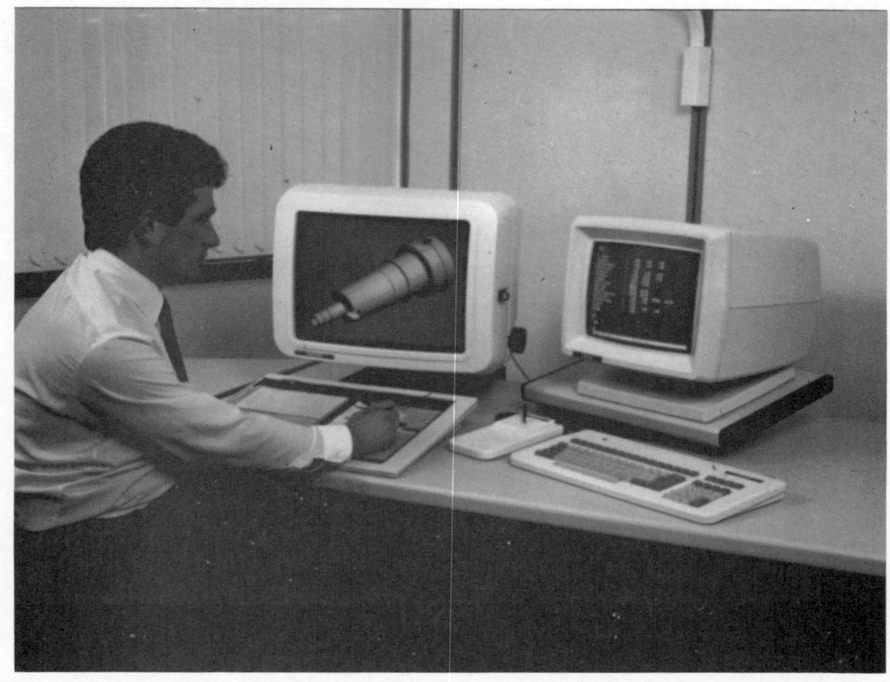

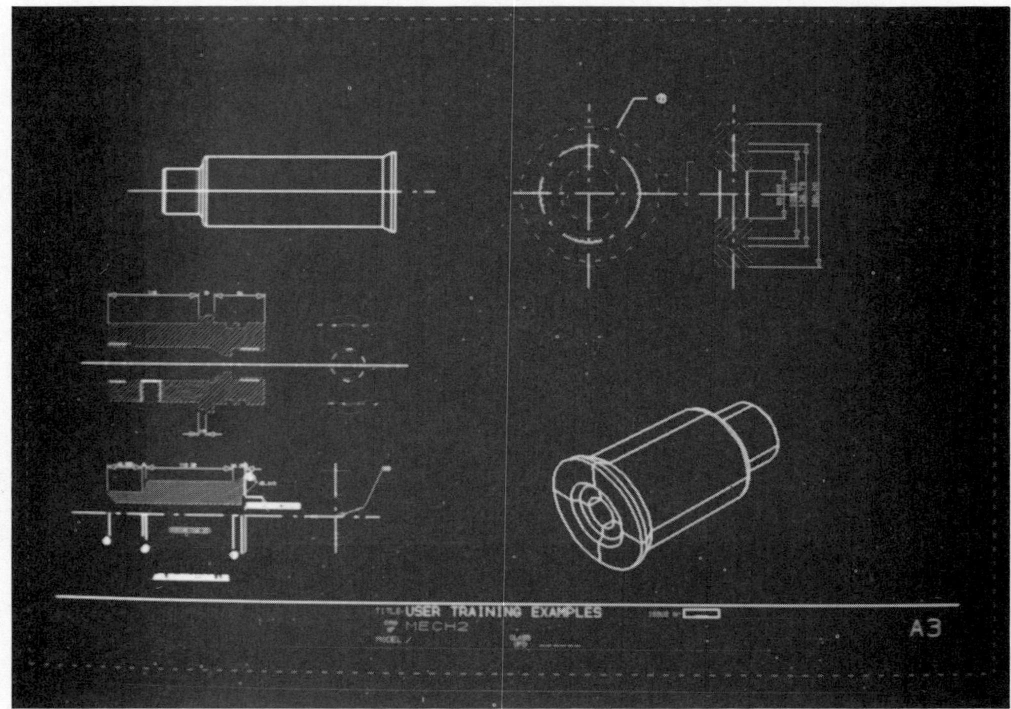
USER TRAINING EXAMPLES
MECH2
A3

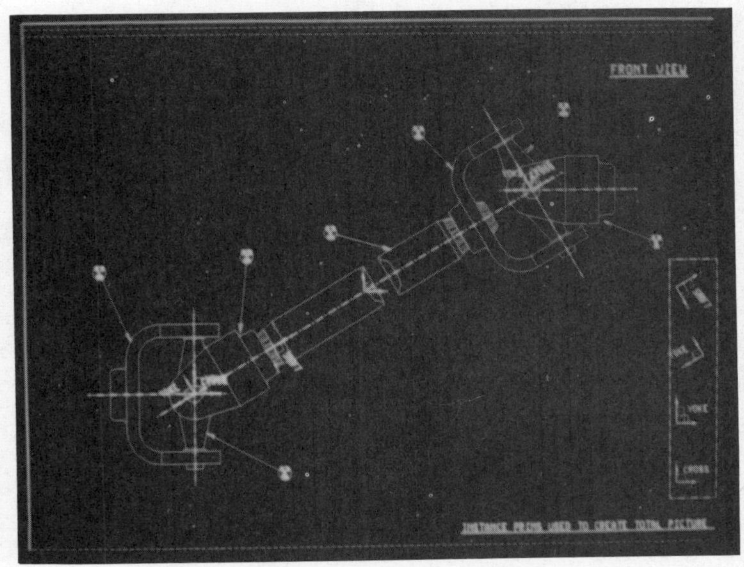
FRONT VIEW
YOKE
CROSS
INSTANCE PRIMS USED TO CREATE TOTAL PICTURE

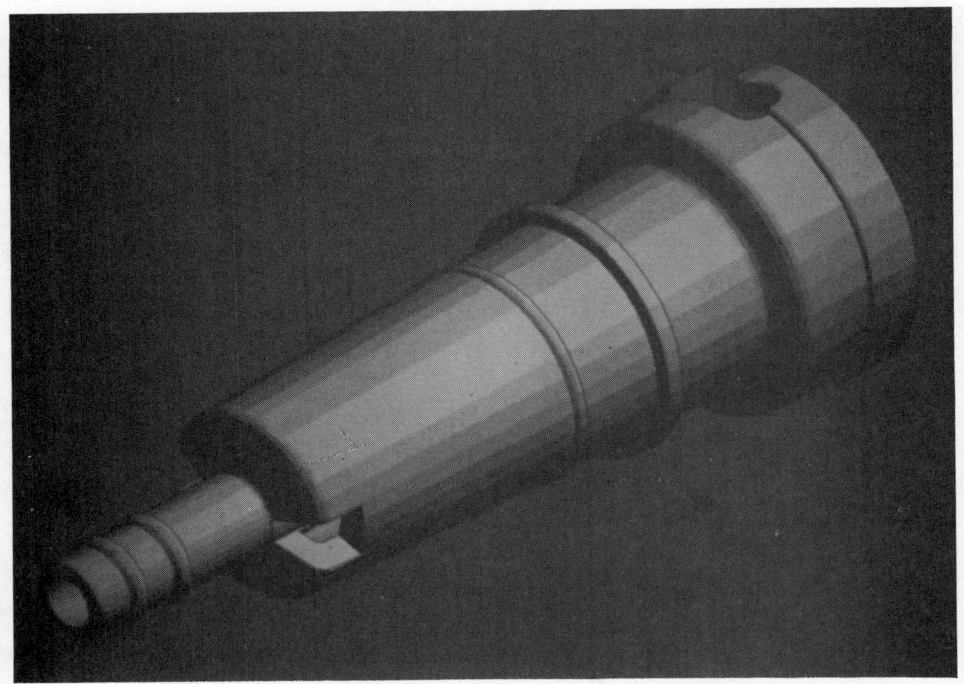

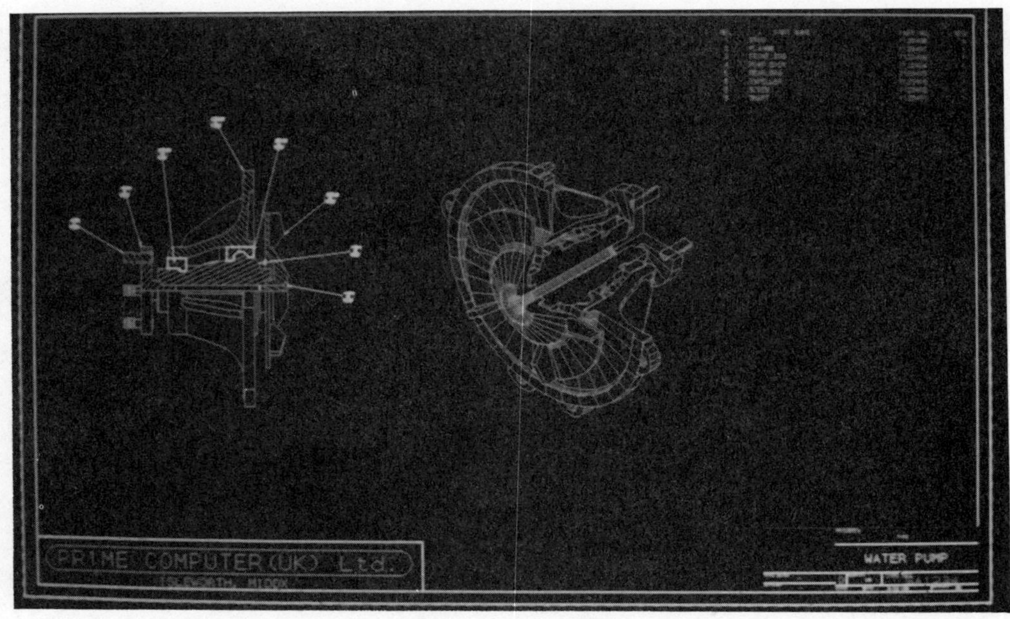
PRIME COMPUTER (UK) Ltd.
WATER PUMP

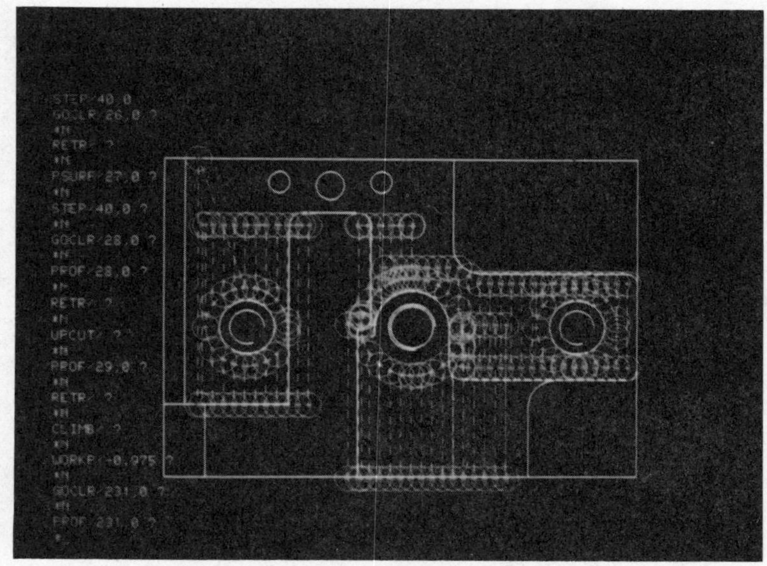
STEP/40,0
GOCLR/26,0 ?
*N
RETR/ ?
*N
PSURF/27,0 ?
*N
STEP/40,0 ?
*N
GOCLR/28,0 ?
*N
PROF/28,0 ?
*N
RETR/ ?
*N
UPCUT/ ?
*N
PROF/29,0 ?
*N
RETR/ ?
*N
CLIMB/ ?
*N
WORKP/-0,975 ?
*N
GOCLR/231,0 ?
*N
PROF/231,0 ?

PROREN 1 & 2

Isykon Software GmbH, West Germany

1. GENERAL DESCRIPTION

1.1 PROREN, THE CAD/CAM SYSTEM FOR DESIGN AND MANUFACTURING

The CAD System PROREN is a product of ISYKON Software GmbH. Isykon developed and enhanced this product based on research of the Institute of Engineering Design at University Bochum/Germany.

Especially taken into consideration are the suggestions of PROREN users, which among others are harmonized with the researching of Isykon to enhance easy and productive use of PROREN. The resulting enhancements are at the users disposal as part of the maintenance contract.

Isykon offers its customers also CAD consultancy and CAD training. Customized solutions based on PROREN are also part of Isykon's services.

The software package PROREN allows the entrance to CAD with a minimal risk using different levels of parametric, adaptive and new design.

With PROREN parts can be entered drawing-orientated (2-D, views, cuts) as well as part-orientated (3-D model) generation of parts is done by linking lines, planes or volumes in an interactive dialog supported by a menu technique.

2-D geometries can be transformed to 3-D volume orientated geometries. Any views and cuts of a part entered three-dimensional can be provided for further two-dimensional processing.

User specific requirements like calculations are easily embedded into PROREN. The user program modules or macros are entered in interactive mode or via the system program interfaces. Also interfaces from PROREN to NC or FEM are available. There are general FORTRAN and IGES interfaces as well as specific interfaces to EXAPT for NC, to GENFES, FEMGEN for FEM and others.

The CAD workstation consists of a graphic terminal with tablet for the graphic interactive dialog, as well as an alpha-terminal for the user assistance, the output of data and alphanumeric functions. Various types of graphic terminals may be used; storage, raster, monochrome and colour.

1.2 PROREN 1 - THE EXTENSION FOR 2-D APPLICATIONS

PROREN 1 is a 2D software. With this software parts are stored and reproduced drawing-oriented via their two-dimensional image. The part is described through linewise generation of the contours or by connecting plane-elements. By this and through powerful dialog functions (alphanumeric, graphic, interactive, menu technique) maximum ease of use with minimum input is achieved. Besides the capability to divide complex assembly drawings in up to 10,000 layers, PROREN 1 allows the definition of any number of so-called priority levels. Utilizing those priority levels PROREN 1 automatically removes non-visible areas in drawings of assemblies or subassemblies. Therefore given geometries can be used without any changes for drawing complete assemblies as well as for drawing single parts. As a result PROREN 1 provides true to scale drawings of assembled parts and individual parts with all necessary information for manufacturing, and if needed bill of material and edited geometrical information for other areas (e.g. FEM, NC-manufacturing, see figure 1).

PROREN 2 - THE SOFTWARE PACKAGE FOR 3-D DESIGN

PROREN 2 contains an exact analytical 3-D model in space which fits homogeneous into the CAD system PROREN. An advantage of the volume model is that all changes in design translate immediately in all views and perspective displays. Any cuts, including recessed ones, are generated automatically. Hidden lines are also removed automatically by the system.

Working fully interactive directly at the 3-D model via a comprehensive set of functions, which are activated via menu fields on the graphic tablet results in maximum ease of use.

Besides the part description by boolean operations on geometrical volume elements there are available a number of manipulation possibilities at the existing model as well as the utilization of 2-D contours from PROREN 1. Negative forms can be derived directly from the model. Output of detail, group and explosion drawings can be done in any view (see figure 2). Collisions for fitting into or addition to existing environment are analysed automatically. Analytical functions calculate thickness of walls, centre of gravity, volume, weight.

2. 3-D DESIGN WITH PROREN-2

2.1 INTRODUCTION

PROREN2 is a software that renders possible a definition and representation of components and assemblies in the computer. It is based on the so-called workpiece-orientated principle, i.e. that the geometrical information of a component part is represented analytically in three dimensions. Unlike the line drawing-orientated principle where components are stored in the computer only by their two-dimensional images, perspective and arbitrary cutaway views can be generated with the help of the three dimensional information. Furthermore, the information can be used for additional output routines like producing no-punch tapes or calculating volume or weight. The main problems of three-dimensional part description are to minimize the extensive data input and to give the designer a simple way of modifying the data. In this paper will be analyzed the possible optimization/minimization of input provided by PROREN2 and subsequently the computer internal representation of objects in this system.

2.2 STRUCTURE OF PROREN2

Figure 3 demonstrates the structure of the PROREN2 system. The input of the designer is interpreted by the geometric processor and translated into the internal representation. The processor provides the possibilities of object definition, modification and detailing. The individual modules of the processor will be explained later in this paper.

The internal representation is a lot of data organized in a certain manner, the so-called data structure.

As mentioned above, the representation can be used for data output in several ways. For example, the designer is able to control his progress at any stage of design with the help of screen drawings and to modify or expand the design through the geometric processor.

2.3 DATA STRUCTURE

In contrast to the aircraft industry or body design, regular surfaces such as planes, cylindrical and conical surfaces predominate in engineering industry. They are manufactured by cutting methods.

Besides these analytic surfaces, only castings, forgings and deep-drawing sheets contain a certain amount of surfaces of a higher degree that cannot be represented analytically in an economical way.

According to this geometric characteristic of engineering design, PROREN2 separates analytically described elements, i.e. planes and surfaces of second degree (quadrics) and their plane sections like straight lines and conic sections, from non-analytically described elements, like intersections of quadrics and higher degree surfaces. The analytic elements are stored and treated by their characteristic analytic values, providing a small amount of storage and fast processing. Only those surfaces that cannot be described analytically are generated approximately and processed by methods of surface patches.

Figure 4 shows two intersecting cylinders and the rounding off surface of one intersection through surface patches.

In this paper only the way to handle analytical elements is described, but thereby even more complex engineering parts can be represented. The completion of PROREN2 to parameter surfaces is the subject of our current research work and will be published in the near future.

Figure 5 shows the data structure of PROREN 2 in detail. The information of an object can be subdivided into two parts. The analytic part stores the characteristic values of vertices and surfaces. The relations between the elements of the three dimensional space like edges, surfaces and solids are listed hierarchically as addresses in the organizing part of the structure. The main information is the edge list. All edges of an object, like straight lines, curves (conic sections) and polygons (approximation of intersections of two quadrics), are stored as addresses there. They refer to the analytic part of the data structure, where information for calculating operations can be drawn from. As a whole, the data structure contains all analytical information to represent the work piece exactly.

This kind of structure allows fast access to every information and guarantees high processing speed.

2.4 GEOMETRIC PROCESSOR

As mentioned above, one main point of PROREN2 is the geometric processor that connects the user's input and the data structure. The input should be as compressed and simple as possible and similar to the designer's familiar way of thinking.

The way to achieve this differs a lot in publications. One group of authors start from the principle that the designer is able to think in three dimensions during layout. Therefore, their proposal for a geometric processor is based on the three-dimensional fusion of volume elements (solids). Other authors state that the designer thinks only in face plans and cutaway views, as he is used to from line drawings. According to this fact, work places are described two-dimensionally, and then transposed into a space object depending on certain regularities.

In contrast to the afore-mentioned procedures, the PROREN2 geometric processor connects different ways of known procedures and adds some new ones. All procedures are combined to a flexible system, in which the user can choose which way he prefers. Figure 6 shows a survey of the available procedures. As mentioned above, the processor is split into three sections: object definition, modification and detailing. These procedures are themselves composed of several sub-procedures, which will now be presented in detail.

2.4.1 Object Definition

The main point of layout is the procedure defining the object. It generates a provisional layout of a component part. Two principle methods are available: fusing volume elements or defining plane contours that execute a translational or rotational movement and hereby generate volumes.

The volume fusing methods places at disposal two procedures. Both are based on a catalogue of modular stored primitive solids and technical elements that are provided by the system. Figure 7 shows a summary of this catalogue. The space elements are supplied with dimensions by parameters that can be taken from the user's manual.

The parameter list of a cube consists of positions and dimensions. The parameters of position are the x-, y- and z-coordinates of one reference vertice and the three angles of space α, β and γ that define the site of the cube. The values A, B and C are the lengths of the edges. All elements can be combined to the complex component representation by the fusing algorithms that allow an adding or subtracting of the elements.

One procedure controls the fusion of volume elements at juxtaposed flat faces as demonstrated in figure 8. The algorithm is based on the fact that two juxtaposed flat faces are joined together to one new face, identical edges being deleted from the data structure. All other faces and edges remain unchanged. In particular, no new vertices or edges arise that were not vertices or edges of the initial elements.

This algorithm can be performed very easily by a program but it has the disadvantage that only those representations of objects can be generated that can be split up exactly into a sum of basic elements. Only regular shapes satisfy this restriction.

In figure 9 the presented element is to be generated by the principle of fusing elements at flat faces. The small element has to be subtracted four times from the cylinder, but this element may not be provided by the software development firm and will have to be programmed by the user. So, in most cases this procedure will fail.

The other fusing algorithm uses the principle of general intersection. The way of this procedure can be compared with the proceeding of manufacture (figure 10). Like a cutting tool performs a certain chip removal from a work piece, PROREN2 performs an intersecting operation between two volume elements.

For subtracting, the procedure automatically determines the common region of both elements and subtracts it from the reference part without an exact definition of the subtracting volume by the user.

For fusion by addition, the overlapping volume is calculated and added to the reference part (figure 11).

The basic algorithm of this method can be split into three parts. First of all, the intersections of all surfaces of both solids are calculated (figure 12). The range of definition of any intersection is restrained to the common region of the intersecting surfaces. The intersections, such as straight lines, conic sections or polygons form the intersecting contour of both solids.

In the second step (figure 13) the remainder of both solids is calculated by intersecting the appropriate edges with the surfaces of the other solid. The points of intersection perform regions of edges that lie either inside or outside the other solid. According to the mode (adding or subtracting), the edges lying outside are preserved and the others deleted, respectively vice versa.

In the third step, the results of the two first steps are combined to one new solid in the data structure. In contrast to the flat surface method, it cannot be foreseen which surfaces will be changed by the fusion. Furthermore, new vertices and new edges are generated in any case.

Despite the enormous expenditure of programming technique, this procedure is absolutely indispensable for the definition of complex objects.

Figure 14 demonstrates an example without any technical implication. A cylinder is subtracted from a polyhedron under an arbitrary angle. The result cannot be obtained by any other known principle in such an economical way.

Both plane-orientated procedures (figure 15) are preferred whenever objects are complex in themselves but geometrically regular in one dimension. This feature occurs very often in the engineering industry. In this case, the characteristic contours are described in two dimensions by a line drawing-orientated principle like PROREN1.[5]

All these four sub-procedures of the geometric processor can be combined arbitrarily. Thus, very complex objects can be designed by a minimum of input data (figure 16).

2.4.2 Modification

Two kinds of operations render it possible to modify the previously designed object.

First, the user is given an indirect access to the internal representation by modular-available procedures. In that way, he can alter each element of the three-dimensional space by, for example, shifting vertices, edges or surfaces.[6]

Moreover, each input sequence can be revised and restarted from the user's terminal. This means that the input sequence is stored automatically on a disc file and can be altered and re-read by the user's command.

2.4.3 Detailing

The component can be completed by the detailing procedure. In the current version of PROREN2 two procedures are available: "chamfer" and "fillet".

In certain publications[8] this phase of operation is realised by fusing volumes of appropriate shape that are added to or subtracted from the reference part. Like the flat faces fusion, this will work only when the shape of the required chamfer or fillet is regular and stored explicitly as a module. Therefore, PROREN2 contains individual procedures for "chamfer" and "fillet" that up-date the data structure, as the kind of modification is known in advance. The faces that share the edge to be machined are changed and the object is extended by the new chamfer or fillet surface.

2.5 CUTAWAY METHOD

Finally, one procedure is to be mentioned that cannot actually be classified in the field of input: the procedure generating arbitrary cutaway profiles (figure 17). This is required not only for line drawings, but also to suppor additional processing.

For example, simple cuts through an object at level planes help determine automatically the cutting for the no-punch tape (2 1/2) dimensional milling).

The cutaway drawing can also be computed by the volume intersecting procedure. After the designer has fixed the cutaway plane and the direction of view, the program generates a polyhedron in such a way that the remainder after subtraction is the desired view. The cutaway plane is marked to be hatched when plotted.

2.6 APPLICATION

2.6.1 Economy

The question of economy of such a system cannot be answered completely It depends on several factors of which two are to be mentioned in detail:

First, it is vitally important how much information can be obtained fr the internal representation. With the increasing amount of processing programs and output programs the profit of the computer internal representation will increase too. The application programs may consist of general programs for plotting, no-punch tape or calculating weight, but also of typical programs for specific firms or specific branches.

The second point of economy features the frequency of repetition of geometric objects in the stages of the designing process.

Repetitive objects may be parts of a component, components themselves or assemblies. They are formulated in advance by the volume elements and their fusion and by the modifying and detailing procedures. Hereafter, they are stored as so-called macros waiting to be called up with a set of actual parameters like certain dimensions, positions etc.

2.6.2 Handling

PROREN2 can be used in two different ways during the designing process.

As all modules of the geometric elements and all procedures of the geometric processor are FORTRAN-subroutines, they provide an opportunity to be installed in design algorithms or calculating routines. Depending on certain design results the calculated values or dimensions are transposed into a computer internal representation of the work piece.

On the other hand, a command language can control the PROREN2 software by an interactive dialogue on a screen to handle free designs of a component part or an assembly.

2.7 EXAMPLE

The industrial application of the PROREN2 system is demonstrated by designing housings of wall sockets for the electrical industry. The computer internal representation is of use not only for generating line drawings of the work piece but also for computing the die-casting mould including the amount of fading. Finally, the no-punch tape of the mould is generated automatically.

The actual design is preceded by the preparation of macros, in this case depending on electrotechnical standards. Such a macro, i.e. the holder with the guides of the two-pin contact, is shown in figure 18.

With the help of the intersecting procedure, the macro is defined by the subtraction of four cubes from a cylinder. The synthesis of the new object starts with the command "CALL MONT2 (0,1)" which means that all elements ("0") are to be fused by subtraction ("1"). The FORTRAN subroutine technique was chosen to formulate a macro, that in this case consists of fixed dimensions only. By calling "STECK" and entering the values of position, this macro can be used in an interactive design.

After creating all macros required the actual design process can be started.

The figures 19a and 19b show one of the possible types of wall sockets and its defining sequence for the internal representation. First, the complex back of the socket is reproduced (figure 19a). The expense of formulation is reduced extremely by the use of two macros ("VERST" and "BOHR").

In this example, the importance of the principle of fusion by intersection becomes evident. The ribs, for example, are generated by cubes only. They adapt themselves to the previously defined structure so that resulting edges of the ribs - partial conic sections - are computed automatically.

Figure 19b shows the front of the socket that results from the subtraction of the macro "STECK" only. In the stage of detailing, several edges of the component are now rounded off (figure 20).

Arbitrary views and cutaway views are reproduced in figure 21. In figures 22 and 23 other types of examples are shown. The hidden line removal is automatically determined by a new kind of algorithm[2]. All drawings of this example are original plotter drawings.

2.8 REFERENCES

1. Bargele, N - PROREN2 - Eine Graphik-Software zur dreidimensionalen rechnerinternen Darstellung von Bauteilgeometrien, Dissertation, Ruhr-Universitat Bochum, 1978

2. Fritsche, B. und Nitsche, M - Automatische Visibilitatsermittlung von dreidimensional erfassten Maschinenbauteilen, Angewandte Informatik, 10/78 Friedr. Vieweg & Sohn, 1978

3. Seifert, H - Moglichkeiten des Rechnereinstatzes bei Entwurfsarbeiten im allgemeinen Maschinenbau, Konstruktion, Heft 24/72

4. Herold, W.-D -Der Einsatz der graphischen Datenverarbeitung in den Konstruktionsphasen des Entwerfens und Detaillierens, Dissertation, Ruhr-Universitat Bochum, 1974

5. Fritsche, B., Harenbrock, D. und Stracke, H. J. - PROREN1 - Eine Software fur die Zeichnungserstellung von Variantenkonstruktionen des Maschinenbaus, Benutzerhandbuch, Lehrstuhl fur Maschinenelemente und Konstruktionslehre, Ruhr-Universitat Bochum, 1975

6. Altjohann, H. - Ein Beitrag zum Problem der Graphischen Datenverarbeitung im Rahmen der Neu und Anpassungskonstruktion Dissertation, Bochum 1975

7. Seifert, H. - Fortschritte bei der graphischen Datenverarbeitung im Konstruktionsbereich des Maschinenbaus, VDI-Z, Heft 1/1977

8. Braid, I. C. and Lang, C. A. - Computer-Aided Design of Mechanical Components with Volume Building Bricks, Automation, Vol. 10, pp 635-642, Pergamon Press, 1974

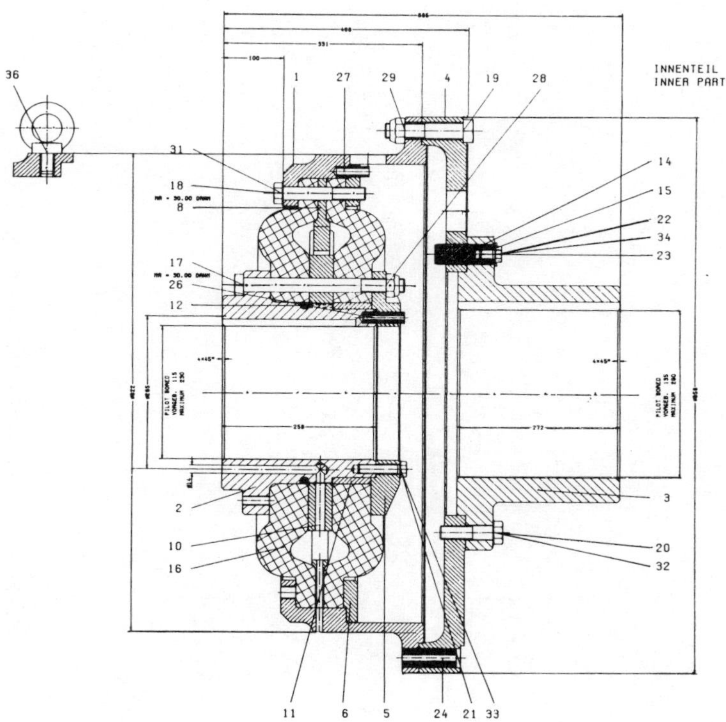

Figure 1. Typical manufacturing diagram provided by PROREN 1

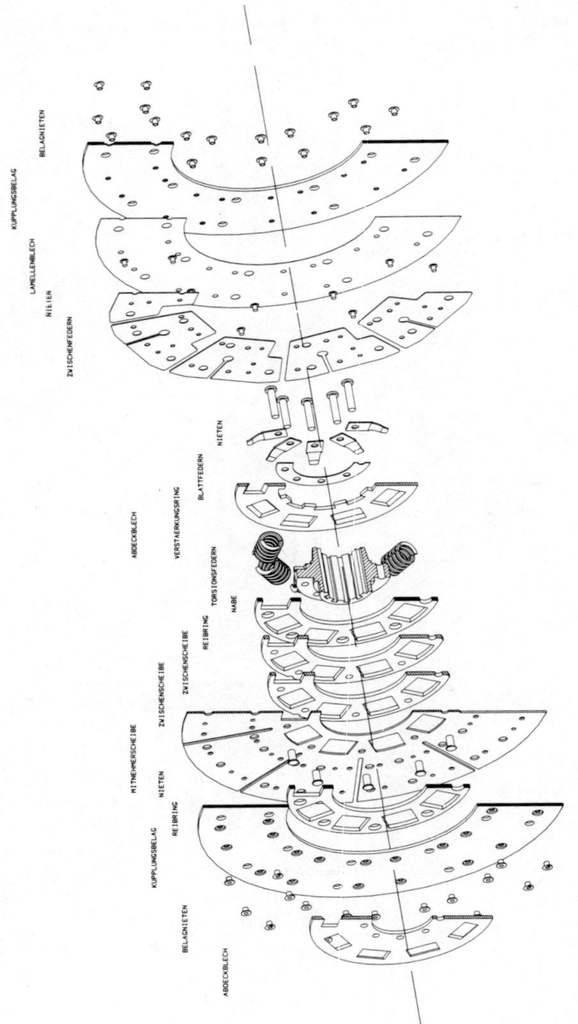

Figure 2. Exploded diagrams provided by PROREN 2

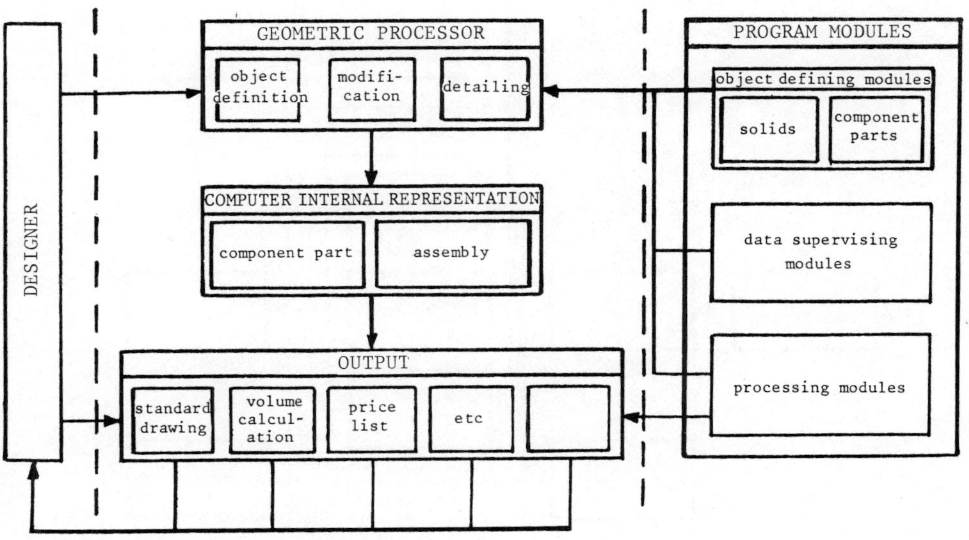

Figure 3. Structure of PROREN2 sysyem

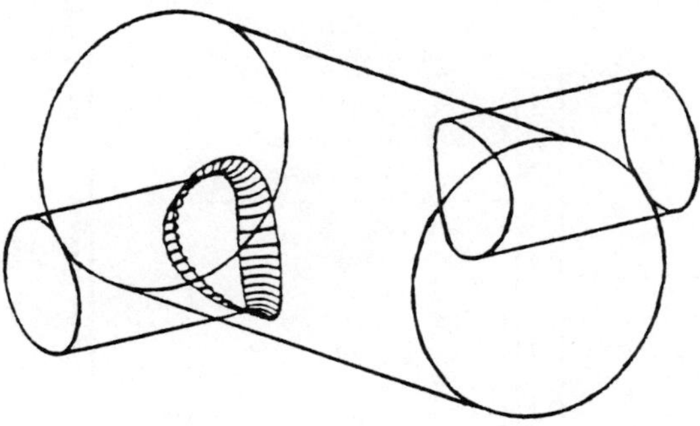

Figure 4. Intersections of two cylinders

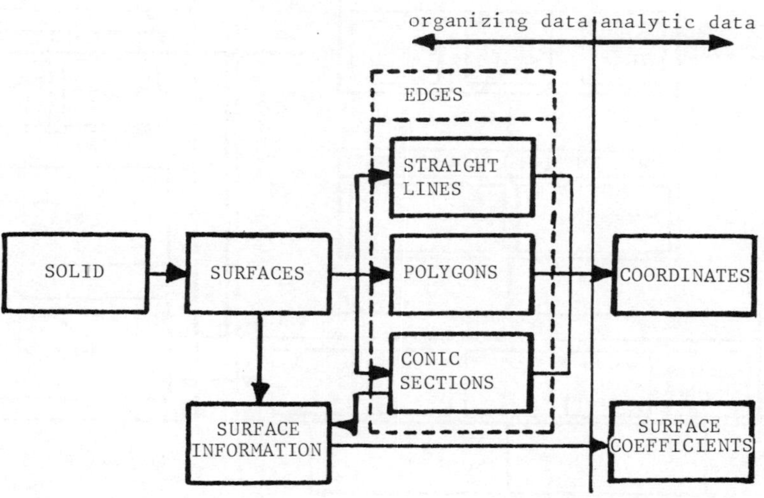

Figure 5. Data structure of PROREN2

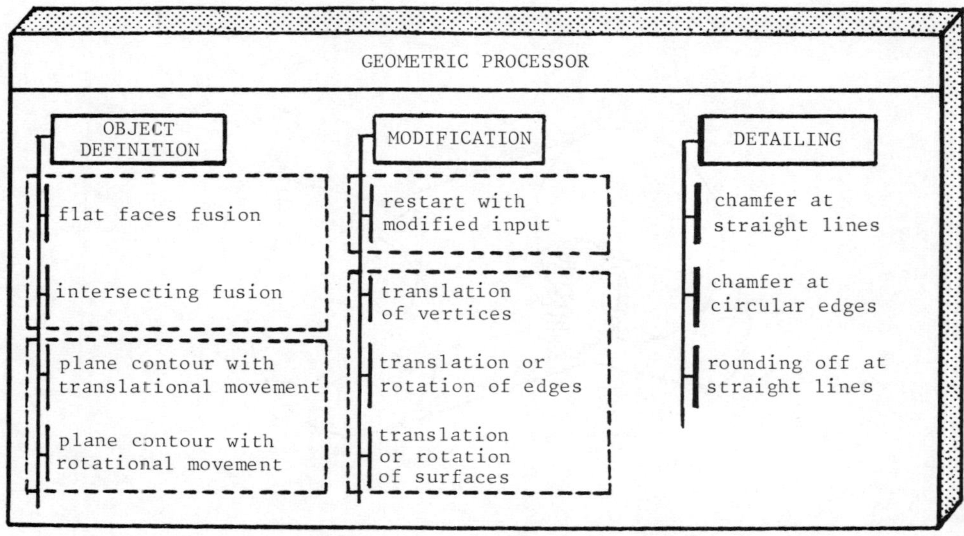

Figure 6. Procedures of the geometric processor

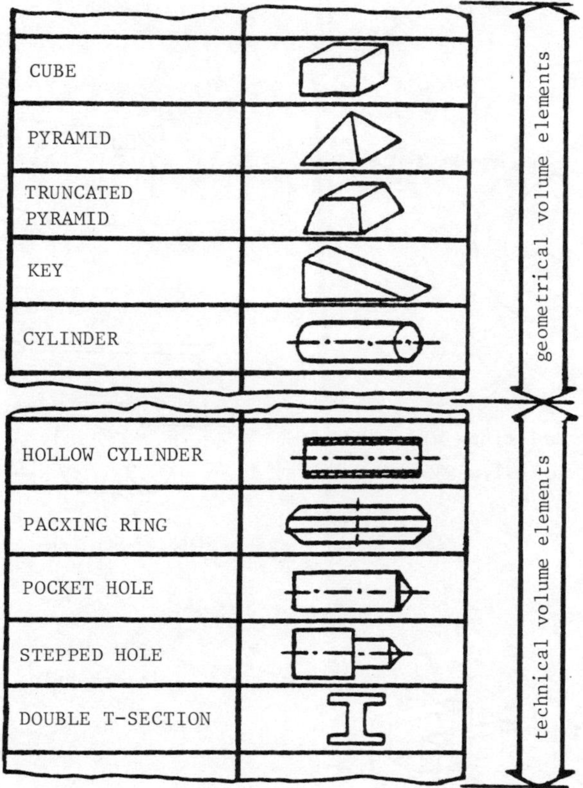

CUBE
PYRAMID
TRUNCATED PYRAMID
KEY
CYLINDER
HOLLOW CYLINDER
PACXING RING
POCKET HOLE
STEPPED HOLE
DOUBLE T-SECTION
geometrical volume elements
technical volume elements

Figure 7. Abstract from the User's Manual

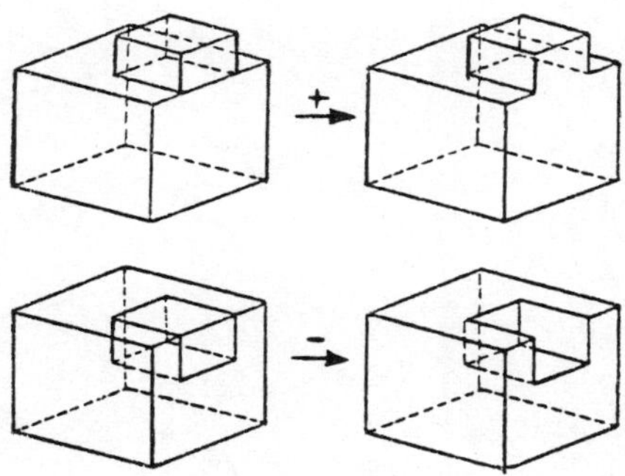

Figure 8. Fusion at joint flat faces

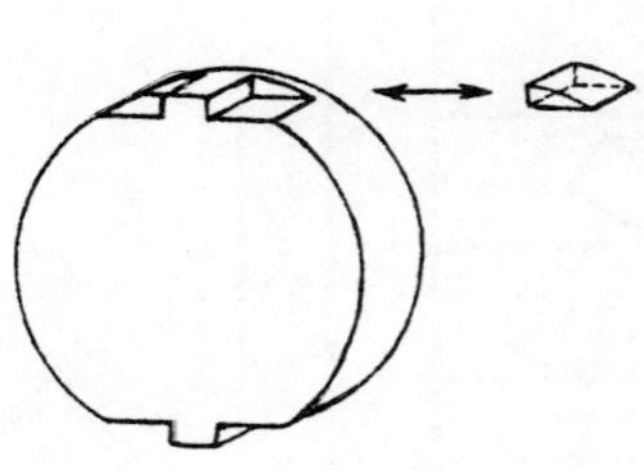

Figure 9. Restrictions of the flat face fusion

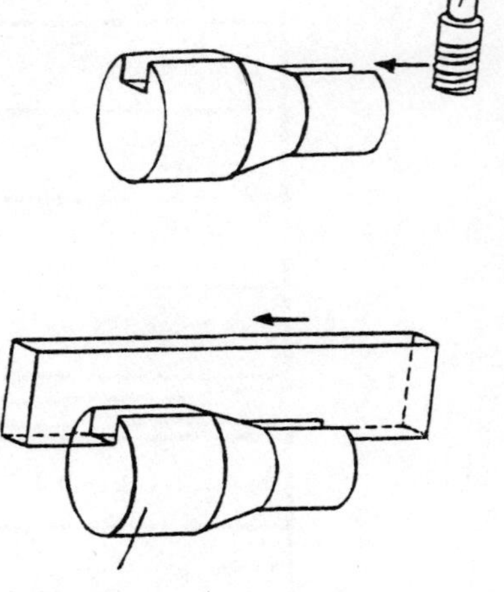

Figure 10. Fusion by intersecting volumes

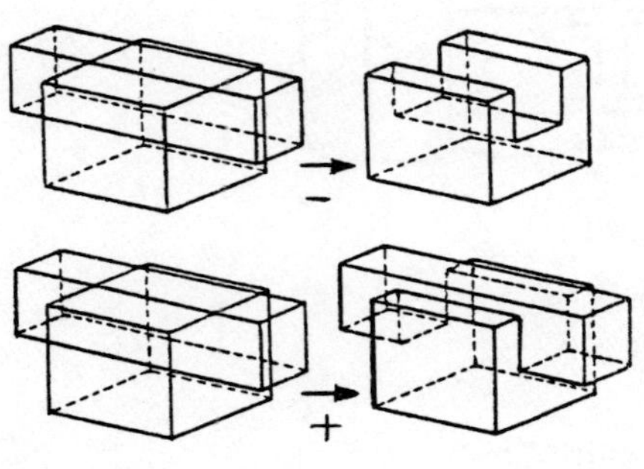

Figure 11. Fusion by intersecting volumes

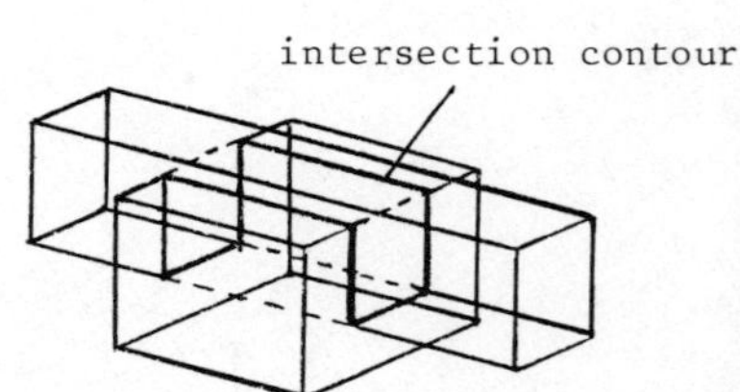

Figure 12. Definition of TRACES

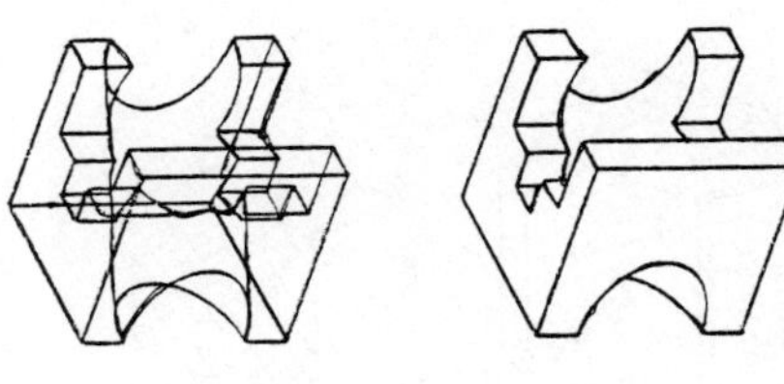

Figure 14. Complex Intersection

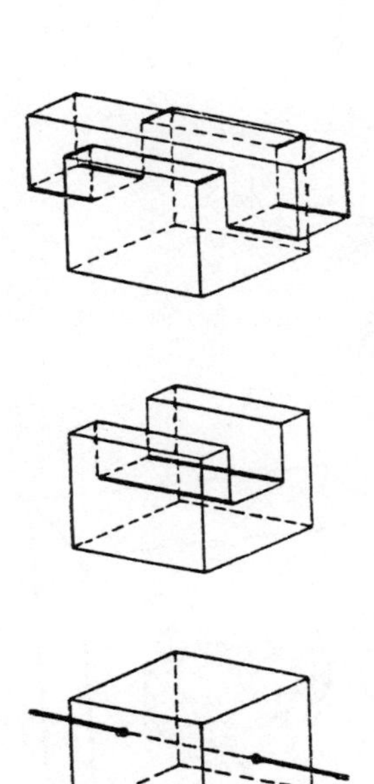

Figure 13. Definition of remaining volume

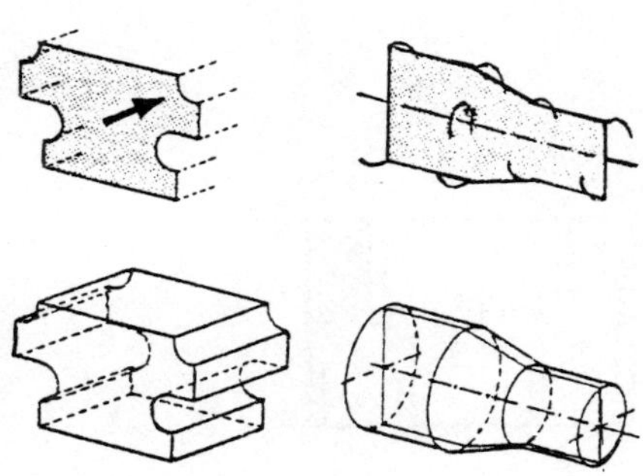

Figure 15. Plane contour executing a space movement

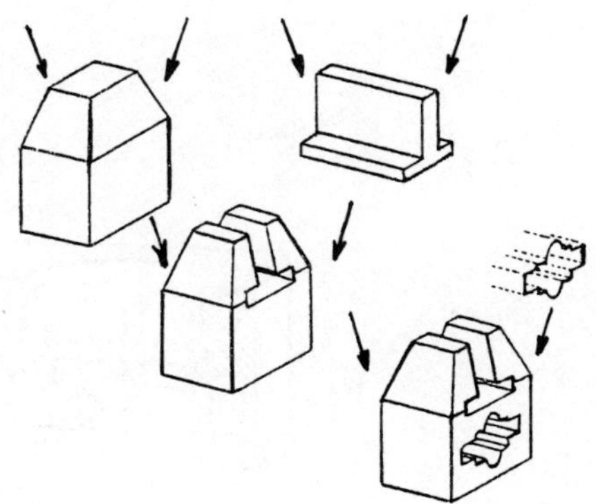

Figure 16. Combination of different input procedures

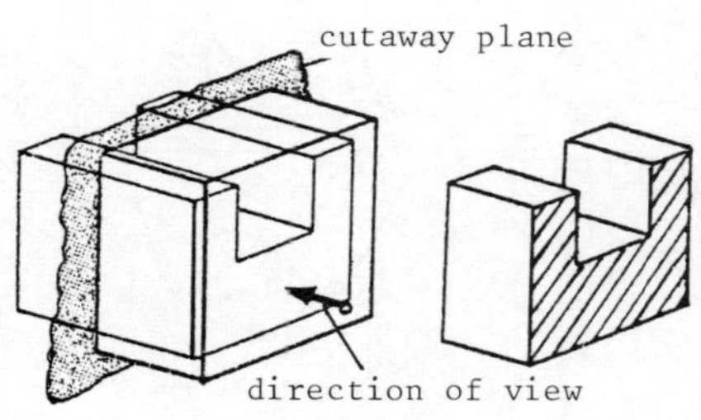

Figure 17. Cutaway view

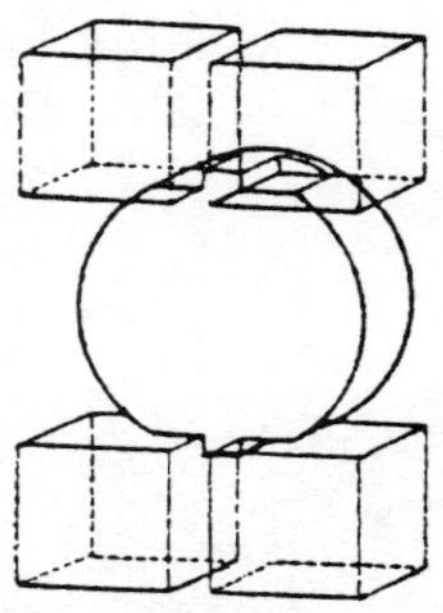

Figure 18. Formulation of a Macro

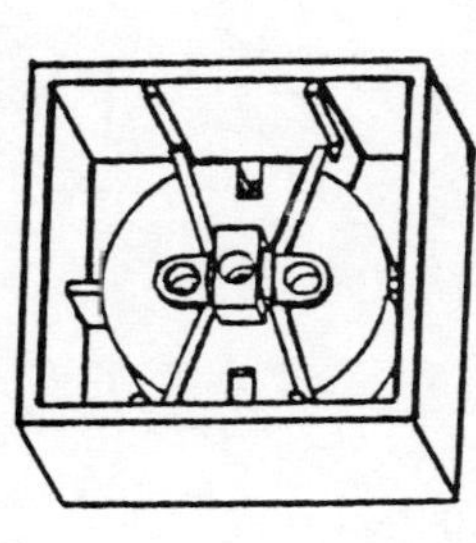

a)

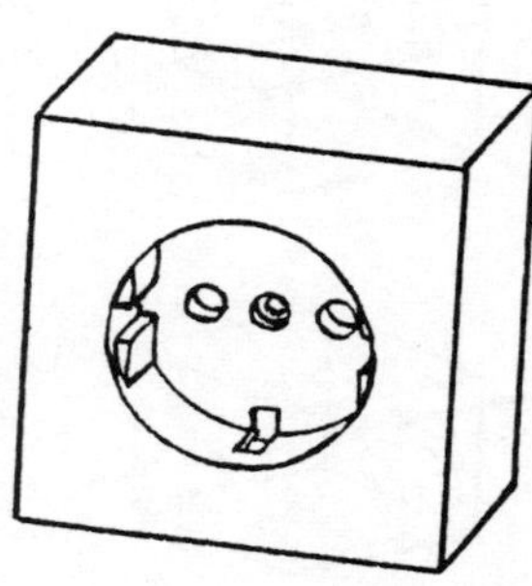

b)

Figure 19. Example

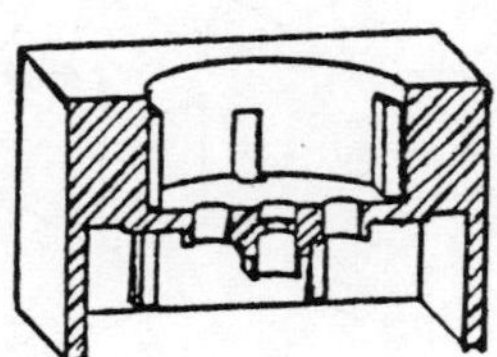

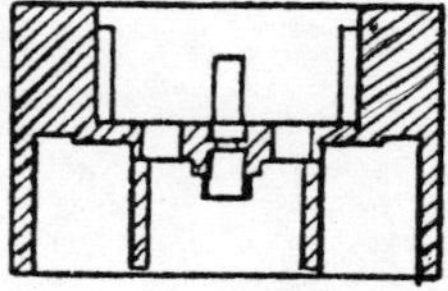

Figure 20. Example. Cutaway view

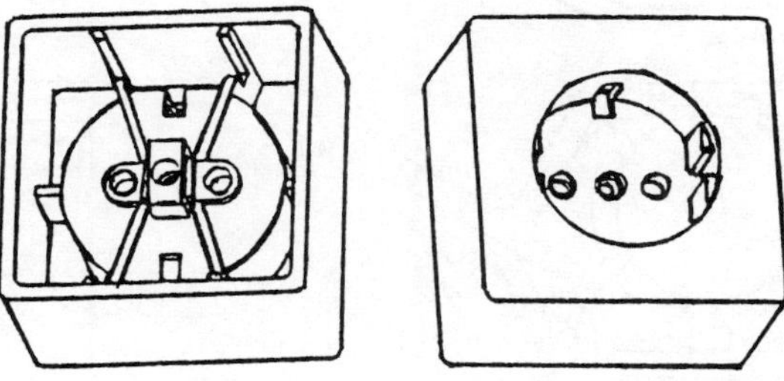

Figure 21. Example with rounded off curves

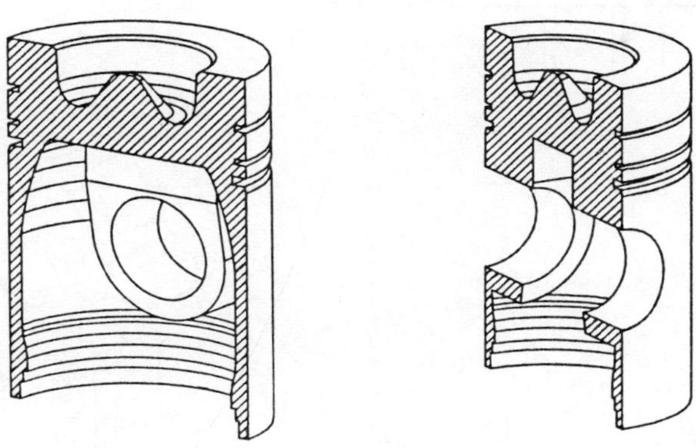

Figure 22. View of a piston generated using PROREN 2

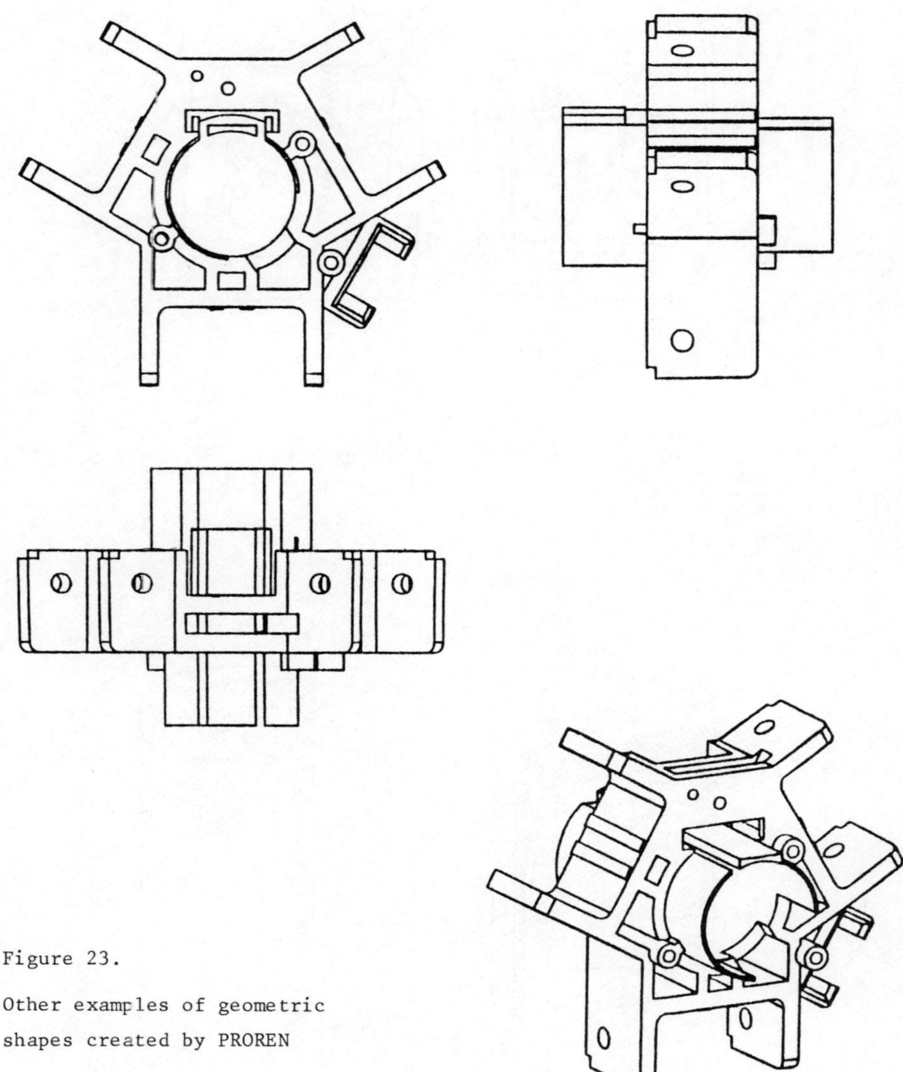

Figure 23.

Other examples of geometric shapes created by PROREN

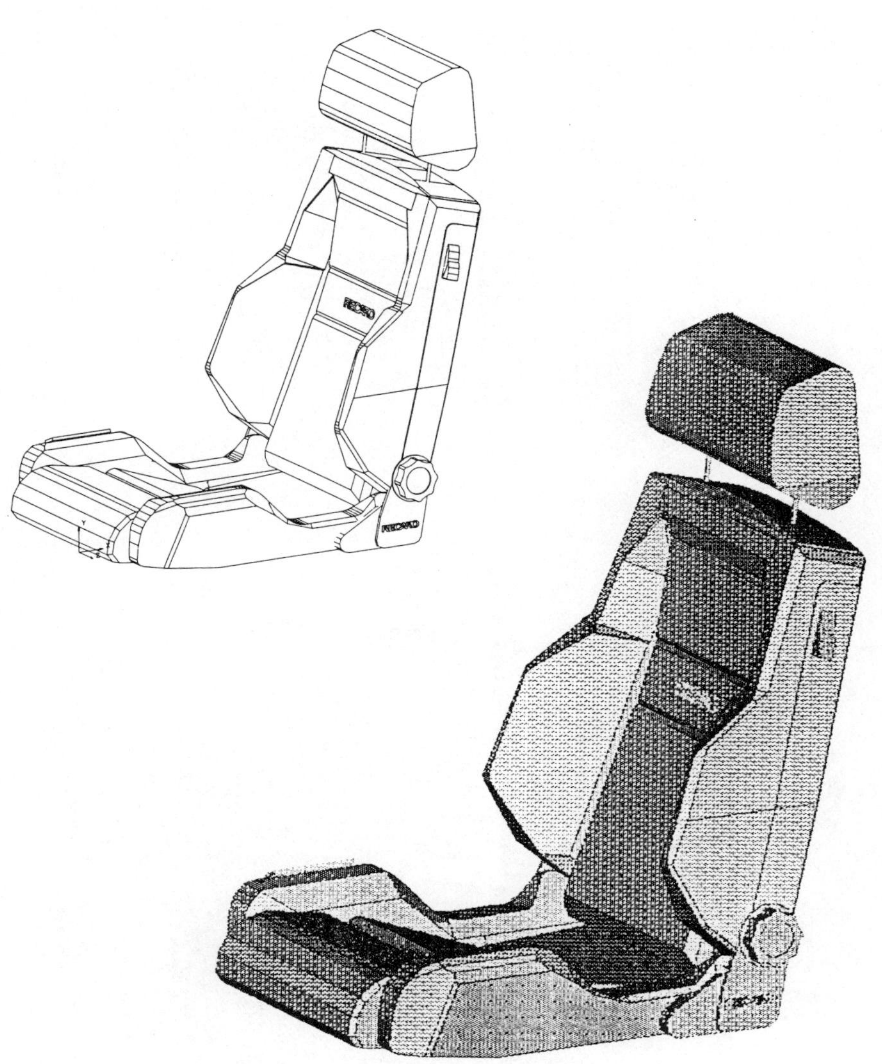

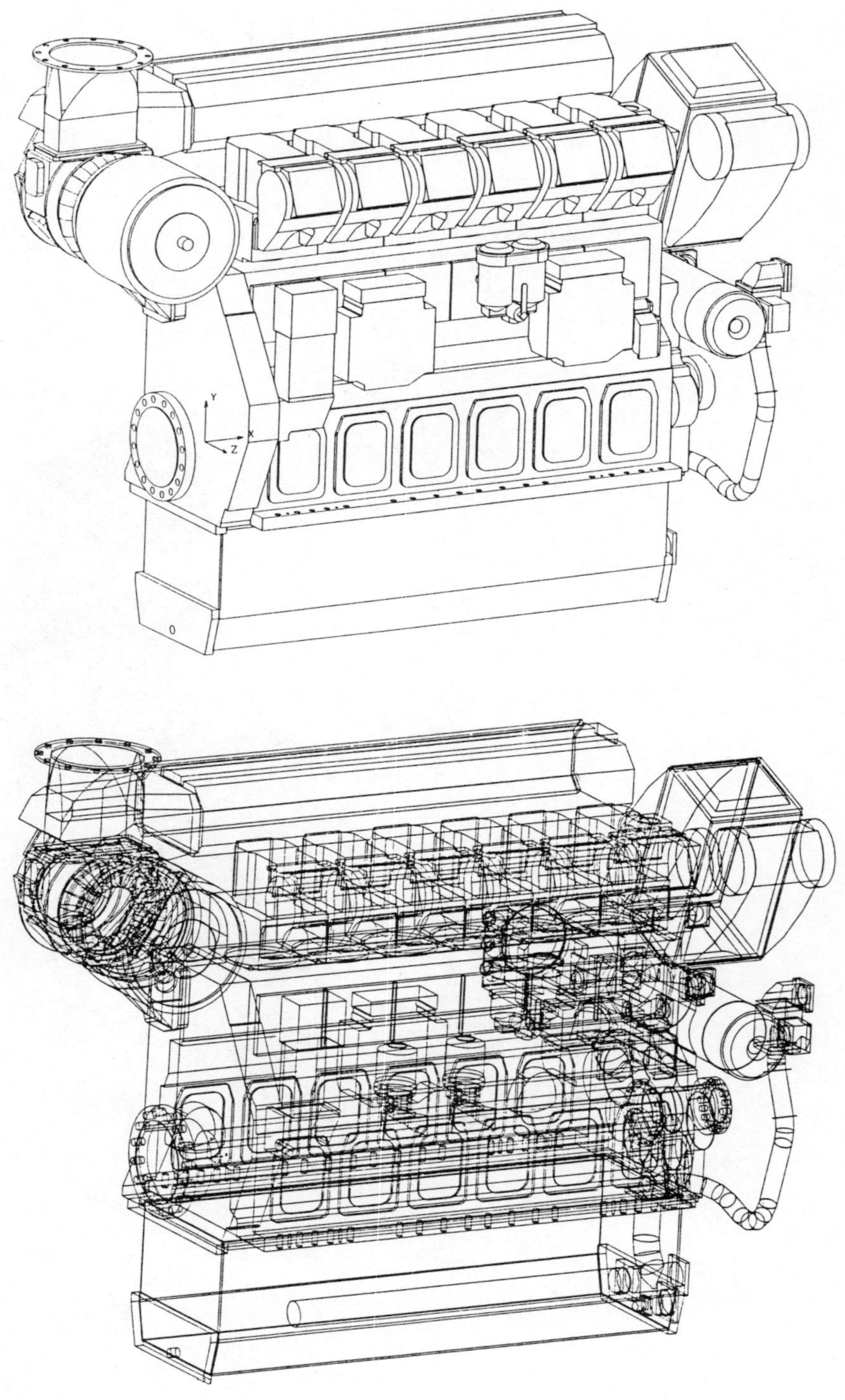
Y
X
Z

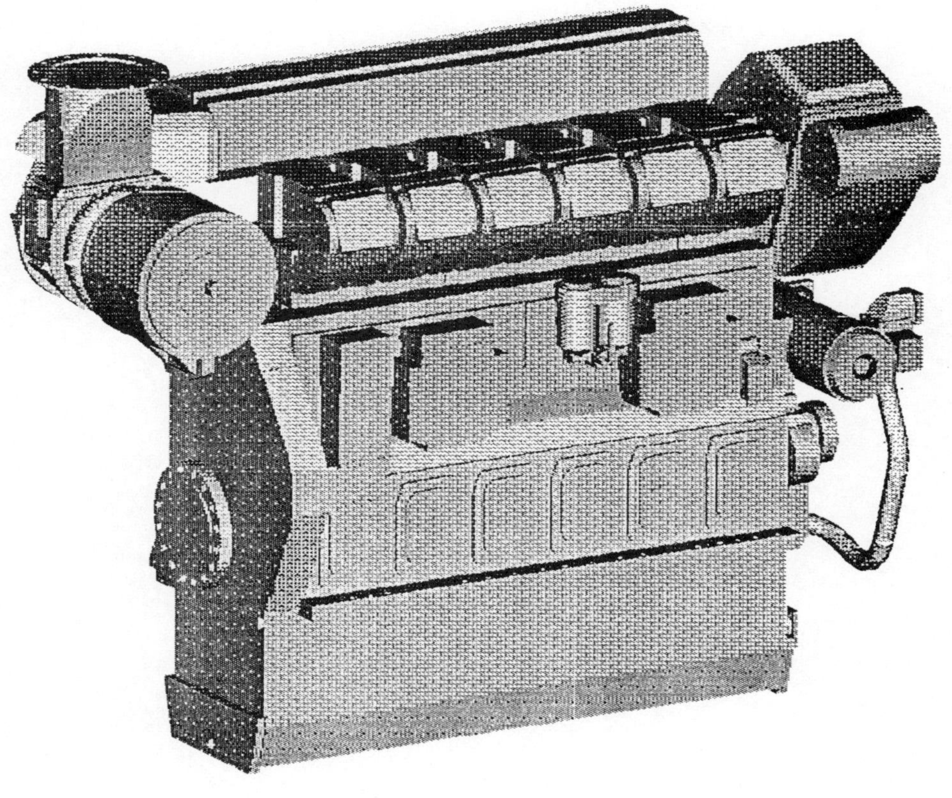

ROMULUS-D™

Evans & Sutherland, U.S.A.

1. GENERAL DESCRIPTION

Romulus-D[TM] is a general purpose solid modeling system with the following features:

Easy to learn and easy to use - Graphical, menu oriented interaction minimizes training time and cost. Romulus-D is an efficient and comfortable tool for the mechancial designer.

Solids-based product definitions - Accurate solid modeling guarantees complete representations of products. Drawings are created semi-automatically.

Modeling of assemblies - Many parts and assemblies can be worked on at the same time. Parts are designed and modified in the context of an assembly; changing the part changes the assembly. Components fit perfectly the first time because features of the assembly are used to design parts.

Integrated product information - Modeling, drafting and design management are fully integrated. Drawings of parts or assemblies are always accurate and in step. Bill of material reports are generated automatically.

Networked design management - Designers work with a central database where information is readily exchanged across a high-speed network. The database also provides a secure archive for all important information.

The system has been made specifically for mechanical design engineers. There's no command language to learn. Menus put everything needed within easy reach. Informative prompts guide the user throughout the system. If the user runs into trouble, sensible error messages are displayed. Extensive help is available on any topic.

Information in the models is readily available for design tasks. Select functions from menus and point at features of parts and assemblies. Pick data from parts and assemblies to use with the full-function on-screen calculator. 'Forms' are displayed with prompts for entering text or numbers from the keyboard.

Romulus-D follows the designer's way of thinking. Minimum constraints are imposed on design methods because the systems allows the user to switch between functions at will. The user can 'undo' a task or go 'back' several stages in a work session, so the user can try something and then change his/her mind.

A range of versatile techniques puts the power of solid modeling at designers' fingertips. Construction geometry is available for work in 3D as well as 2D. Outlines can be spun or swept to create solid material. Material can be made or modified using simple 3D shapes such as cylinders and blocks. Change parts by adding, subtracting and copying material or by moving and changing features. Position material easily by pointing at surfaces and edges.

There's no limit to the number of different parts that can be worked on at one time. Views of parts and assemblies each appear in their own 'window'. Develop different parts and assemblies simulataneously while also displaying reports, drawings, and mass properties.

Romulus-D never approximates. Part definitions are accurate to one micron in a kilometer. The user can be confident that every feature seen is a true and accurate representation of the design.

Romulus-D lets the user work on parts and their assembly at the same time. Display as many parts as required, each in its own window. Position components exactly in the assembly by aligning edges, abutting faces, moving parts and rotating them. Check for interference between components. Use the geometry of components in the assembly to design other parts.

Design the assembly constraints and configuration first. As detail is added to components during the process, the assembly is kept in step automatically.

A part exists only once in the database, no matter how many time it is used in assemblies. Make design changes to a part once only. Romulus-D propagates the change automatically through all assemblies that use the part.

Use the constraints of the assembly to redefine the shape and location of its components. Modify the dimensions of a part by altering features, such as the location of a face, using other geometry in the assembly to achieve an exact fit.

Whenever changing an assembly, Romulus-D keeps track of the old version and new version. Changing the version of a part can change the version of all assemblies that use it. Current bills of material and where-used reports can be produced whenever needed.

2. NETWORKED DESIGN MANAGEMENT

Coordinating work within a project or across departments is time-consuming. Romulus-D provides a design management network that administers the corporate database as well as individual work-in-progress. During a work session, each designer has a dedicated Apollo workstation, which is linked via a high-speed network to all other designers and to the central database. Information anywhere in the network can be accessed as if it were the designer's own.

Romulus-D supports the flow of design information for work-in-progress and group development and production pools. Each designer has a private work area. All changes in release levels are recorded. Current versions of assemblies always use the correct release of components.

Romulus-D maintains a single product definition for each design from initial concept through release, revision and re-release.

Flexible security allows any company to establish as much control over the database as it needs. Passwords to use Romulus-D supplement the Apollo security system.

Designs that are obsolete can be archived on tape and retrieved at any revision level.

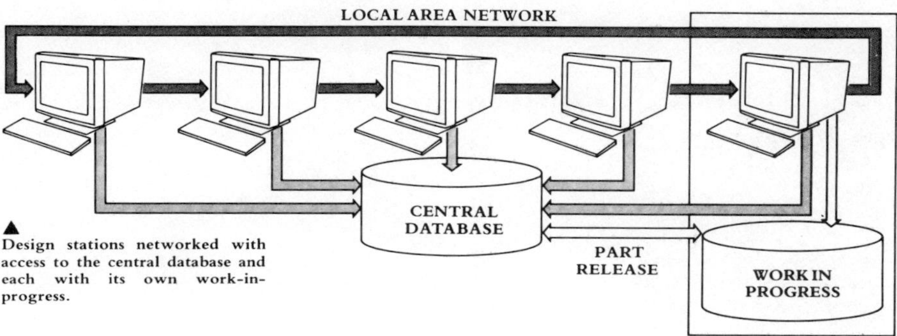

▲ Design stations networked with access to the central database and each with its own work-in-progress.

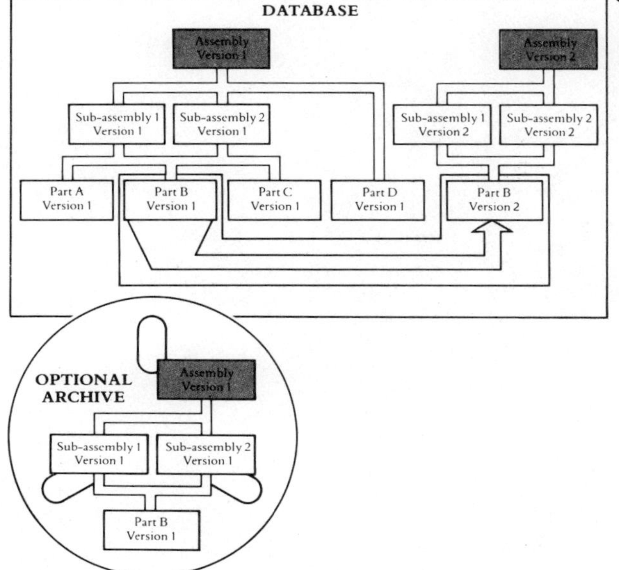

◀ An assembly tree structure in the database showing modification of a part and the resulting change in subassemblies and the top level assembly. Also shows optional archiving of the old assembly configuration.

3. INTEGRATED DRAFTING AND REPORTS

Romulus-D integrates design, drafting and reporting. They all use the solid model definitions as their primary source of information. This integration keeps all elements of a design, from part definitions to engineering drawings and bills of materials, consistent at all times.

Engineering drawings are easily created using views of parts and assemblies. Integration with the solid models means that when a design change is made, the drawings change automatically.

A wide range of annotation forms and dimensioning styles are available. Full annotated and dimensioned engineering drawings can be produced to company standards.

Reports reflecting the current state of any design can always be generated. Romulus-D can produce and print bills of material and where-used reports in a variety of formats. A history can be generated for any part or assembly showing all the design changes it has undergone.

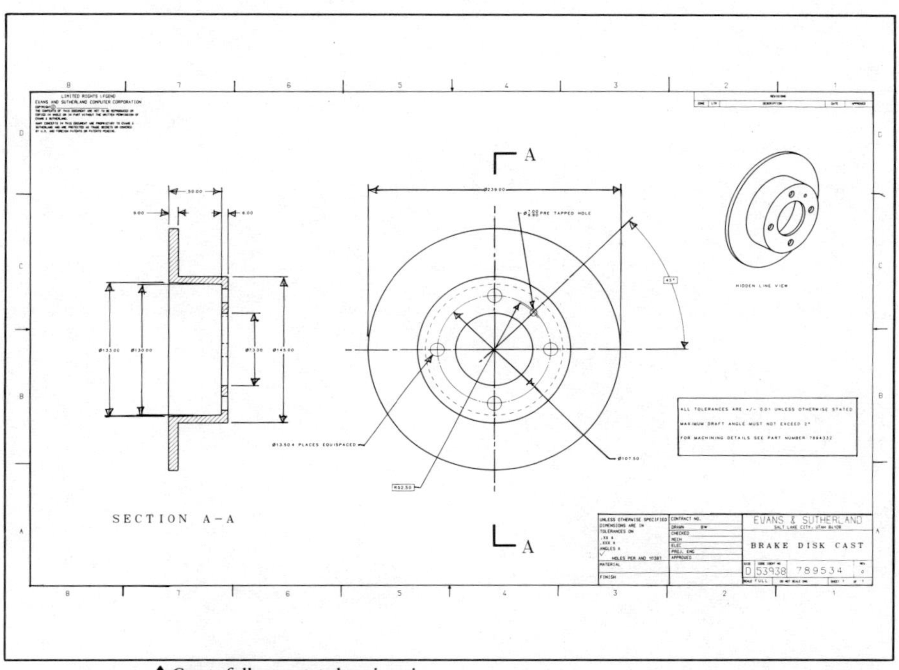

▲ **Create fully annotated engineering drawings from views of parts and assemblies.**

Parts explosions are easily created ▶ from part and assembly models.

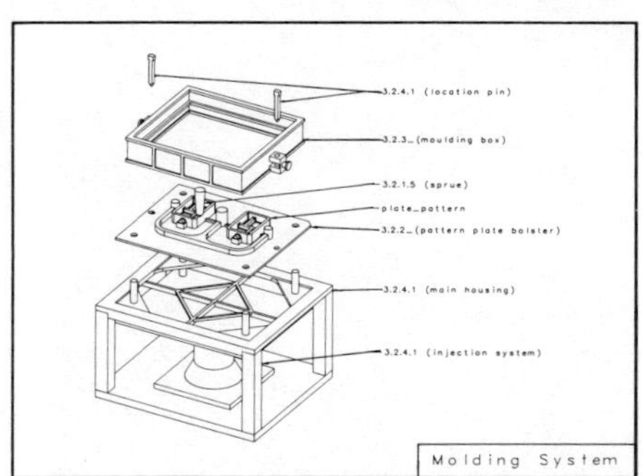

SABRE-5000

Gerber Systems Technology International
(UK), U.K.

INTRODUCING SABRE-5000

Now Gerber Systems Technology presents a new generation of computer aided design and manufacturing technology ... SABRE-5000.

SABRE-5000 embraces the very latest workstation technology, offers excellent CAD/CAM applications software, and can be configured to meet your price and performance requirements.

All SABRE workstations feature 32-bit CPUs, virtual memory, floating point accelerators, and double-precision arithmetic for fast, versatile operation. Plus, they offer super-fast graphics processors, high resolution colour raster displays, industry-standard UNIX® operating system, and the productivity enhancing SABRE-5000 user interface.

SABRE-5000 is also upward compatible with previous GST systems, with re-engineered software to give you greater performance, ease of operation, and support.

Advanced Performance at an Affordable Price

Choose from a broad range of affordable SABRE-5000 systems with the CAD/CAM solution that's right for you.

At the high end, we can configure powerful engineering workstations with multiple CPUs, multiple graphics displays, and advanced software modules for solid modelling, design engineering and analysis, and computer-aided manufacturing. You can even use SABRE-5000 to develop your own software.

Or, if you require only a basic design or manufacturing capability, we can configure a cost-effective SABRE-5000 system you can put to work immediately to boost productivity.

Whichever SABRE system you choose, you are never locked into a fixed capability. SABRE-5000 grows with you as your needs change. You can add an unlimited number of workstations or a shared resource manager without affecting your present SABRE system.

® UNIX is a trademark of Bell Laboratories

High Productivity Workstation Puts 32-bit Power at Your Fingertips

A single, modern keyboard and cursor control put the SABRE's 32-bit power right at your fingertips. Dual screens separate menu and graphics for clean operation and fast, uninterrupted graphic display.

SABRE provides operating modes for any user level. If you are a first time user, you will be amazed with your professional results using step-by-step menu prompts. With some experience, you will learn to work even faster by typing ahead to anticipate the prompting messages. Later you will really fly using macros and the SABRE command language.

SABRE-5000 is not only smart, but smart looking too, making an attractive addition to any environment. Its contemporary, ergonomic design gives greater operator comfort and convenience. Plus you have a choice of either an integrated unit, or a free-standing desk and individual components.

CAD/CAM SOLUTIONS

There is a wide, versatile range of practical SABRE-5000 software which can help you go from concept to machined part. Display your designs as wireframes or with the realism of vivid colour and shaded solid models - or both at once. Then, prepare design documentation and send manufacturing data directly to your machine tools on the shop floor.

Complete Mechanical Design Solutions

Add a whole new dimension to your mechanical designs with SABRE-5000. Powerful curve surface, and solid modelling programs let you create, change, and refine models of simple to complex parts. The most complex aerospace and automotive parts, dies, and moulds are created quickly and precisely.

SABRE-5000 is a very fast system for colour rendering. Automatic hidden line and surface removal lets you create striking lifelike images to help you visualise design and speed design cycles. High-speed colour shading and multiple light sources even simulate metallic surfaces. SABRE solid modelling software helps you sell your ideas and products without high-cost hand artwork and models.

Design documentation is a snap with SABRE's software for dimensioning and detailing, parts lists, layout and plotting.

Powerful Engineering Analysis Tools

Increase engineering productivity even more with SABRE's engineering analysis programs for design verification and optimisation.

Mathematical computations used in product design, such as volumetric and mass properties, are standard functions in SABRE-5000 software.

Finite element modelling and analysis packages perform more advanced engineering design tasks. And for designing thermoplastic injection moulds, we offer programs that analyse material flow and cooling.

Outstanding NC Machine Tool Programming

GST has earned an enviable reputation worldwide for cost-effective, highly productive solutions for the metalworking industry.

The tradition has been continued with SABRE-5000. Here is software that generates tool paths for a broad range of NC machine tools for simple profiling, pocketing and lathe work, as well as for multi-axis machining of complex, sculptured mould surfaces.

Machine tool paths up to 5-axes can be generated graphically. Produce machine code using GST generic or dedicated post-processors, APT or COMPACT II source output.

Distributed Network Puts Capabilities Where You Need Them

Locate your SABRE-5000 workstations, plotters, file servers, and peripherals where they are used most effectively. then, link them with SABRE's Ethernet local area network and standard communications gateways. Designers, Engineers, and Machine Operators can share design and manufacturing information - within a faculty or from remote locations via phone lines - under full management control.

CUSTOMISE YOUR SABRE SYSTEM

SABRE-5000 can be enhanced with special GST software, by writing your own application software or by selecting from the many available third party packages.

Unique Software Solutions For Your Special Applications

GST CAD/CAM solutions extend beyond versatile prepackaged software. We also supply solutions for your special applications. We have simplified work for the aerospace, automotove and plastic industries by developing unique application software for complex components.

When the aerospace industry wanted to automate the design and manufacturing of complex turbomachinery components, GST developed a dedicated impeller machining package.

When auto subcontractors needed an efficient means to transfer and receive part design information from major car makers, GST provided the proper interface capabilities to their CAD data bases.

When tool makers sought a faster way to make moulds, GST developed software which automated the creation of draft surfaces. This software innovation has since found wide acceptance among glass, thermoplastic, and die cast mould makers.

But, that is not all. We have also helped sheet metal fabricators boost productivity with software which automated flat pattern layout and NC punch press output.

Ask us how we can help you cut the time needed to go from concept to machined part with a SABRE-5000 software solution tailored to your special application.

User Programming Made Easy

SABRE's open architecture, modular design, industry-standard UNIX operating system, and standard compilers for all commonly used engineering programming languages let you customise your system for even more productivity. With SABRE-5000 software your programming staff can take advantage of SABRE's advanced user interface and graphics utilities by developing software for your special or proprietary applications.

Build an Electronic Library with Data Security and Control

With SABRE-5000 archive library software it is easy to manage your design, drafting and manufacturing files.

Just set up your own secure, parts design library. You can store complete part groupings and project or department files in one centralised location. You control the access to this information by assigning security levels. You even track part files and control design changes after files have been stored on magnetic tape.

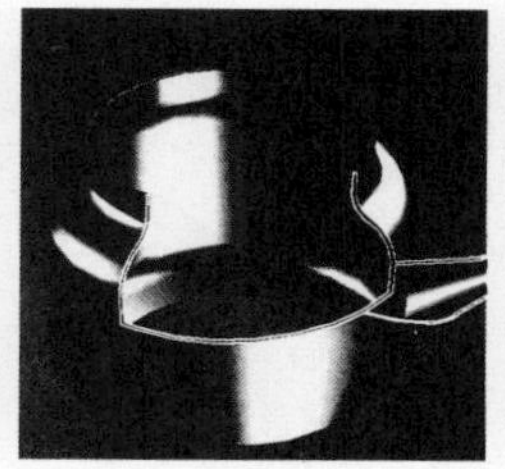

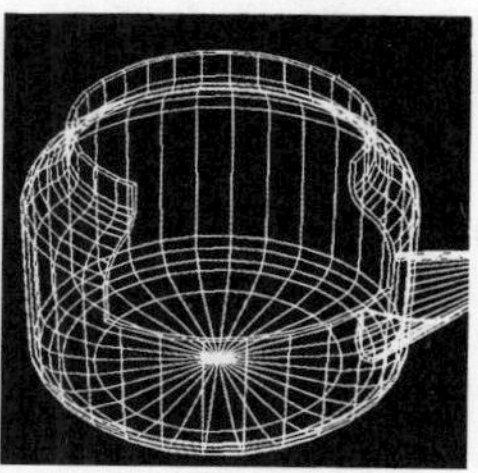

Software for conceptual design using solid modeling

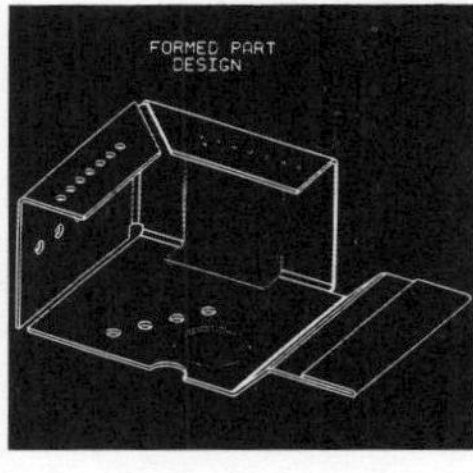

Special application software

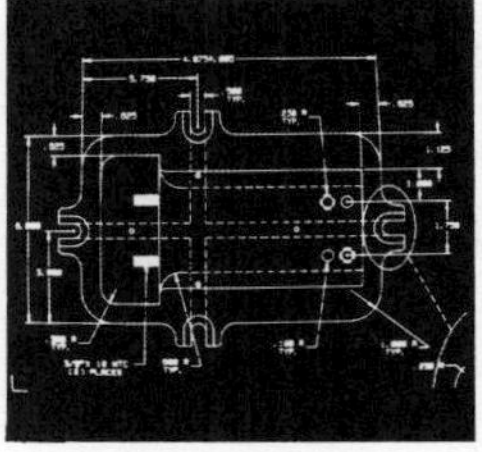

Complete design documentation

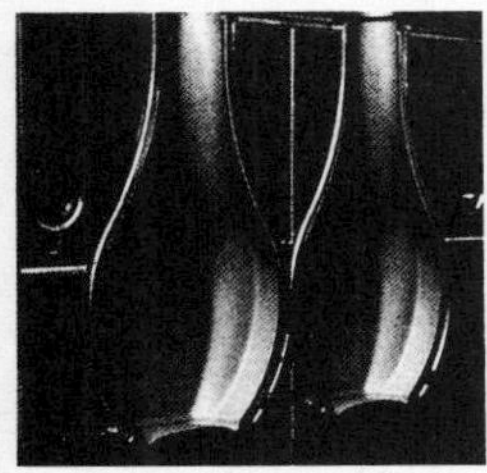

SABRE-5000 -
a must for moldmaking

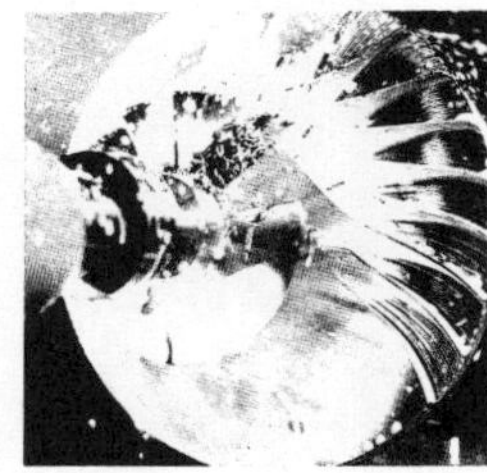

Simplify 5-axis machining

Create lifelike solids

SYNTHAVISION®

MAGI – Mathematical Applications Group
Inc., U.S.A.

INTRODUCTION

The SynthaVision® System frees engineering design from the cost and delays of constructing physical models, and frees the CADAM system operation from the constraint of two dimensions.

The integrated SynthaVision CADAM system allows you to design solid models, using familiar CADAM system construction techniques. You work with your design in three dimensions, build it part by part and alter it, as though it were an unending succession of physical models - but with much greater accuracy, and in a time frame that shrinks days to minutes.

Once you store the data that describes a solid object, the System "knows" both its shape and the position at which you want to see it in three-space. It not only gives you the three-dimensional isometric view you want (including sections, compound sections, exploded views) but any other view you want in seconds.

It can present your design as a monochrome wireframe, or a wireframe in multiple colours - with or without hidden lines

Its capabilities are even more remarkable. Because the wireframe image is really the outline of a surface for which the System has data, it can give you a complete visual representation: full colour photographic images. The most obvious result is elimination of all ambiguity.

When your design is completed, the selected views are stored as normal CADAM system drawing files. Using the power of the CADAM system, finished drawings can be created by adding dimensions, crosshatching, annotation etc.

ENGINEERING CAPABILITIES

Makes you a model builder

SynthaVision software literally lets you build at the design station and you see your model as you construct it, stage by stage.

Your building blocks are a full set of "primitive" shapes, more shapes than any other system offers. Although these alone permit construction of just about any design, you are not limited to them. The System's database permits the combination of two or more primitives into one super-primitive which you can handle as a single shape.
SynthaVision has complete Boolean capabilities including intersection, difference and union.

Because discrete dimensions are assigned to each piece as you construct your model, each can be independently manipulated and modified in the computer. It not only can be dimensionally changed but also scaled, rotated, translated or otherwise reoriented.

Automatically measures clearances, checks for interference

The SynthaVision System knows where each part you create is positioned with respect to any other. The System therefore, not only can check clearances but - with one command - will check the total model for the clearances you require.

You don't have to ask for clearance between specific parts (unless you want to) because all possible combinations are checked.

Interferences are automatically - and separately - flagged. The area of interference can be displayed and its volume calculated.

Gives you mass properties, in minutes

Because the System's software knows everything there is to know about the dimensions of your model, it can calculated its surface areas and volume. Enter the specific gravity of the materials and the System will give you weight, centre of gravity, moments of inertia and fifteen additional mass properties of any component subassembly or the whole model.

Gives you a complete boundary file

The System automatically stores a complete file of solid modelling data for numerical control of machining and finite element mesh generation.

All data you enter, or that the SynthaVision System generates during the design process are stored automatically. Any part of the data, or all of it, can be re-used, changed, or output in a format suitable for documentation.

PRODUCTIVITY AND CREATIVITY IMPLICATIONS

If your current procedure is to make physical models, the time saved by eliminating the would, alone, quickly repay the investment in the SynthaVision® System

But, the System steps up productivity at CADAM® system installations in several more ways.

Unlike the CADAM system, which demands new data for each view, the SynthaVision System can present an infinite number of views, automatically, from one set of data, including sections and cutaways.

The SynthaVision System's 3-D output is more quickly "read" and understood. Enhanced by colour and removal of hidden lines, SynthaVision images eliminate the need to penetrate and comprehend complex orthographics.

The value of additional accuracy and reduction of errors defies calculation. Further, the System's 3-D representations can lead to shortcuts and be of great help in process planning.

There are many engineers whose creativity and innovativeness are bottled up for lack of tool that can give them play and expression.

The SynthaVision System is such a tool. Because it can increase productivity, save time and reduce costs so dramatically, its potential for giving design groups the means to make significant, fundamental advances is easily overlooked.

For example, by eliminating the need for actual interim models, the SynthaVision System reduces the time between design steps by a significant amount. The creative process is telescoped; it does not stagnate waiting for models. Ideas are tried, checked and compared in a time frame short enough to allow them to illuminate each other. And, the designer no longer has to depend on his mind's eye. His vision is externalized. It is cast into three dimensions on the CRT.

Training on SynthaVision packages, at your location of MAGI corporate offices in Elmsford, N.Y., is included in their price. Length of training varies by package but in every case MAGI will make sure your people achieve mastery of the programs. We have the experience to help them reach that goal in minimum time.

Support and Service

MAGI is committed not only to support its software, but also to establish and maintain a sound interface between our products and our customers' operations. This requires more than just basic training of your personnel, troubleshooting, fixes, and the revisions and updates provided in maintenance arrangements.

In addition to these , we make ourselves available for "postgraduate" consultation and technique development.

We will also supply customized software to interface our basic packages with your unique programs.

HARDWARE

SynthaVision is run on exact CADAM® system configurations. They include the following:-

- IBM® 5080 Graphics System, IBM 3250 and their compatible design terminals
- System 1250 and System 1500 Multi-station, trademarks of Spectragraphics Corporation

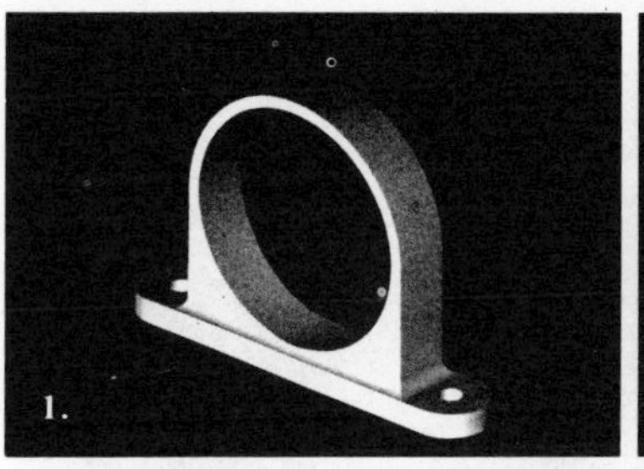

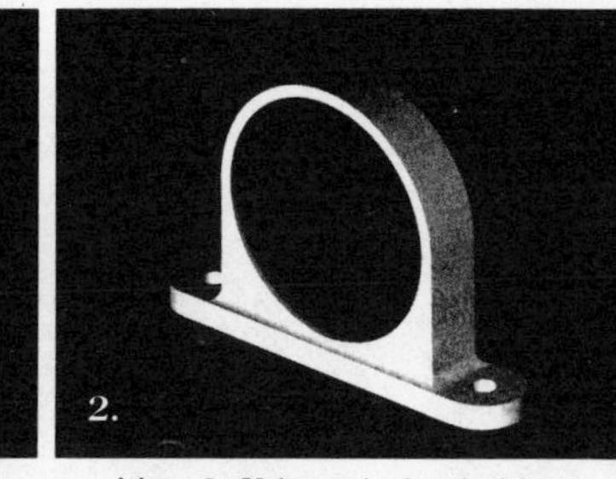

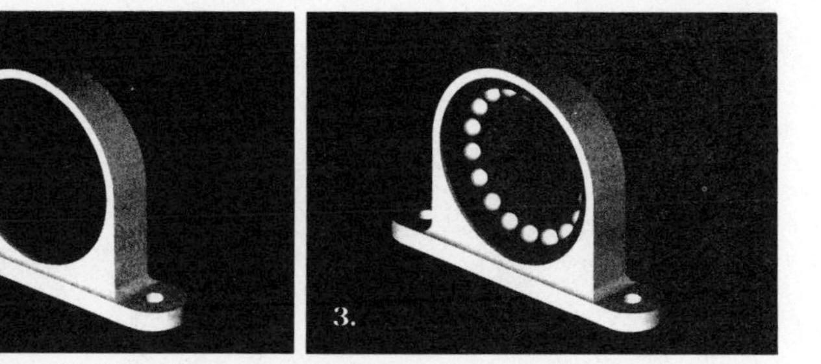

1. *Full-color, shaded picture of the housing in a pillow block bearing assembly composed of multiple prim-* 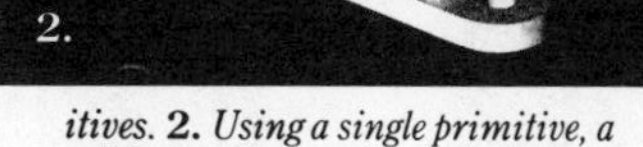 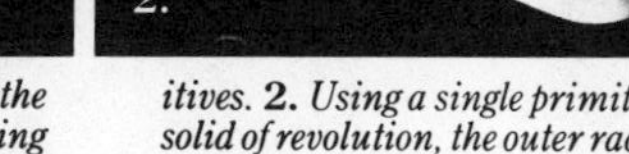 *itives.* **2.** *Using a single primitive, a solid of revolution, the outer raceway has been created and set in place.*

3. *Each sphere representing a bearing is created and placed using calculator and instance functions.*

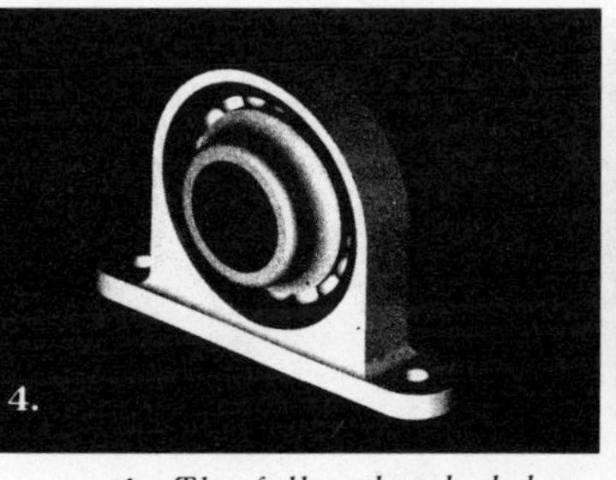

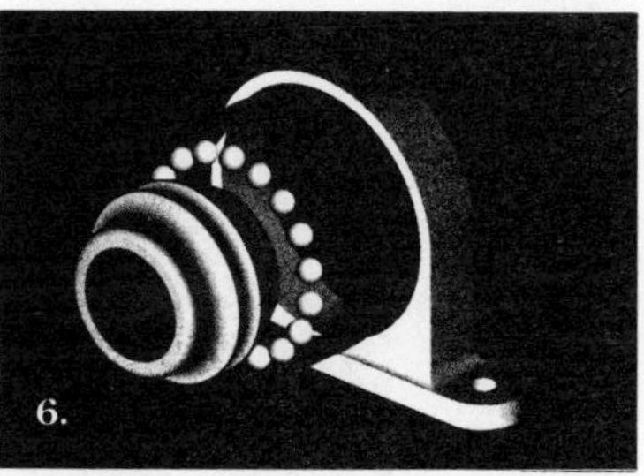

4. *The full, color-shaded assembly, including the inner raceway which is a single, solid of revolution,* **5.** *cutaways and sectioning, such as this one-quarter cutaway, and exploded views,* **6.** *improve visualization of the assembly for technical publications, reports, communication to manufacturing, etc.*

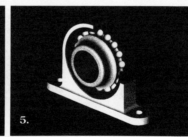

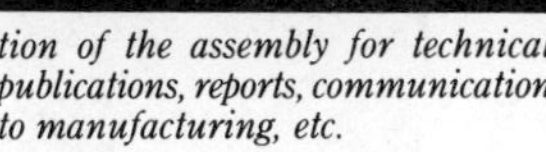

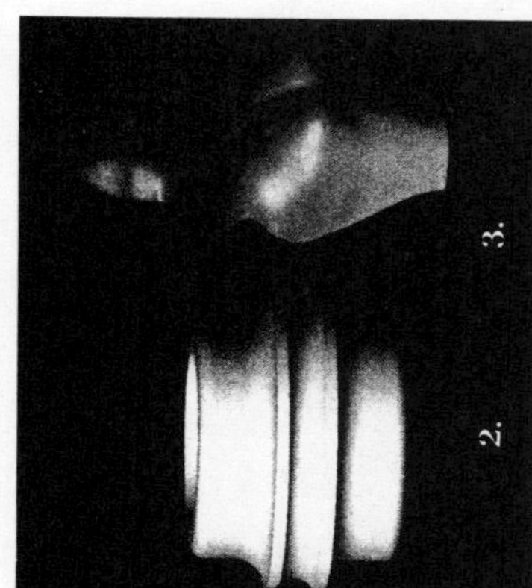

1. *The system has a complete set of solid modeling primitives, including all standard geometric shapes,* **2.** *swept-solids (such as the arbitrary slab and solid of revolution, above),* **3.** *plus free-form objects, constructed with our general solid primitive.*

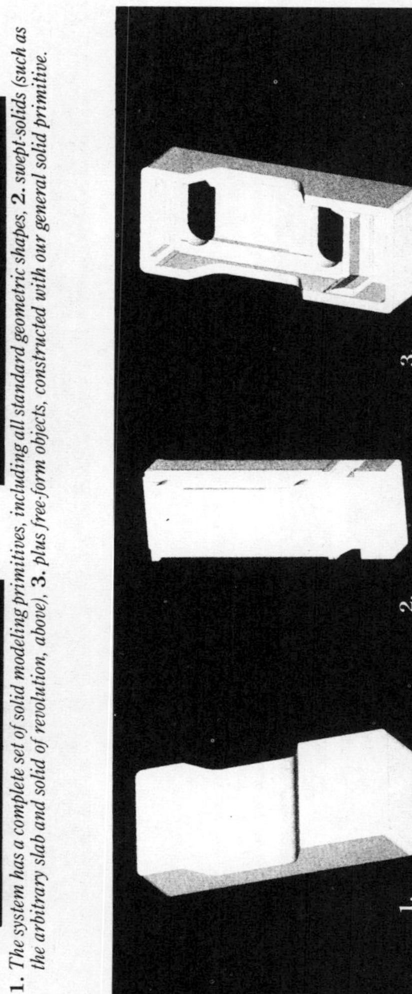

1. *Any combination of primitives can be used as a primitive and* **2.** *can be Booleaned with any other complex primitives to* **3.** *achieve your final design as shown in this sequence.*

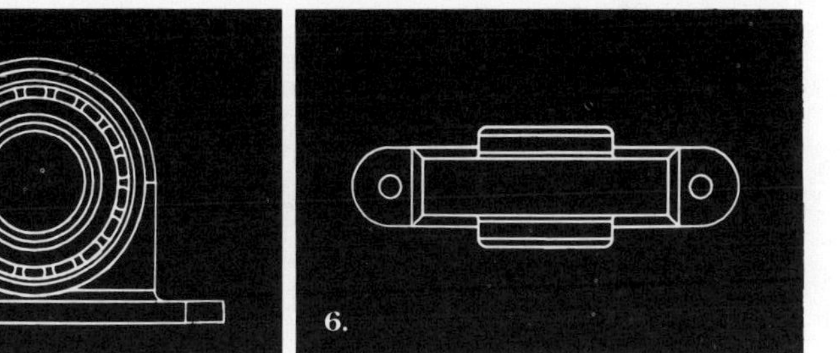

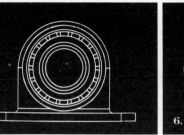

4. *The completed assembly, shown as a 3-D wireframe drawing of the isometric view with hidden lines removed. The orthographic views,* **5.** *front,* **6.** *top,* **7.** *end, are created. This combination of SynthaVision's accurate boundary file and its automatic hidden line removal, lets you quickly create all of the views of the part or assembly necessary for drawings.* **8.** *The data are then passed to the CADAM system where the same terminal supplies the drawing format, dimensioning and annotation.* **9.** *The integrated SynthaVision/CADAM system provides a more productive method of creating the output, the finished drawing.*

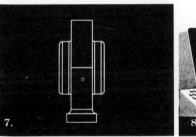

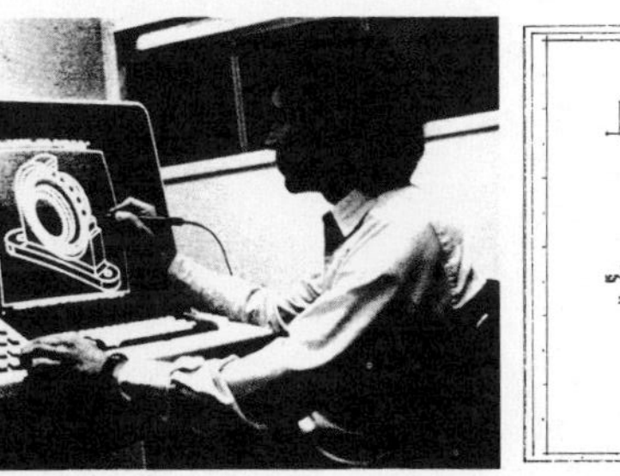

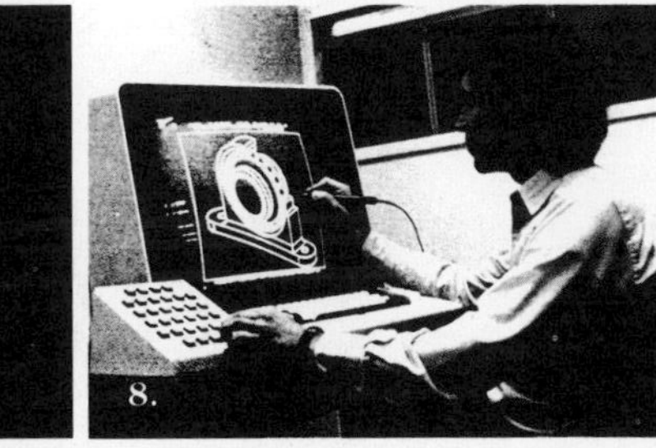

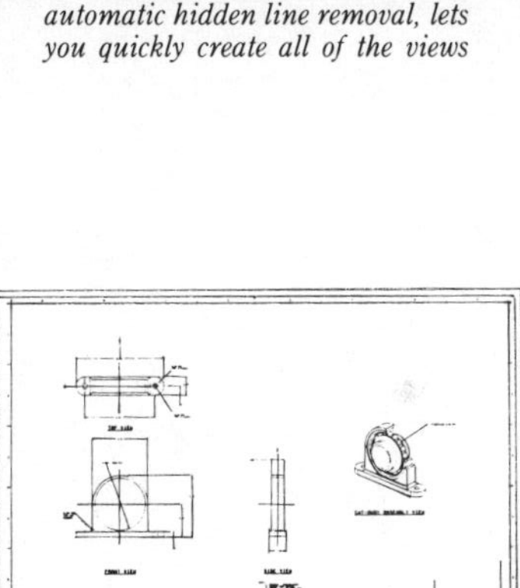

TIPS-1

Faculty of Engineering, Hokkaido University,
Japan

TIPS-1 (Technical Information Processing System-1) is one of the oldest Solid Modellers whose development started in 1967 and the first publication was made in 1973 at PROLAMAT (1) including a concept of solid modelling defined by set operation and simulative approach to CAD/CAM. A major objective of the development of TIPS-1 was to demonstrate the proposed process for CAD/CAM (2) shown in Figure 1 in which there are 3 steps for the simulation process; input step, modelling step and application step. In correspondence to these steps, the current TIPS-1 system structure has been constructed and is shown in Figure 2.

A part and an assembled shape model defined interactively or in batch by set operation using half space primitives are stored in the data-base and converted to CSG and B-Reps data structure. Three types of computer graphics technology of wire, shaded and grid pictures from CSG are developed and another wire picture routine with automatic dimensioner was made from B-Reps for correct drawing. (Figures 3 and 4).

For simulation process, some analyzers which are able to apply any shape are prepared as follows;

Mass property calculator: Volume, weight, center of gravity, moment of inertia and surface area can be calculated in a three digit accuracy by using the Monte-Carlo method.

FEM, BEM Analyzer: Every characteristics of a design object, i.e. stress, strain deformation, temperature distribution, flow analysis and others are analyzed.

Assembly Simulator: Assembled parts are built up, while being confirmed by the graphic processors and interference checker.

NC Command Generator and NC Simulator: Delta volume approach and a search method were applied for NC command generator. Graphic simulation of NC cutting is to compare the difference between the model and shape after cutting. (Figure 5).

Robot Simulator: Robot motion defined by robot language can be seen on a CRT display with interference check.

References

1) N. Okino, Y. Kakazu, H. Kubo, TIPS-1; Technical Information Processing System for Computer-Aided Design, Drawing and Manufacturing, Proc. of PROLAMAT'73 (1973).

2) N. Okino, Y. Kakazu, H. Kubo, TIPS-Technical Information Processing System for CAD/CAM, JARECT Vol.7, North-Holland Publishing Co.,(1983).

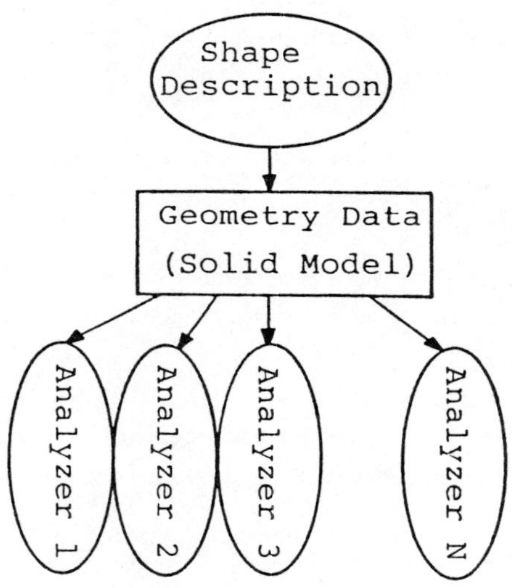

Figure 1. Basic Process for simulation

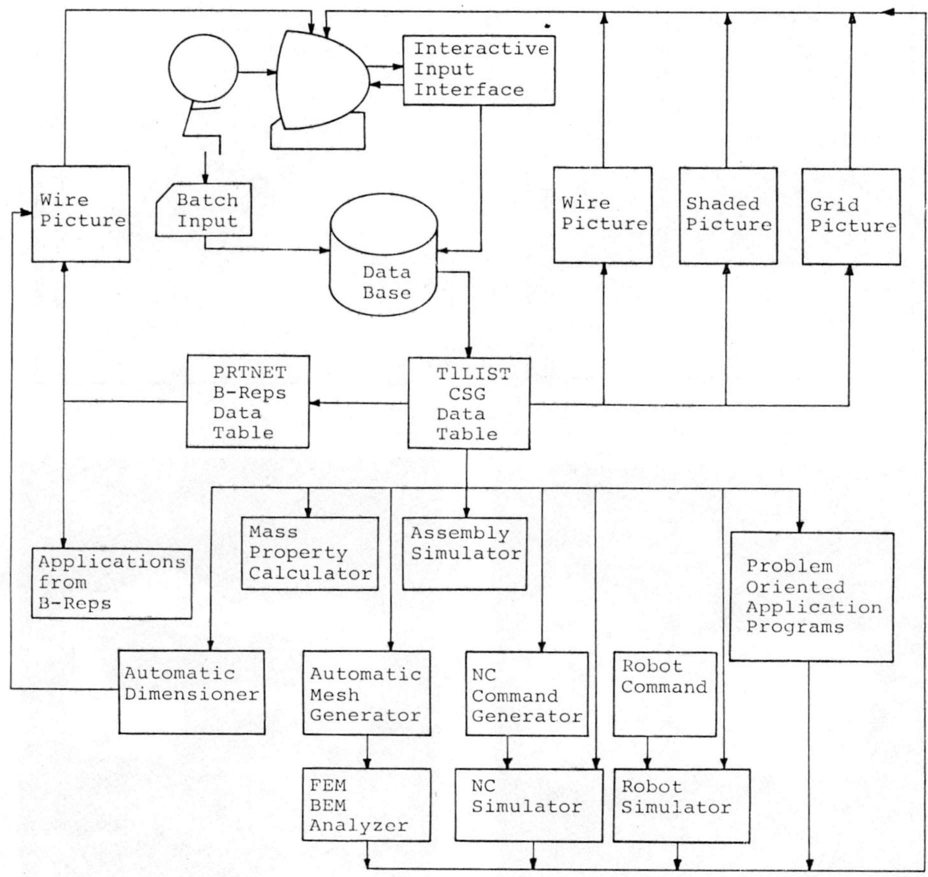

Figure 2. System structure of TIPS-1

GRAPHIC EXAMPLES OF TIPS-1

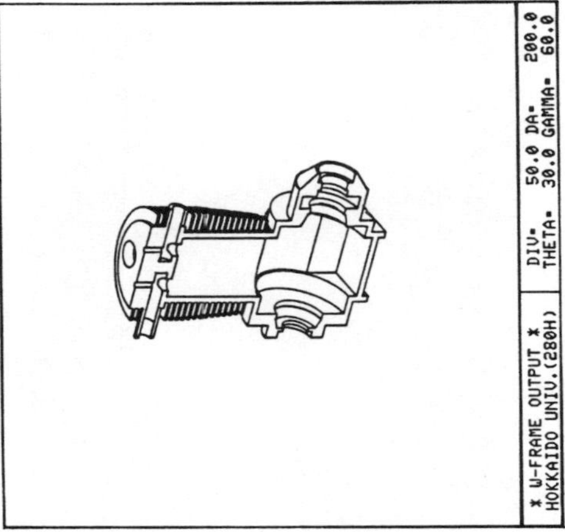

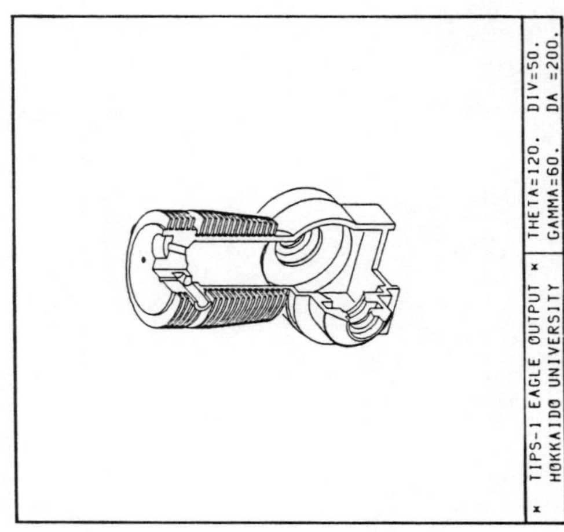

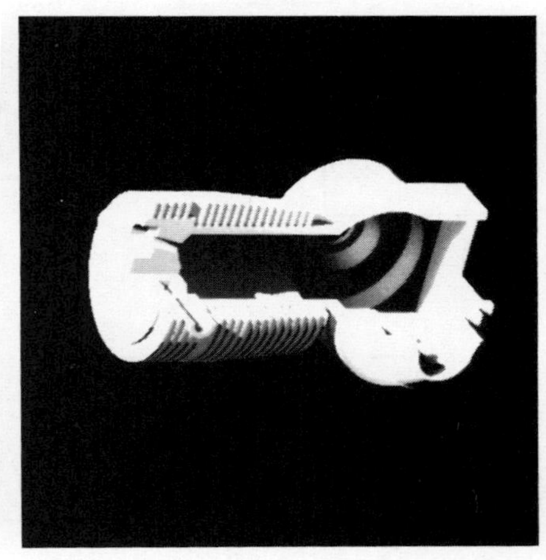

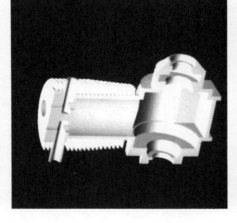

Figure 3 Wire frame and shaded pictures of an engine

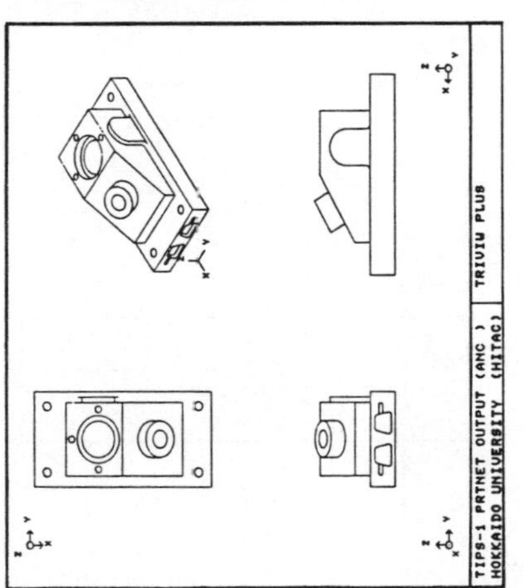

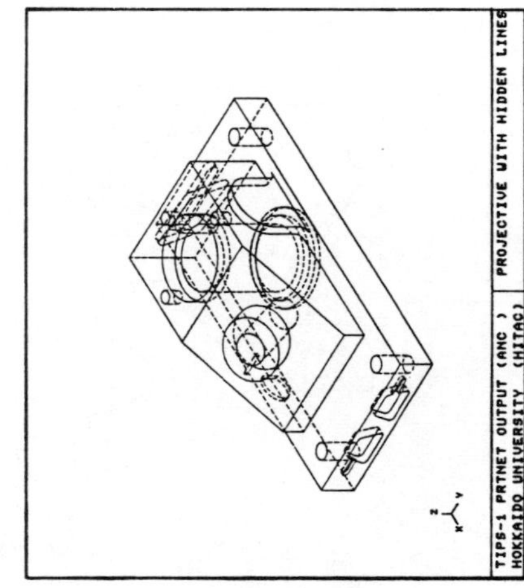

Figure 4 CAM-I Europe test shape

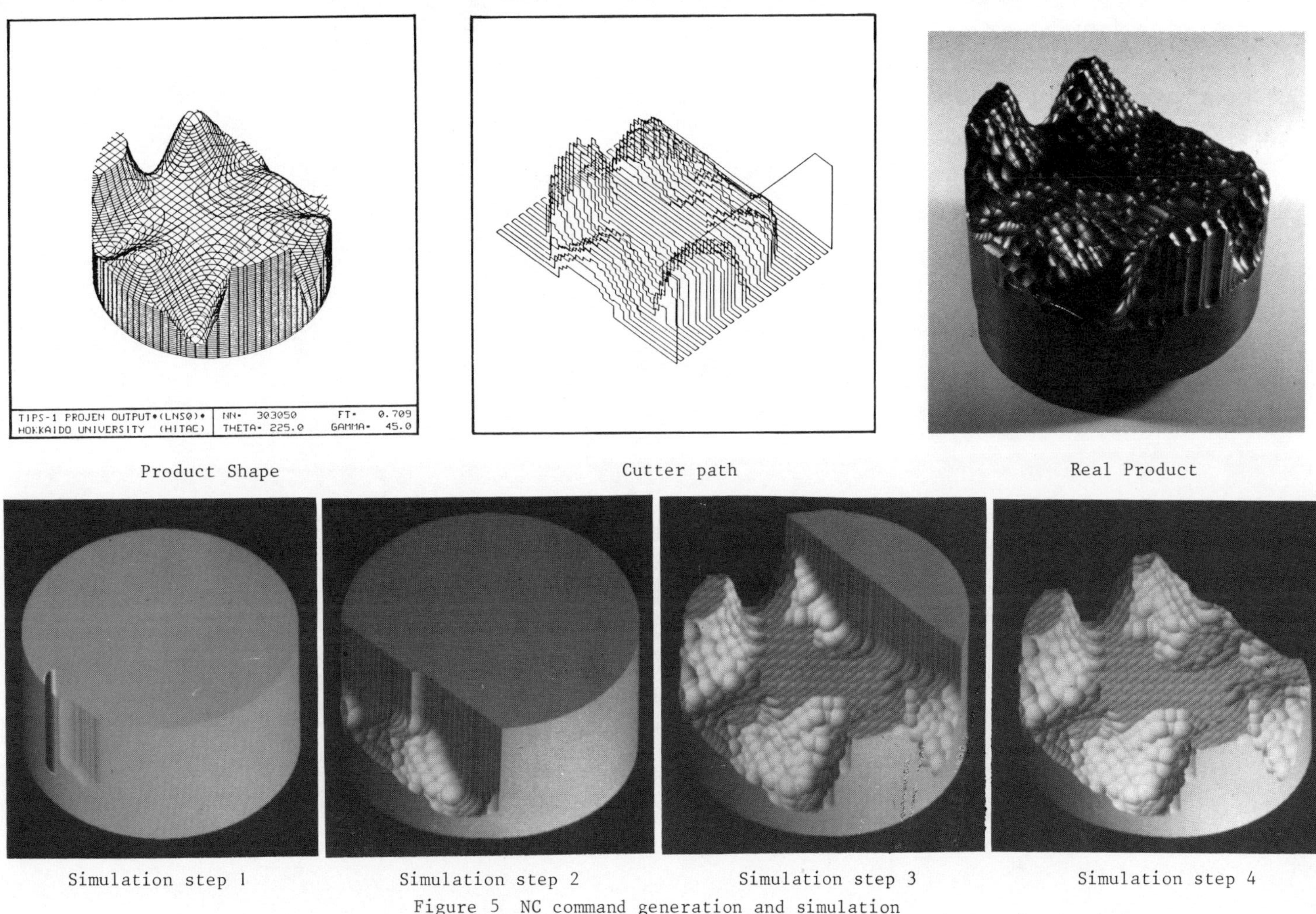

Figure 5 NC command generation and simulation

UNIGRAPHICS II/UNISOLIDS™

McDonnell Douglas Information Systems Ltd.,
U.K.

1. UNIGRAPHICS II

1.1 Introduction

McDonnell Douglas Corporation have been pioneers in the development and use of interactive graphics systems for computer-aided design and computer-aided manufacturing (CAD/CAM). Consequently, a variety of systems has been in use throughout the Corporation for more than 24 years. Many years of system development and involvement with users within our own company have given McDonnell Douglas a level of experience that is unique in the CAD/CAM vendor community.

UNIGRAPHICS II is the result of years of market research and customer input that has enabled us to produce the type of CAD/CAM system needed in the marketplace today. Our commitment to the development of advanced hardware and software technology led to UNIGRAPHICS II. McDonnell Douglas has designed a system that can be tailored to fit each user's specific needs. A large number of user-defined parameters along with customer-specific data make it easy to customize UNIGRAPHICS II to a particular application. With UNIGRAPHICS II, McDonnell Douglas has automated many manual tasks as well as carefully tailored the design, analysis and manufacturing features.

UNIGRAPHICS II is an advanced interactive graphics system with applications in many phases of the product development cycle, including engineering design and analysis, drafting, and generation of NC data for manufacturing. By providing a common data base for all of these activities, UNIGRAPHICS II facilitates a smooth and rapid transition from initial concept to finished product. What does this mean to you? It means your new products can reach your market in record time.

As an idea begins to take shape in the mind of a designer, its potential can be determined in a few moments on a UNIGRAPHICS II workstation. During the design iteration process, UNIGRAPHICS II allows you to constantly analyze your design and make changes where necessary. The speed and convenience of UNIGRAPHICS II allow you to investigate many design alternatives in a short period of time, and serious downstream problems can be uncovered early without the expense of building physical prototypes.

The end product of the design cycle traditionally has been a set of drawings. But after all, the part is the final product that you are interested in completing in a more productive and cost-efficient manner. A part design developed on UNIGRAPHICS II is much more than a drawing, it is a complete and accurate three-dimensional model of the part, a design data base that serves as the focal point for a host of further activities.

The wide variety of truly three-dimensional curves and surfaces allows all the features of a part to be faithfully modeled, and the user of double precision floating point arithmetic ensures that the data are accurate for even the most demanding applications. Various forms of engineering analysis can be performed, and NC instructions can be generated for manufacturing. By providing a common data base for all of these tasks, UNIGRAPHICS II promotes the integration of engineering and manufacturing activities that is so vital to increased productivity.

A friendly system becomes productive quickly, since people accept it easily and are eager to use it, rather than being afraid of it. Users come up to speed quickly, and do not need constant retraining. Ongoing benefits are significant because a wide variety of people can use the system themselves without having to work indirectly through operators.

User interface design is one of the most important features of any computing system. Like our other systems, UNIGRAPHICS II is completely tutorial; it constantly prompts you by displaying messages and menus written in plain English. You respond simply by pressing a button. And time can be saved by encoding frequently used button-push combinations in macros. Since the system always initiates the dialogue, there is never any doubt as to what options are available at any given moment. There is no cryptic command language to memorize, and very little typing is required.

1.2 UNIGRAPHICS II CAD Functions

The UNIGRAPHICS II CAD package includes all the capabilities necessary to describe the geometry of a mechanical part or assembly and produce finished engineering drawings. The curves available in UNIGRAPHICS II are lines, arcs, conics, and splines. Each of these curves can be constructed by a variety of methods; for example, there are 14 basic techniques for constructing a line. UNIGRAPHICS II surfaces include tabulated cylinders, analytic surfaces, fillet (blending) surfaces, and free-form sculptured surfaces.

Following are brief descriptions of some of the major functions being offered in UNIGRAPHICS II:

Attributes

One of the most important uses of this function is the ability to extract information from UNIGRAPHICS II for input to other programs, such as process planning or inventory control. UNIGRAPHICS II attributive features enable you to assign nongeometric data to the system's entities and parts. Because attributes are user-defined, there is flexibility in their range of values and applications. There also is an interactive report generator which produces a keyed summary of attribute values.

Dimensioning and Drafting

UNIGRAPHICS II provides automated methods for posting different types of dimensions and tolerances in a variety of industry-standard formats. Dimensions of cylinders, holes, and arc lengths are among the many included in UNIGRAPHICS II. Since all drafting entities are linked to the geometry used in defining them, any modification of the defining geometry causes an automatic recreation of the associated drafting entity. UNIGRAPHICS II editing features make it possible to change the location or size of drafting entities with just the push of a button.

Drawing Layout

Drawing features include complete screen layout capabilities, among them addition, removal, and relocation of views on the screen. The drawing creation function allows an unlimited number of views to be produced on a drawing as well as drawing layouts to be edited.

Viewing Capabilities

Perspective viewing allows you to examine models from a more realistic viewpoint. Display features, such as dynmaic rotation, give you the capability to examine the appearance of a model from any viewpoint and to "zoom in" on areas of special interest.

File Management

File management in UNIGRAPHICS II is simplified by the use of dynamic file space allocation. You can create your own directory structure tailored to individual organizational needs. Distinct file protection classifications assure system security. Each user is assigned a distinct set of privileges to control file access and system resource use. Complete records of system use and access violations are automatically compiled. File management is designed to operate on alphanumeric terminals and, therefore, need not tie up graphic workstations that are expensive to operate.

Part Merge

Part Merge allows you to place your commonly used components in different assemblies with the touch of a button. You do not have to recreate each component, a significant time-saving benefit. Using UNIGRAPHICS II, you can merge any geometry with an existing part and file an assembly subset as a component. The subset is then merged into another part, where all of the component geometry is linked together into a group structure which will inherit the attributes of the component part.

Groups

UNIGRAPHICS II provides the means of linking associated geometry in collections called groups. These groups can be multileveled, and extensive editing can be performed to add and remove group members. Once a group is created, you are given the option of performing operations on the entire group or on individual group members. By using multileveled groups, complex assemblies can be modeled. And by taking advantage of the attribute capabilities of UNIGRAPHICS II, these assemblies can contain the information needed to describe the structure, contents, and order of assembly.

Transformation and Editing

These functions allow any portion of UNIGRAPHICS II models to be duplicated, moved, or modified in various ways. For example, a block of text may be relocated, two curves may be trimmed at their intersection point, or the shape of a spline may be changed by moving a defining point. It is possible to transform different types of entities, including surfaces and groups. These functions also give you the ability to reproduce repetitive or symmetric geometry,

OPTIONAL MODULES

GSM

The optional Graphics Schematics Module allows you to create complex electrical and piping schematics. You create symbols that can be saved and then easily retrieved for placement on the schematic. At any time, the system can generate a bill of materials recording use of the various symbols and a connector list describing how they are linked together. These lists can be processed by GRIP

(Graphics Interactive Programming) programs for such applications as circuit analysis as well as pricing information. They also can be used as input to McAuto's UNIPCB^{TM} system for printed circuit board design.

Flat Patterns

Flat Patterns is an optional UNIGRAPHICS II module that gives manufacturing users access to information built into the design model. This module allows you to generate triangulated flat patterns and unfold a three-dimensional model. The geometry can then be used to help determine individual manufacturing resource requirements.

1.3 UNIGRAPHICS II CAE Capabilities

Engineering analysis can be time-consuming. With UNIGRAPHICS II, it doesn't have to be. A wide variety of analysis programs is available for use in predicting the properties and behavior of a part without the time and expense of building a physical prototype. If the analysis results indicate that the design needs improvements, it can be quickly modified and reanalyzed. The use of UNIGRAPHICS II in design iterations can result in dramatic improvements in product reliability and material use.

Traditionally, the input for these analysis programs has been prepared using tedious and error-prone manual coding techniques. UNIGRAPHICS II provides automated methods that are faster and more reliable since they operate upon existing design geometry. Two optional modules are available : GFEM and the MOLDFLOW^{TM*}/UNIGRAPHICS interface package.

GFEM

The Graphics Finite Element Module represents state-of-the-art integration of design and analysis. GFEM allows you to easily create elements and nodes on UNIGRAPHICS II surfaces for input to ANSYS, NASTRAN, or your own analysis program. The finite element entities are in the same file as the part geometry, and therefore make the editing of both a simple process. After analysis, GFEM reads the results directly

* Moldflow Australia Pty, Ltd.

from a file generated by the analysis program. The results can then be displayed using contour lines and deflected shapes.

MOLDFLOW

UNIGRAPHICS II is supported on 32-bit processors from Digital Equipment Corporation and Data General, giving you access to many third party software packages. MOLDFLOW is just such a package. Many companies are turning to the MOLDFLOW package as a means of avoiding repetitive trial and error in the design of plastic injection molds. With the MOLDFLOW/UNIGRAPHICS interface, existing UNIGRAPHICS II geometry can be used to generate the input to the MOLDFLOW programs. After element mesh generation, you can enter material, temperature, and other data needed for the analysis. MOLDFLOW calculates total volume, flow rates, and temperature and pressure ranges; pressure contours can then be graphically displayed for easier interpretation.

1.4 UNIGRAPHICS II CAM Capabilities

UNIGRAPHICS II CAM capabilities eliminate the amount of costly waste material associated with repeated shop floor tryouts. The machining functions provide an interactive graphics alternative to conventional NC programming techniques. After engineering has constructed and verified the geometry of a part using UNIGRAPHICS II design functions, that same geometry is used as input to the machining modules. After input of such manufacturing data as tool dimensions, speeds, feeds, and tolerances, the system automatically generates and displays the tool motions simulating the machining of the part.

The basic UNIGRAPHICS II system provides point-to-point machining capabilities and an editor for manipulating Cutter Location Source Files (CLSF). More advanced manufacturing functions are available in four optional modules - Graphics Lathe Module, Graphics Mill Module, Graphics Multi-Axis Module, and Nesting.

GLM

The Graphics Lathe Module is an optional enhancement to the powerful UNIGRAPHICS II machining system that allows you to automatically create two-axis lathe motion with an immediate display of the tool path for inspection and approval. The interactive procedures are presented in a logical sequence and in terms familiar to the lathe machinist. GLM prompts you for information about tool descriptions, machining parameters, part and material contours, and postprocessor parameters to be inserted into the CLSF. Rough, finish, groove, thread, and drill are turning operations that can be performed using GLM.

GMM

The Graphics Mill Module provides capabilities for two- through five-axis regional milling. Its functions are single- and multiple-pass profiling, and zig, zig-zag, and follow pocketing. These modules support the machining of regions that can contain an unlimited number of islands.

The pocketing functions provide automatic clearance of any region that has a planar floor and is bounded on the sides by curves. The zig and zig-zag features provide an efficient method of removing large amounts of material. Zig machining consists of unidirectional linear cuts across the part surface, thus performing either climb or conventional milling. Zig-zag machining consists of bidirectional linear cuts across the part surface.

GMAX

The Graphics Multi-Axis Module provides three- through five-axis machining capabilities by way of the following functions: Surface Contouring, Parameter Line Machining, and Roughing-to-Depth.

Surface Contouring allows you to machine any UNIGRAPHICS II surface, including complex sculptured surfaces. Parameter Line Machining produces cutter motion across a rectangular grid of UNIGRAPHICS II parametric surfaces (except for planes, which can be machined using GMM); its capabilities include gouge checking and correction, tolerance checking, and scallop height control. Roughing-to-Depth automatically clears out cavities one layer at a time.

Nesting

The UNIGRAPHICS II Nesting module is an optional machining module that allows you to optimize material usage. Patterns on the screen can be individually translated, rotated, or flipped manually, and any interference between patterns can be checked. Effective and actual material use is calculated, and sheet metal can be cut with a minimum of waste.

1.5 GRIP: A Powerful User Language

The functions that are performed interactively in UNIGRAPHICS II may also be performed automatically by executing a program written in the GRIP (Graphics Interactive Programming) language. For example, GRIP has commands to create geometry or drafting aids, interrogate the UNIGRAPHICS II data base, manipulate attributes, generate part programs for NC machine tools, or perform file management operations. Commands are also available for performing text manipulation, vector arithmetic, and other scientific calculations. A GRIP program can display messages and menus, interacting with you as it is operating. In addition, GRIP in UNIGRAPHICS II allows you to retrieve, create, and file parts.

A complex design and NC procedure can be encoded as a GRIP program. In this way, the talent and expertise of the person who devised the procedure are captured and stored in the system. Less experienced designers or programmers can then take advantage of this stored expertise. The GRIP program leads them through the procedure, prompting them for input only when necessary. "Family of Parts" programs, are a good example of this approach; a specific-size part can be generated simply by inputting values for certain critical parameters.

All GRIP programs can be interfaced to FORTRAN programs. By using even the simplest of GRIP programs, remarkable productivity increases can be achieved. For power, flexibility, and ease of use, GRIP is the state-of-the art in CAD/CAM user languages.

1.6 INTERFACING

IGES

The Initial Graphics Exchange Specification translator is capable of pre- and post- processing the following UNIGRAHICS II entity types: points, arcs, conics, splines, all dimension and drafting entities, and all surface types.

User Programming

A flexible subroutine package is available for user-written programs to access the UNIGRAPHICS II data base, perform file management functions, and interact with UNIGRAPHICS workstations. These routines are FORTRAN-77 compatible.

Telecommunications

Transfer of UNIGRAPHICS files among UNIGRAPHICS II systems is supported on asynchronous, DECnet, and XODIAC communication links. UNIGRAPHICS II file transfers involving Digital Equipment Company (DEC), International Business Machines (IBM), and Data General systems will include options for data coversion.

Postprocessors

A Generic Postprocessor Module (GPM) is being offered with UNIGRAPHICS II. McDonnell Douglas developed with GPM to answer the need for standard, fixed-cost alternatives to custom numerical control software, eliminating the expense of custom postprocessors. Postprocessors written in FORTRAN are also available.

2. UNISOLIDS

2.1 General Description

UNISOLIDS™ from McDonnell Douglas is a solid modeling system specifically designed for mechanical engineering and manufacturing based on 10 years of proven research and experience.

Creation and manipulation of a wide variety of mechanical parts and assemblies are possible with UNISOLIDS. These same models can then be transferred automatically to the McDonnell Douglas UNIGRAPHICS CAE/CAD/CAM system to form the basis for additional applications such as drafting, engineering analysis, and generation of NC data for manufacturing.

Modern CAE/CAD/CAM systems are designed to provide a common central source of data for all associated applications. Solid modeling systems store complete, unambiguous descriptions of the geometry of physical parts. The richness of the geometric model has a profound effect on the capabilities of the CAE/CAD/CAM system; if more complete information is stored, then more applications can be addressed.

Conceptual design, the origination of an idea, has an outlet in UNISOLIDS. Shape, structure, or characteristics of a particular mechanism, or any variety of parts, can be rapidly constructed by creating simple building blocks, known as primitives, or creating sweeps using sweep construction methods. These can be combined to form more complex parts, a rapid method of producing a three-dimensional solid model.

Characteristics change most frequently during this concept stage. Redefinition, editing, and altering elements are easily executed in UNISOLIDS, and thus are extremely appropriate tasks for the software.

Not only is a quality representation of an idea achieved, with the aid of features such as hidden-line removal and shaded images, but the designer is able to communicate his or her ideas to others in a concrete way early in the design phase. Technical illustrations for management presentations or as aids in the competitive bidding process are by-products of this type of design work.

In many ways, the solid model may take the place of a physical prototype. However, unlike a physical prototype, a solid model can be changed quickly and easily so that many design alternatives can be investigated in a short time. The end result is that your products work better and cost less.

The core of UNISOLIDS is the PADL-2 system which was developed in cooperation with McDonnell Douglas by members of the Production Automation Project at the University of Rochester, New York, a major center for research in solid modeling and programmable automation.* The basic techniques and concepts of UNISOLIDS have been tried and tested during more than 10 years of work by one of the foremost research teams in the field.

Highly reliable geometric calculations characterize UNISOLIDS. Both boundary representations and constructive solid geometry (CSG) are available. Boundary representations are used to create rapid displays, while most other UNISOLIDS applications use constructive representations which are models stored as combinations of primitives. CSG and its flexible architecture give UNISOLIDS unparalleled reliability. With CSG, geometric calculations work without exception, even when objects have tangent or coincident surfaces. CSG prevents the user from designing an object that is not physically possible. The use of CSG by UNISOLIDS provides a vital link to future automated applications.

* Development of PADL-2 under the Production Automation Project of the University of Rochester was sponsored by McDonnell Douglas, certain other industrial firms (names supplied on request), and the National Science Foundation.

UNISOLIDS has adopted the highly interactive, menu-driven user interface proven to be so successful in the UNIGRAPHICS system. Tutorial in nature, UNISOLIDS prompts you by displaying messages and menus written in ordinary English. Each operation is selected by simply pressing a button. Since the system initiates the dialogue, you always know which options are currently available. Memorizing a cryptic command language is not necessary, and little typing is required. Thus, both casual and dedicated system users can easily access UNISOLIDS.

2.2 Design Process

UNISOLIDS construction begins with the creation of simple primitives or the use of sweeps. Either primitives or sweeps may be combined to form more complex parts and assemblies using the Boolean operations of intersection, union and difference.

Boolean operations are analogous to common, everyday processes. For example, the union operator simply merges or fuses several objects. Similarly, in a different operation, one object is used as a tool to carve out a cavity in a second object. An uncombine option undoes the Boolean operation.

A single Boolean operation can often do the work of several-dozen lower-level functions used in wire frame and surface systems. A simple, one-step procedure will automatically section an object to reveal its internal details. Major part changes may be made with a few steps.

UNISOLIDS is particularly effective in capturing the design elements of machined parts since the primitive shapes are similar to those most often produced in machining operations.

Both linear and rotational sweep solids can be created. Functions are provided to define two-dimensional sweep outlines which are used to create sweep solids. These outlines may be used to create linear (or extruded) sweeps or to create rotational (solids-of-revolution) sweeps. These powerful sweep functions are provided to construct solids of constant cross section, especially those with tangent cylindrical and/or planar surfaces.

The use of part merge allows the UNISOLIDS part to reference geometry in an external UNISOLIDS part file. This capability is especially useful for referencing standard components since all parent parts will be automatically updated when changes are made to referenced parts.

Editing Features

Strong editing capabilities are inherent in UNISOLIDS with such construction aids as the transformation function to move objects to new positions. The multiple-copy option allows repetitive features to be modeled very quickly in a step-and-repeat fashion.

Instancing, another editing capability, is similar to copying a solid, but an instance maintains its associativity with the original solid. Any geometric change to an instance solid will be reflected in all associated instances. As a result, identical components may be instanced throughout a part for easier update and more compact data storage. Both primitives and more complex solids may be instanced.

Model Analysis

Since UNISOLIDS maintains a complete description of the geometry of the part, mass properties can be calculated automatically in a single step. For example, the system computes volume, weight, center of gravity, or moments of inertia about any axis. The user controls the speed and accuracy of the calculations so that rough estimates may be obtained quickly. A unique error analysis feature indicates exactly how rough the answers are so that closer calculations may be requested if necessary.

UNISOLIDS also calculates mass properties of an entire assembly of solids. The density of each of the solids in the assembly may be specified. Additional analysis functions allow you to interrogate the model to determine point locations, angles, distances, clearances, and edge properties. Interference checking may be performed visually, or the intersection operator may be used for an analytical check.

Capture Concepts and Communication with UNISOLIDS

UNISOLIDS provides a variety of functions that control the way a part is displayed on the screen. You may examine the appearance of a model from any angle and zoom in on details of specific areas. More than 30 standard views are built into the system and either orthographics or perspective images are available at the touch of a button.

Dynamic viewing capabilities are available with selected design stations to manipulate models in real time.

High-resolution line drawings together with automatic hidden-line removal can be used when maximum clarity is important. Edge displays include visible, invisible, and dashed hidden lines.

More life-like images can be obtained with continuous-tone shading and highlighted edges. Add to this partial shading for refining a small area of an image or selectively modifying an image.

These sophisticated display functions help the designer visualize the shape and structure of a part and understand how it will function. Life-like shaded images, either used alone or in conjunction with engineering drawings, can be tremendous aids to effectively communicate ideas and concepts.

Interface UNISOLIDS/UNIGRAPHICS

After a model is developed with UNISOLIDS, it may be transferred automatically to UNIGRAPHICS and used to produce annotated engineering drawings, finite-element models or NC instructions for manufacturing.

The UNISOLIDS/UNIGRAPHICS interface has a number of advantages.

UNIGRAPHICS is able to handle all of the downstream requirements in drafting, engineering analysis, and manufacturing, from UNISOLIDS data.

Both systems run on the same hardware and employ similar user interfaces. Users are able to work on UNISOLIDS easily after using UNIGRAPHICS, and vice versa.

UNISOLIDS and UNIGRAPHICS data are maintained under the same file management system. System managers and users who know the tasks required to maintain UNIGRAPHICS can perform the same tasks for UNISOLIDS. No new system management training is necessary.

An IGES preprocessor is also available for interfacing with other CAE/CAD/CAM systems that support IGES.

Support

Users of McDonnell Douglas CAE/CAD/CAM products are fully supported with financial assistance, professional training, and full-service maintenance.